Robert Penn Warren's Circus Aesthetic
and the Southern Renaissance

robert penn warren's

Circus Aesthetic
and the Southern Renaissance

patricia L. bradley

THE UNIVERSITY OF TENNESSEE PRESS
Knoxville

Copyright © 2004 by The University of Tennessee Press / Knoxville.
All Rights Reserved. Manufactured in the United States of America.
First Edition.

This book is printed on acid-free paper.

Library of Congress Cataloging-in-Publication Data

Bradley, Patricia L., 1952–
Robert Penn Warren's circus aesthetic and the Southern renaissance /
Patricia L. Bradley.— 1st ed.
      p. cm.
Includes bibliographical references and index.

ISBN 1-57233-311-1

1. Warren, Robert Penn, 1905—Knowledge—Performing arts.
2. American fiction—Southern States—History and criticism.
3. American fiction—20th century—History and criticism.
4. Southern States—Intellectual life—1865–
5. Warren, Robert Penn, 1905—Aesthetics.
6. Southern States—In literature.
7. Circus—Southern States.
8. Circus in literature.
 I. Title.
PS3545.A748Z625 2004
813'.52—dc22   2004012280

For Joe,
who joined me from across
Warren country

Contents

Acknowledgments

In the earliest stages of this project, when I was struggling not only for a direction but also for a critical voice, I was guided by two people who, perhaps, little knew the results their advice to me would have. I am immensely grateful to Art Eaves for introducing me to Robert Penn Warren's under-read novella "The Circus in the Attic" and to Steve Ryan for the illuminating discussions in his office that helped me begin to understand the possibilities of that text. About that same period, even as I was still formulating my ideas, I was fortunate enough to meet, through the Robert Penn Warren Circle, the very scholars who had written the most and the best on Warren. As a group, and to a person, they welcomed me among them and encouraged my study.

At a later stage, when I needed guidance of a different sort, Dorothy Scura provided exactly the right balance of structure and latitude that suited my short-term requirements and my long-term aspirations. Without her vision, her willingness to consider my efforts as more than mere process, this book would have been much longer in the making. I am also grateful to her colleagues and my friends—Chuck Maland, Mary Papke, and Ted Hipple—whose engaged, informed readings and insightful suggestions at this most crucial stage tested and refined my ideas. I truly realized the vast worth of their collective efforts on my behalf when my eagle-eyed editor, Joyce Harrison, brought my manuscript to the attention of Warren scholars John Burt and David Madden. They proved as enthusiastic and supportive of it as Joyce earlier had been, and I am pleased to include the three of them among the many who have helped me develop this work to its present form.

My friends and family have been witnesses to and participants in the day-to-day effort a project of this sort demands. My daughters Jennifer Davis, Jocelyn Bradley, and Joanna Bradley can barely remember when I have not been thinking and talking and writing about Warren and the circus; I hope some day they will know to what extent this effort was for them and how much they contributed to it. My mother Letha Petty and my sisters Susie Lankford and Sandra Lankford have stood four-square with me in this and every goal I have pursued; just as important, my grandmother Callie Lankford and my friend Bessie Bradley have steadily voiced their confidence in my abilities. My friend and colleague Gina Rossetti listened many times over to my ideas, bringing empathy and encouragement where they were much needed. Mine was never solitary effort.

And finally, the one constant over these many years has been my husband, Joe Millichap. Himself a Warren scholar, Joe's critical comment that "The Circus in the Attic" was the matrix for Warren's fiction led me to question why, fired my critical thinking about the novella, and ultimately inspired this book. What began abstractly, however, evolved into more concrete service as he offered his talents, his example, and his wisdom for the duration—when acting as my steadying force was no easy accomplishment of his effort, energy, and commitment. For these gifts—and so much more—I am very grateful.

Introduction

> *[T]here is no* one, single, correct *kind of criticism—no* complete *criticism. You only have different kinds of perspectives, giving, when successful, different kinds of insights. And at one historical moment one kind of insight may be more needed than another.*
>
> —Robert Penn Warren
> "Warren on the Art of Fiction," 1957

Robert Penn Warren is twentieth-century America's most distinguished person of letters. He has been honored in the course of his career with a Pulitzer Prize in fiction for *All the King's Men* (1946), with two Pulitzer Prizes in poetry for *Promises: Poems 1954–1956* (1957) and *Now and Then: Poems 1976–1978* (1978), and in 1986 with the designation as America's first official poet laureate. His career as poet, novelist, biographer, literary critic, essayist, editor, and teacher spanned over five decades and kept pace with the century's passage through literary, political, and cultural changes, all of which Warren observed and remarked upon in his voluminous canon. Recognized steadily throughout his career as an artist of unmistakable stature, Warren has earned a central place among twentieth-century American writers as well as among the authors of the Southern Renaissance.

This study will examine Warren's identity as an American writer and as a writer of the Southern Renaissance through the window of the circus trope. Circus and carnival references appear with arresting regularity in Warren's early prose works, including his unpublished novels, his biography of John Brown, and two of his first three published novels. By the time he writes his 1947 novella "The Circus in the Attic," Warren is ready to develop the circus trope to the degree that it gives added significance to the prose in which it had originally appeared and lends greater depth of meaning to his later novels, essays, poetry, and reminiscences. His use of the circus trope, including such figures as the clown, the ring master, and the girl acrobat, is formalist in that it reveals not only Warren's New Critical preoccupation with image and symbol but also his desire to establish links of influence with validating literary fathers; on the other hand, the trope is intertextual in that it aligns Warren with other writers of the Southern Renaissance whose experiences are culturally consonant with his own.

In turn, Warren's circus trope can be read psychologically in its reflection of his characters' conflicted interpersonal relationships; these relationships are particularly meaningful when viewed through the interpretive lenses of the Freudian and Lacanian family romance, René Girard's concept of triangular desire, Eve Kosofsky Sedgwick's concept of male homosocial desire, and Richard King's theory of the southern family romance. Finally, Warren's circus trope is modernist in that it illuminates his perception of himself as an artist whose yearning toward pure art must be informed by impure elements; conversely, the trope is antimodernist in its interrogation of elitist attitudes by folk wisdom.

In Warren's canon, however, as well as in the works of other authors of the Southern Renaissance, circus references cannot always be read, as one might expect, as transgressive carnivalesque elements. Cultural and historical examinations of the role of the American circus during the decades of the 1920s, 1930s, and 1940s—decades that roughly correspond with the height of the Southern Renaissance—reveal instead how the circus supported conservative American ideologies.

The circus and the modern south

Social and cultural historians such as John Culhane and Don Wilmeth note that although the circus was a popular form of entertainment throughout the nineteenth century, America experienced its circus heyday during the second decade of the twentieth century.[1] The surge in popularity of this form of mass entertainment may well explain the abundant circus references in the works of American authors who came of age during that period. This trend is especially evident in the works of several authors generally associated with the Southern Renaissance, which extended roughly between 1920 and 1950. Certainly the circus was a fitting modernist trope as a low culture version of traditional theatrical art forms.[2] Additionally, southern writers may have identified in the circus their own post–Civil War region, forced as it was to a status of otherness and yet honored all the more by its constituents for the very qualities that set it apart from the modern, mainstream North. This attitude, for example, along with the growing sectionalism of antebellum America, is succinctly demonstrated by an ad for G. N. Eldred's Great Southern Show, which advertised itself in an 1856 Tallahassee paper as "Southern Men, Southern Horses, Southern Enterprise Against the World."[3]

A quick survey of the Southern Renaissance authors considered in addition to Robert Penn Warren in this study reveals that they either were children or actually had come of age during the crucial years of the circus heyday. A brief examination of the literary manifestations of the circus in works by such authors as Katherine Anne Porter (1890–1980), Caroline Gordon (1895–1981), William Faulkner (1897–1962), Thomas Wolfe (1900–1938), Eudora Welty (1909–2001), and Ralph Ellison (1914–1994) will further reveal the cultural relevance of Warren's use of the circus in his works, thus establishing him within a frame of southern intertextuality. Furthermore, as each of these authors began in the 1920s, 1930s and 1940s to effect the distinctive literary flowering of their region, the circus itself came to reflect the three defining cultural moments of the Southern Renaissance: World War I, the Great Depression, and World War II.

Circus historian John Culhane records that America's entry into World War I in 1917 caused a great manpower shortage among the ranks of circus workers. At that time, even the two most famous circus shows, the Barnum & Bailey Circus and the Ringling Bros. Circus, found their regular activities hampered when great numbers of their able-bodied male employees enlisted in the armed forces. Since most shows traveled their circuits by rail, the circuses' mobility was also threatened as the military need for railroad transportation grew. In fact, World War I was indirectly responsible for the formation of the "Greatest Show on Earth"—the Ringling Bros. and Barnum & Bailey Circus—in 1919. The consolidation, which had been effected on paper much earlier, reflected the owners' fears of a longer war and their mutual decision to pool their limited wartime resources (177–78).

This loss of young men to the war effort will explain in part why women aerialists were prominent among the glittering array of performers in this history-making 1919 season, the debut for which was announced on the front page of the *New York Times*. The placement of such free advertising indicates the contemporary popularity of the circus, and the persistence of the spectacle in the face of a devastating war shows as well the public's need for some reaffirmation of the continuity of life. Culhane describes one act in which three troupes of women aerialists, dressed in colorful butterfly costumes, hung and spun by their teeth from the top of Madison Square Garden. Another woman acrobat, part of the Cromwell double-trapeze act, swung suspended by her feet from the feet of her male partner. Still another woman, billed as Miss Tiny Kline, stood rigid on a metal trapeze in which she executed 360° swings. Finally, in an act so popular that it commanded the center ring and required that the other two remain darkened and empty (management's assumption was that no one would watch them anyway), wire walker Bird Millman executed steps from popular dances of the day from one end of the high wire to the other. Her showstopper was when she coyly sang "How Would You Like to Spoon with Me?" (Culhane 179). Millman's rendition hinted at the greater freedoms women would experience in the decade that followed World War I while at the same time reaffirming expectations of womanliness that existed prior to the war.[4] Any of these performers, but especially Bird Millman, could have provided a source for Robert Penn Warren's often-used figure of the girl acrobat—daring but demure, capable yet vulnerable, self-determining yet fulfilling masculine definitions of womanly appeal.

The death in 1931 of one of the most beloved and glamorous of the woman aerialists of the 1920s seemed timed to announce the reassertion of masculine controls on women's postwar freedom, the culmination of the Jazz Age, and the staying power of the Great Depression. Ringling Bros. and Barnum & Bailey Circus billed Lillian Leitzel as the "Queen of Aerial Gymnasts" for her ability to perform as many as one hundred (and on one occasion more than two hundred) swingovers as she hung by one arm over her audience. Her act, which required the strength necessary to throwing her entire body head over heels with her shoulder socket as a fulcrum, was replicated by Betty Hutton in the 1952 blockbuster movie *The Greatest Show on Earth*. Not even Leitzel's equally famous husband, trapeze artist Alfredo Codona, could draw bigger crowds than she (Culhane 186). When Leitzel died of a fall in 1931, Codona succumbed to melancholy and in 1933 suffered an injury that ended his circus career; he committed suicide in 1937 and was buried next to Leitzel's ashes beneath the twelve-foot monument he had erected in California after her death. The monument, called *The Spirit of Flight,* depicts a woman embraced by a creature with angel's wings (Culhane 199–200). It is suggestive of a minor character in Warren's *All the King's Men* who is in turn a psychic double for his protagonist Jack Burden. This character, in mourning for his aerialist wife, the "flying angel" in a circus troupe, seeks release from his grief-inspired emotional paralysis by molding angels from masticated bread dough.

Perhaps Warren was alluding to this character in a 1966 interview with Frank Gado about the background sources of *All the King's Men*. Warren equates Willie Stark's southern Depression regime with Roosevelt's New Deal, remarking that in a vacuum of power or even in a vacuum of social goods, "somebody has to provide the bread and circuses; if not, there's going to be real trouble."[5] Notwithstanding his debt to Juvenal for the sentiment, Warren's words suggest he may have been aware of what few presently know: from 1935 to 1939, the federal government supported WPA (Works Progress Administration) circuses, giving jobs to unemployed circus workers who in turn performed free shows for hospitals and poor children (Culhane 214). In this way, the circus, ordinarily considered a site for social transgression, was used to attest to the country's basic stability in the face of what many hoped would be a temporary economic collapse. As one historian has put it, the "circus as 'reassuring constant' represented an era of shared values and principles, before the details of everyday life became . . . so involved and problematic. For this reason the circus would be included in the cultural nationalism of the New Deal."[6]

Conversely, another New Deal program, the PWA (Public Works Administration), provided comic fodder for Emmett Kelly, who was forced by the Great Depression to exchange his aspirations to trapeze stardom for a career as a clown (Culhane 215). His hobo persona was a fitting image for the 1930s, becoming almost as famous as Charlie Chaplin's Little Tramp had been.[7] Kelly captured the country's attention when a publicity still of him leaning on a shovel next to a PWA sign was published nationwide. The PWA Shovel Routine prompted disgruntlement from Roosevelt Democrats and gratification from Republicans (Culhane 213–14), demonstrating that despite the circus's reputation for transcending "race, gender, class and occupational distinctions," it played a cultural role in shaping and reflecting social and political hegemonies.[8] Especially demonstrative of the circus's social and political roles during the 1930s were the series of strike actions staged by animal handlers and roustabouts against circus management in 1938.[9]

By the time of World War II, the federal government realized what it had not fully exploited during World War I: the value of the circus in maintaining public morale during the dark days of war.[10] The rail transport restrictions of 1917 and 1918, which had severely curtailed circus activity and forced the consolidation that later became known as "The Greatest Show on Earth," were not repeated in 1941, although worker shortages were inevitable as many enlisted in the armed forces. Instead, the Office of Defense Transportation, with the support of President Roosevelt, made it possible for circus trains to continue to travel the United States and thus for the circus to make its home-front contribution to the war (Culhane 241). In 1943, the Ringling Bros. and Barnum & Bailey Circus returned the favor by loaning their general manager George Smith, an acknowledged expert in circus logistics, to facilitate troop movements in the United States to various points of embarkation to the front.[11] In the darkest early days of the war, however, the public looked to an even more humble source of inspiration when *Time* heralded the animated character Dumbo, the circus elephant, as one of the first of the war heroes, declaring that "among all the grim and forbidding visages of A.D. 1941, his guileless, homely face is the face of the true man of good will" (qtd. in Culhane 242). In these ways and many others, the circus proved itself a valid source for patriotic resolve.

Historically, the twentieth-century circus and its performers have confirmed American nationalism and helped create American identity rather than subverting it, as critical studies of the Bakhtinian carnivalesque might suggest. For example, John Culhane speculates that the antebellum clown Dan Rice, "tall, lanky, bearded, dressed in red-and-white stripes like an American flag, [and] calling himself Uncle Sam," was Thomas Nast's model for the country's unique national symbol (47). Rice was also a genius at what every successful clown does best—defining his audience to itself.

Fred Bradna, the ringmaster for forty years, first for the Barnum & Bailey Circus and then later for the Ringling Bros. and Barnum & Bailey Combined Shows, recalls escorting no fewer than four American presidents to their front-row seats at the circus: Woodrow Wilson (1913–21), Warren Harding (1921–23), Calvin Coolidge (1923–29), and Herbert Hoover (1929–33). Reportedly, Wilson used the occasion of his visit to the circus to announce his candidacy for reelection in 1916, literally throwing his hat into the center ring. On another occasion, according to Bradna, Wilson was only barely dissuaded by his closest advisers and Secret Service agents from accepting John Ringling's offer to ride an elephant.[12]

During World War II, the Ringling Bros. and Barnum & Bailey Circus overtly addressed the war effort in both its acts and spectacles as well as in its advertising. The combination of the show's patriotic theme and America's need for diversion and self-affirmation made 1942 the most successful year ever for the RBB&B.[13] That year's finale, for example, included lowering giant pictures of Franklin Delano Roosevelt and General Douglas MacArthur into the center ring. In 1943, two of the featured spectacles were titled "Let Freedom Ring" and "Drums of Victory." Representative circus posters bragged "Coming Soon! To Tokyo and Berlin" and carried the requisite admonition to "Buy War Bonds" (Culhane 245–46).

Implicit recognition of the Ringling Bros. Barnum & Bailey Circus's admirable wartime service came in 1945, after the tragic big top fire in 1944 in Hartford, Connecticut, killed 168 spectators. Economically crippled by costly litigation and anticipating that the public henceforth would be too fearful to attend performances of the circus under canvas, the RBB&B management invited Gen. George C. Marshall to its Washington, D.C., show, and Marshall accepted. Not only was the circus the first public function Marshall attended after the end of the war, but the general also brought his grandson to shake hands with Emmett Kelly, a gesture captured in a publicity photograph and picked up by newspapers all over the country. In this manner, public faith in the safety of the circus under canvas was restored and the continued economic viability of the Greatest Show on Earth ensured.[14]

The history of the circus has ever been a paradoxical mixture of the respectable with the outlandish, witnessed in countless cultural juxtapositions. Consider, for example, the previously mentioned circus origins of our national symbol, Uncle Sam (Culhane 51); the experience of "Yankee Robinson," who in 1859 fled a southern mob protesting not his daily circus performances but his nightly staging of what his audiences perceived as an overly propagandized version of *Uncle Tom's Cabin*; the 1858 campaign speeches of Abraham Lincoln and Stephen A. Douglas, which were delivered to a gathered crowd in the tent of the Spalding & Rogers Circus (Culhane 60); "son of the circus" Henry Ringling North, whose elite Yale education led to his suggestion of the name "Gargantua" for the huge gorilla exhibited for twelve years by the Ringlings (Culhane 228); and, finally, the reputation the Ringling Bros. and Barnum & Bailey Combined Shows had in the business as a "Sunday school show," adjudged suitable for even the youngest and most tender-minded audiences.[15] The culmination of this steady "rehabilitation" of the circus has, in recent years, been its partnership with such respectable (and exclusively male) groups as the Shriners and Rotary and Lions clubs in order to facilitate community acceptance and to draw profitable crowds. In just this way, the two communities—the peripatetic circus and the fixed audience it cultivates—find themselves representing and complementing the activities of the other.[16] Once considered antithetical to orderly hegemony, the twentieth-century American circus progressively became more of a force for social balance than for social change.

вакhтin аnd тhe сircus

This gradual twentieth-century rehabilitation of the American circus consequently discourages the cultural application of the Bakhtinian carnivalesque, not only to Warren's "Circus in the Attic" but also to many other works of the Southern Renaissance in which circus references appear. In fact, Warren's unmistakable tendency to seek out patriarchal influence rather than avoid it, to confirm hierarchy even as he wages an ironic rebellion against it, casts his circus in a distinctly ideological role. Unlike such latecomers to the Southern Renaissance as Carson McCullers and Flannery O'Connor, whose circus and carnival references reinforce the grotesque and carnivalesque in their works, Warren's symbolic circus becomes the antithesis of Bakhtinian carnival.

Thus, my study will foreground the tradition of the "official feasts" that Mikhail Bakhtin recognized in *Rabelais and His World* (in Russian, 1940; first English translation, 1965) as antithetical to carnival. As Bakhtin noted, the "official feasts of the Middle Ages, whether ecclesiastic, feudal, or sponsored by the state, did not lead the people out of the existing world order and created no second life. On the contrary, they sanctioned the existing pattern of things and reinforced it." Starting as early as the nineteen-teens and World War I, the American circus is more and more the modern model of the Middle Ages' official feasts, upholding "the triumph of a truth already established, the predominant truth that was put forward as eternal and indisputable."[17]

Robert Penn Warren's use of the circus in "The Circus in the Attic" (1947)[18] confirms the novella's place in the tradition of Bakhtin's "official feasts." For one thing, this work lends itself to a type of literary analysis favored by many of the so-called New Critics: the image study. Even before the introduction of the novella's protagonist Bolton Lovehart, Warren's circus image is a recurring and unifying element. Initially, the circus connotes war and rebellion, experienced domestically between the North and the South as well as between parent and child. With the resolution of the Civil War, however, the circus develops into an expression of Bolton Lovehart's yearning for the patriarchal model that can aid the son in his assertion of identity and in his escape from maternal domination. By the conclusion of the novella, Bolton's circus and its major figures—the clown, the girl acrobat, and the ring master—approach a symbolic status that reaffirms the patriarchal myth of southern history, "the truth people have to believe to go on being the way they are" ("Circus" 8).

Even as Bolton seeks that patriarchal model, however, a close reading of "The Circus in the Attic" as well as Warren's additional criticism, fiction, poetry, and memoirs reveals a multiplicity of fathers located within this most enigmatic of Warren's creations. First, Warren's analyses of Nathaniel Hawthorne as an artist and a man reveal meaningful conjunctions of biography and subject matter between Warren's literary father and Bolton Lovehart. On the other hand, Bolton's Bardsville neighbors neither appreciate nor understand what his attic circus has meant in terms of personal conviction and self-sacrifice. In this sense, Bolton is the image of Warren's own father, Robert

Franklin Warren, who was deeply loved by his son but whom, in his most fearful moments, Warren recognized as another failed artist. Furthermore, the proximity in time during which Warren composed *All the King's Men* and "The Circus in the Attic," as well as their strikingly similar uses of the figure of the girl acrobat, adds a dimension of Jack Burden's distant and disaffected persona to the characterization of Bolton Lovehart. Finally, Bolton reveals aspects of Warren himself since creator and creation are each a compendium of many fathers.

The psychology of the circus

For Warren, the more vehement a son's rejection of the father, the more certain their subsequent reconciliation, be it physical, psychological, or ideological. Nowhere in his canon is this trend better illustrated than in "The Circus in the Attic," in which father and son relationships are symbolically reiterated to the point that Bolton Lovehart ultimately plays both roles in the family dynamic. Somewhat predictably, Warren's novella replicates Freud's Oedipal model in which the mother's initial importance to her son's life is displaced by the son's obedience to his ideological bond to the father.

Not quite so predictable is the role Richard King's concept of the "southern family romance" plays in Warren's "Circus in the Attic." As Joseph Millichap has noted in making this application of King to Warren, "Southern myths and ideologies, in both their popular and literary manifestations, are in a Freudian sense the family romances of a neurotic culture."[19] And yet, the key to King's southern formulation of Freud lies in a particular patriarchal response to women and black slaves. Thus, Warren's novella is a family romance several times over not only in its multiplicity of mothers and fathers and sons but also in its foregrounding of the myth of southern history—one version of which King calls "the plantation myth"—through the sentimentalization of women and blacks.[20]

Without a doubt, "The Circus in the Attic" speaks to Warren's career-long troubled engagement with the gendered and racial other. Clearly, Mrs. Parton is not the woman her husband Bolton thinks her to be; this ostensibly demure southern lady has a secret sensual dimension that reveals her as the death-defying aerialist in Bolton's imaginary circus. Her son Jasper is an even more mysterious presence in this text. His characterization as the "sinister ring master" is effected through the kind of minstrel show stereotypes that once defined "negroid" behavior to white audiences, making Jasper's appearance in the novella as culturally subversive as that of the sexually liberated Mrs. Parton.

Nevertheless, the myth of southern history triumphs in the end as these two fulfill the individual destinies ordained by Bolton's circus. Their sudden, untimely deaths leave Bolton to return to his attic circus, leaving unresolved the question of his greater enlightenment into their true natures.

Despite Jasper's eventual death, however, his relationship with Bolton as son to father repeatedly supersedes Bolton's marital relationship with Mrs. Parton, bringing the reader to the novella's final reworking of the Freudian family romance. This reworking is revealed by way of René Girard's concept of triangular desire, which has its purest manifestation in the putative rivalry of father and son for the mother's attention. As Girard points out, however, any such sexual rivalry merely serves to mask the bond produced between the two male rivals, a bond more intense and meaningful than any that exists between either of the rivals with the female beloved.[21] Speaking of a similar bond between Hawthorne's famous rivals Arthur Dimmesdale and Roger Chillingworth, Warren voices his own version of triangular desire: "In the end, the two men are more important to each other than Hester is to either; theirs is the truest 'marriage.'"[22]

Warren's canon contains many such "marriages": homosocial bonds created when male characters vie for a female character, not necessarily to consummate a relationship with her but more likely to effect stronger links between themselves. In fact, Warren's canon is a litany of the son's search for the father—a search often hampered by the intrusive presence of the (m)other. The erotic triangle for which the ring master, the girl acrobat, and the clown provide a model appears in such Warren novels as *At Heaven's Gate* (1943), *All the King's Men* (1946), *World Enough and Time* (1950), and *A Place to Come To* (1977), as well as in such autobiographical works as *Portrait of a Father* (1988). It was a model that would command Warren's fascination for his entire career.

modernism and the circus

When Robert Penn Warren enrolled at Vanderbilt in 1921, the news of modernism had just found its way to that small Methodist university in Nashville, among the most conservative educational enclaves of the South. Allen Tate, older and more experienced than his Guthrie, Kentucky, companion, had also communicated to him his own appreciation for T. S. Eliot and modern poetry. Tate and fellow Fugitive John Crowe Ransom remained diametrically opposed on the issue of the viability of the modernist aesthetic. Warren, however, was not slow to take up the torch. His early poetry was distinctly influenced by Eliot,[23] and Warren biographer Joseph Blotner has interviewed students and colleagues who recall Warren's reciting *The Waste Land* in its entirety from memory.[24]

Warren's preoccupation with the sensibilities of the privileged white male and his conflicted depictions of the feminine and the racial other are traits consistent with the high modernist tendencies of his early career. And yet, even as Warren clings to this modernist tunnel vision so consistent with his conservative southern upbringing, he is aware, as were other modernists, of the diminished stature of his men of privilege and the limited world in which they move. Warren's clown/artist, a version of the modernist hero/artist, also finds himself with a diminished capacity to connect with the rest of the world through his art. Ultimately, this is the quality of Bolton Lovehart's attic circus that reveals the weakness Warren perceives in literary modernism.

Warren's sense of the diminished possibilities of modernism is similarly revealed in his judicious comment on fellow southerner Thomas Wolfe. Commenting wryly on the romantic excesses of Wolfe's novels, Warren noted that Shakespeare was content to write *Hamlet*—he did not have to *be* Hamlet. Oedipal considerations aside, Warren's remark speaks to his personal realization that the role of the artist is to speak to the "ordinary citizens of the Republic."[25] Wolfe's admiration for the circus and circus performers is plain in his short fiction collection, *From Death to Morning* (1935). All the same, in *You Can't Go Home Again* (1934), Wolfe's George Webber looks on disparagingly as the artist Piggy Logan, who critic John Idol notes is modeled after the modernist sculptor Alexander Calder, entertains his audience with a miniature circus, appropriating an icon of mass culture to pander to the jaded tastes of the aficionados of high culture.[26] The source of Warren's circus is much more humble and accessible, compounding his view of Wolfe's southern romanticism and speaking as well to the perceived affectations of modernism. Unlike the nobly romanticized circus folk envisioned by Wolfe, the prototypes of Bolton Lovehart's circus were fashioned by John Wesley Venable, from Hopkinsville, Kentucky. Venable's circus figures, currently on display in Hopkinsville's Pennyroyal Museum and in the Robert Penn Warren Birthplace in Guthrie, Kentucky, owe their fame more to the eccentricity of their creator than to his artistic ability: many are little more than cutouts pasted to cardboard.

Similarly, Bolton Lovehart's fictionalized collection asserts the pitiable inefficacy of art and his weakly realized subversion of family and community. When Bolton donates his carefully crafted circus—a trope for his escape from the bonds of family and community—to support Bardsville's wartime effort, the community accepts it, little understanding Bolton's creation or its cost to him. They adapt Bolton's artistry to fit their own requirements for a myth of history and a truth that allows them to continue as they already are.

Ironically, Bolton's privately subversive circus works in a public way to reaffirm the myth of history, to unite the community within that myth, and to reestablish the ideological tenets on which both depend. In another sense, Bolton's circus creations meet the same fate of modernist art within a mass culture: the intensely private language and style of modernism removes it from popular understanding but not from a popular interpretation.

The circus as southern intertext

Clearly, the pervasiveness of the circus in early and mid-twentieth-century literature of the South marks it as a southern intertext. Circus references appear not only in Warren's fiction but also in the fiction of some of the greatest artists of the Southern Renaissance: Katherine Anne Porter, Caroline Gordon, William Faulkner, Thomas Wolfe, Eudora Welty, and Ralph Ellison. Warren's consistent and canon-enveloping use of the circus, however, reveals the trope as a southern intertext essentially at odds with the concept of patriarchal influence.

In their introduction to *Influence and Intertextuality in Literary History* (1991), theoreticians Jay Clayton and Eric Rothstein argue that to impose a framework of influence on a text is automatically to define it in masculine/patriarchal terms. They further assert that the goals of an influence study are ultimately "hegemonic" and "evaluative"; in other words, texts authored by white males typically provide the hegemonic structure and thus set the evaluative standard. Conversely, Clayton and Rothstein define intertextuality in feminine/matriarchal terms, characterizing the critical goals of such a study as "diffuse" and "inclusive."[27] As would befit his status as premier New Critic, Warren's use of the circus balances this very tension between the masculine and the feminine, exclusive and inclusive. The appearance of the circus trope in both his "Circus in the Attic" and his additional essays, poetry, novels, and memoirs can be read traditionally and patriarchally for the influences—both personal and literary—that have guided Warren's artistic consciousness. And yet, as a result of its reiteration throughout Warren's works as well as among the many texts of the Southern Renaissance, the circus trope serves not only as an intertext and matrix in Warren's own individual canon but also places him most compellingly within the circus intertext of modern southern literature. That the seven authors considered in addition to Warren in this study—Porter, Gordon, Faulkner, Wolfe, Welty, Ellison, and their temporally distant though thematically conjoined colleague

Toni Morrison—are broadly diverse in terms of race, class, and gender speaks all the more compellingly to the intertextual nature of the trope.

In keeping with Clayton and Rothstein's theory, then, a critic intent upon writing a classic "influence study" of the circus trope would begin by tracking the image down to its earliest literary manifestation in the works of a group of interrelated artists such as the writers of the Southern Renaissance. As a result, the originator of the trope would receive the distinction of being named its literary father, through whose influence other lesser artists discovered the trope's value. Yet as Clayton and Rothstein reveal, this approach has evolved into a means of granting hegemonic exclusivity and thus canonicity initially to only a select few artists and then later to those equally few who confirm their ideologies and rhetorical emphases.

This study, however, does not seek to posit Robert Penn Warren as a literary father; in fact, using the circus trope to do so would be well-nigh impossible simply because of the pervasive intertextual presence of the circus in all the works of the Southern Renaissance authors. If anything, it would be much easier to establish Warren as the inheritor of the circus trope rather than as its originator, especially in light of the multifaceted role he played among his Renaissance contemporaries as friend, critic, and editor. Warren is the member of the Southern Renaissance whose singularly intense engagement with a voluminous number of texts of the Southern Renaissance has been documented through his editorial record with the *Southern Review*, in his personal and professional correspondence, in his criticism, in his critical introductions of texts, and in his published interviews. But the conjecture that he utilized the circus trope because he observed his Southern contemporaries doing so first suggests a viable circumstance that nevertheless fails fully to explain its appearance in his canon. Obviously, Warren and his literary companions also utilized the circus because of its part in what Clayton and Rothstein term the "cultural surround"; in other words, it was a part of their cultural upbringing long before any of them read the authors who would eventually comprise the Southern Renaissance. The significance of the trope emerges especially through this overarching cultural awareness of the circus and its several remarkably similar, oft-reiterated, and spontaneously observed parallels with the culture of the South of the first half of the twentieth century.

Robert Penn Warren's Circus Aesthetic and the Southern Circus Intertext

This introductory chapter has provided a brief but relevant history of the American circus during the years of the twentieth century that correspond with the lives and careers of several writers of the Southern Renaissance. Chapter 1, "'The Circus in the Attic': The Matrix for Robert Penn Warren's Aesthetic," will explain the centrality of Warren's novella to his canon through several key aspects: first, the novella's publishing proximity with and thematic links to Warren's most highly regarded novel, *All the King's Men*; second, a close reading of the novella and its major image, the circus; third, its intertextual links with other works in Warren's canon in which circus images appear; and finally, the discussion of the several fathers—including Robert Franklin Warren, Jack Burden, Robert Penn Warren, and, especially, Nathaniel Hawthorne—whose identities inform the character of Bolton Lovehart.

Chapter 2, "Robert Penn Warren's Clown, Acrobat, and Ring Master: 'The Circus in the Attic' as Personal Myth," provides several varied but ultimately interrelated readings of Warren's triangulated characters, the clown, the acrobat, and the ring master. These readings are informed by the social and/or psychological narratives formulated by Sigmund Freud, Jacques Lacan, René Girard, Eve Kosofsky Sedgwick, and Richard King. Readings of the novella in this chapter are reinforced by observations of similar triangular character patterns in additional texts from Warren's canon.

Chapter 3, "'Pure and Impure Poetry': The Circuses of Thomas Wolfe and Robert Penn Warren," examines the materials, methods, and literary programs of two authors of the Southern Renaissance whose contrasting artistic approaches are revealed by their mutual uses of the circus in their canons. The contrast between Robert Penn Warren and Thomas Wolfe is best typified by their choices of real-life models on whom to base their fictional commentaries on literary modernism: sculptor Alexander Calder, who is the inspiration for Piggy Logan in Wolfe's novel *You Can't Go Home Again*, and the eccentric Kentucky hobbyist John Wesley Venable, who inspired Warren to create Bolton Lovehart, the protagonist in "The Circus in the Attic."

Chapters 4 and 5, "The Circus as Southern Intertext: The Myth of History and Initiation into Time" and "Ralph Ellison and Toni Morrison: African American Writers and the Southern Circus Intertext," examine the widespread appearance of the circus in works by authors of the Southern Renaissance. In addition to Robert Penn Warren, who had established an editorial, critical, and/or personal bond with all of these southern authors, they include Katherine Anne Porter, Caroline Gordon, William Faulkner, Eudora Welty, and Ralph Ellison. Although Toni Morrison is not technically a member of the Southern Renaissance, she and her novel *Beloved* (1987) are also included in chapter 5 because of her unique handling of some of the same themes of the Southern Renaissance. All of these authors contrast the superficial enjoyments of the literal circus with the thematically realized image of the circus as a staging ground for learning about cultural subtleties that are particular to the South.

This study concludes by examining why the image of the circus was a particularly compelling one for the writers of the Southern Renaissance as they considered their cultural bonds to the Old South and their moral obligations to the New South. These broad-ranging considerations demand an image to which all members of the Southern Renaissance feel they have a claim and of which they can each speak with equal authority; by finding that image in the circus, these several writers achieve a southern intertext that is both diffuse and inclusive in its accessibility by them regardless of their diverse races, genders, and classes.

Chapter One

"The Circus in the Attic"
The Matrix for Robert Penn Warren's Aesthetic

That has always been the appeal of the circus: it is life
as heightened as imagination can make it. It is also, to
be sure, life as carefully controlled as human precision
can make it, but it is not special effects; it is real.

—John Culhane
The American Circus, 1990

Robert Penn Warren's only collection of short fiction, *The Circus in the Attic and Other Stories,* published in 1947, capitalized on the 1946 publication of his Pulitzer Prize–winning novel *All the King's Men.* At the same time, this collection became a labor of love as Warren revised and reconfigured fictional efforts dating back a decade and a half to the early 1930s. Warren would later call his work on short stories "a kind of accident," confiding, "I never had the same feeling for them as I had for poems or novels."[1] At one point, however, he admitted that he "really liked" the two stories included in the collection that were the last, chronologically, to have been composed—"Blackberry Winter" and "The Circus in the Attic."[2]

As it turned out, Warren's foray into short fiction was necessarily brief yet significant; the stories "Blackberry Winter" and "The Patented Gate and the Mean Hamburger," which appeared with his title novella in the collection *The Circus in the Attic and Other Stories,* have since become anthology favorites. Yet, as Warren quickly recognized, the short-story form appropriated many of his best poetic ideas; he noted in retrospect that "when [his poems] were tied more directly to the sort of thing that might become a short story," he would make the conscious decision to create the poetic form instead. Consequently, Warren gave up writing short stories, which he claimed he had taken up in the thirties to produce "the fast buck."[3] Since writing poetry remained his first love, creatively speaking, he could ill afford the luxury of writing short stories. In another interview, Warren states the case more succinctly: "Short stories kill poems."[4] He claimed not to have written any more after 1946. Included among his uncollected stories, however, are fifteen "pre-publication excerpts" from novels. The best known of these is "Cass Mastern's Wedding Ring," which was excerpted from the work-in-progress *All the King's Men* in 1944.[5]

Thus, the collection *The Circus in the Attic and Other Stories* is considered something of an anomaly within the Warren canon, and the title novella, like most of its companions in the volume, has languished in critical obscurity until quite recently. In 1979, Allan Shepherd found "The Circus in the Attic" notable primarily for the proximity of its composition to Warren's final editing of *All the King's Men* in 1946. Writing dismissively that "in characterization, theme, style, and even, initially, in point of view, resemblances between novella and novel may be detected," Shepherd nevertheless concludes that "even [those resemblances] cannot legitimize 'The Circus in the Attic.'"[6] Even the title of Shepherd's article, "Prototype, Byblow and Reconception: Notes on the Relationship of Warren's *The Circus in the Attic* to His Novels and Poetry," reinforces his contention that the novella is, at best, the bastard offspring of the earlier, more successful novel. Randolph Runyon's 1985 analysis again posits that the significance of the novella is primarily within the collection it introduces. Using a term whose multiple meanings he appropriates for his own purposes, Runyon suggests that the function of the novella is to "articulate"— to speak for, to bind together, and to send tissues of connective imagery to— the other stories within the collection.[7] Conversely, Joseph Millichap's 1992 study of Warren's short fiction grants the novella "critical consideration in its own right" by analyzing Warren's psychobiographical approach as well as his theme, the romance of southern history.[8] Seen from this perspective, "The Circus in the Attic" is revealed as a freestanding work whose richly plied allusions, symbolism, and imagery do credit to the New Critic who created it.

"The Circus in the Attic"

A close reading of "The Circus in the Attic" reveals the care and consistency with which Warren initiated and developed the circus imagery that dominates it. To be sure, the novella begins with the very image that introduces the reader to Jack Burden's hypnotic (if not hypnotized, given Jack's predilection for moral somnambulism) prose style in *All the King's Men:* an automobile gliding over a slick black highway. But whereas Jack's narrative transports the reader more deeply into the political landscape of Willie Stark's unnamed southern domain, the narrator of "The Circus in the Attic" describes the literal landscape of Bardsville, Bolton Lovehart's home and "the county seat of Carruthers County" (4). Jack Burden takes fatalistic pleasure in imagining what would happen if the vehicle in which he is riding succumbed to a sleepy inertia (Jack's own moral tendency) and ran uncontrollably from the road. He even imagines the "love vine" that would grow over the skull and crossbones marker the Highway Department would later place to commemorate the site. In Bardsville, on the other hand, a "love vine" grows embracingly around the memorial of a different type of fatal inertia—the war monument raised by Bardsville's United Daughters of the Confederacy, "the defenders of ancient pieties and the repositories of ignorance of history" (5).

The names of Seth Sykes and Cassius Perkins are prominently etched on the monument. Sykes died during the now-distant days of the Civil War because he was foolish enough to think himself safely isolated from the realities of time and sectional strife, preferring to stay home and farm his land as the war was fought around him. Cash Perkins, similarly honored despite his drunken confidence in his invulnerability in the face of time and war, had actually joined Bardsville's home guard, "a few middle-aged men and a rag-tag-and-bobtail of young boys who could ride like circus performers and to whom the war was a gaudy picnic that their tyrannous mothers would not let them attend" (6). These romantic (and later romanticized) heroes little suspect the ignominious deaths that await them; their brash ignorance is ironized by Cash's hasty, drunken retreat from the Union troops who shoot him dead and by the image of Seth Sykes's blood and brains splattered on the boots of a youthful and untried Union lieutenant. According to the novella's omniscient narrator, Perkins and Sykes retain their dubious standing in history because loyal Bardsvillians, like most people, "always believe what truth they have to believe to go on being the way they are" (8). Consequently, Bardsville, resolutely ignorant of the facts of their deaths, prefers to consider Perkins and Sykes the heroic saviors of their hometown and their southern way of life; Warren's narrator later judges them and "all the heroes who ever died for all their good reasons" (61) as fitting members of Bolton's circus in the attic. Thus early on does Warren demonstrate his thematic intersection of circus with the myth of history.

With our introduction to Bolton Lovehart, the novella's protagonist, the significance of the circus expands to include his search for identity. Bolton is caught between a passionately manipulative mother who lives only to control her child as she would "a clever puppet with beautiful chestnut curls and a lace collar on the velvet jacket" (16) and an austerely aloof father, whose disengagement from life dates from his experiences in the war and his consequent possession of a truth that enables him to "live past all passion" (18). As Bolton is alternately smothered by maternal extremes of frantic possessiveness and left neglected by paternal indifference, the boy understandably begins a search for his own truth. At this point in the narrative, the circus images reappear.

One day, the twelve-year-old Bolton wanders from home and finds himself, without conscious planning, in pursuit of a religious "errand." No doubt Bolton's age and the spiritual nature of his subsequent experience are meant to parallel Jesus's disappearance, at age twelve, in Jerusalem and his parents' subsequent discovery of him receiving instruction from the elders in the temple. In the New Testament account, Jesus asks Mary and Joseph, "How is it that ye sought me? wist ye not that I must be about my Father's business?"[9] Significantly, from this point in Bolton's life, the business of the "fathers" takes on an increasingly circus-like aura.

And so Bolton follows the sound of singing voices to the deep spot in the creek where religious conversions are being marked by baptisms. To his childish eyes, the preacher's coat drips and glitters in the sunshine, and "to the shiny black cloth a few gold willow leaves [are] stuck, here and there, like spangles." Bolton's first circus ideal, the ring master,[10] begins to evolve. The young convert's droopy white dress "billow[s] about her like a dancer" (21), and Bolton's girl acrobat is dimly realized as well. Wandering too close to the drama, Bolton is himself snatched up and baptized, comically pledging himself as a clown in the circus that will grant him a measure of independence from his mother and become an integral part of his lifelong identity.[11]

Bolton is punished for his unseemly fall from the Lovehearts' Episcopal propriety, but this early departure from the social standards set by his mother prepares him for his later flight with an actual circus when it visits Bardsville. This time, Bolton is sixteen, and he coolly plans his escape in advance. As he approaches the railroad spur where the circus train is preparing to leave town, Bolton's view of the departing show folk confirms his archetypal expectations: "the tumult [was] like a flame-streaked Dionysiac revelry or like the terror-stricken confusion of a barbarous tribe, rich in colored cloths and jangling metals and garish tinsel and savage, symbolic beasts, making ready to flee before the cosmic threat of fire or flood" (24).

Bolton is ill suited for this world. He hopes to inaugurate new temporal and historical directives in his life, but all he can offer to demonstrate his willingness to do so are a few of his best arrowheads, bloodless relics that, like his father's Confederate sword and faded regimental flag, are merely romanticized and idealized connections with the past. To Bolton's credit, he perseveres in the face of cruel treatment, scanty food, and minimal lodgings. Nevertheless, within a few days of his being hired to feed and water the circus menagerie, his suitcase is stolen and his arrowheads disappear with it, along with his dreams of joining the world beyond Bardsville. His father soon appears to take him home, where he becomes, "for a moment, a kind of hero" (27) among his schoolmates.[12]

But Bolton cannot sustain the identity of the heroic circus ring master even though he clearly covets the role. For example, at age thirty-three, during his two-week idyll as ticket-taker in Bardsville's old opera house cum moving picture house,[13] he performs his tasks with "the air of an impresario" (38), obviously with the forceful ring master as his model.[14] Once again, his mother thwarts his yearning for a life outside the bounds of propriety and pressures him into quitting his theater job.

After long decades of lost opportunities and maternal oppression, Bolton finally stumbles across a plan that will bring the circus within his own limited sphere, secretly flout his mother's authority, and permit him his own identity. Once again, Bolton sees the circus in Bardsville, but this time it is not a real circus but a child's toy circus. He discovers three miniaturized figures displayed in the local hardware store window: "a ring master dressed in black cloth, a girl acrobat with a stiff little skirt and a painted smirk on her face and eyes far too large and blue, [and] a clown swathed in spotted cloth" (40). In this first clearly delineated description of the trio, the character of the clown now joins the cast of Bolton's circus characters. His addition at this point can only mean Bolton's final acceptance that he will never become the capable ring master; instead, he assumes the subordinate role of the clown.

Indeed, as Bolton grows to the knowledge that he is destined to be his mother's constant companion throughout her lengthy and manipulative hypochondria, his physical appearance becomes progressively more clownlike. He is strange looking to his former school companions, who see "a lanky young man with thinning black hair and very clean unfashionable clothes that always looked awry on his nervous bones" (31). He is clearly more clown than impresario as he stands in the moving picture house "with his trousers too short on his bony shanks and his sleeves too short on the wrists" (38). Bolton's final metamorphosis into the clown is effected once he has "no hair on his head . . . no buttons on his wrinkled coat . . . [and] hands [with] liver spots on the thin skin" (16). Bolton's similarity to the storefront clown is completed, right down to the spotted "garment" of his aging skin.

So it is that Bolton begins to retreat every evening behind a locked attic door to fashion with paint and wood and glue the circus figures that give his life meaning. These figures are very much at home as they line the attic shelves alongside the stamp and arrowhead collections of his childhood, articles displayed with his father's cavalry saber and faded regimental flag. Mrs. Lovehart, reassured that Bolton has abandoned all hope of escape from her, imagines that he is writing a book—the history of Carruthers County—and slowly the rest of Bardsville accepts this explanation for Bolton's seeming disinclination to pursue a manly and socially acceptable occupation. Neither they nor Bolton realizes that history, in a form that would suit the myth-believing, monument-building Bardsvillians, is indeed his grand theme.

After years of happy preoccupation with the attic circus, however, Bolton becomes uncomfortably aware of his own mortality when his mother dies. Mindful that "the hateful painted eyes of the creatures he had made" (45) might someday be the only witnesses to his death, and prepared at that moment to repudiate his circus creations, Bolton reenters the world of Bardsville at age fifty-nine and marries the social-climbing Mrs. Parton, also taking her ne'er-do-well son Jasper into his home.

Appropriately, Mrs. Parton is the embodiment of Bolton's masterpiece, "the girl acrobat, with blue eyes and a skirt of silk" (41). Consistent with her circus identity, she carries her head modestly and watches the people around her "out of the corner of her innocent, china-blue eyes" (47). Furthermore, Mrs. Parton recognizes that Bolton's clown persona is the key to her social success: he has received his standing in Bardsville as his birthright and is like the clown in the hardware store display who balances securely "on top of a ladder, held there by a slot in his wooden feet" (40). Conversely, Mrs. Parton is aware that she must "never [take] a step before she [is] sure of her footing. . . . She [has] seen every rung of the ladder, every stage of the ascent" (47).[15] Marriage to Bolton Lovehart becomes the triumph of her social acrobatics. In meaningful contrast to this careful self-control, however, Mrs. Parton periodically retreats behind closed shades to "make herself a shakerful and drink it and go to bed and lie hot and dizzy and shaking in the dark, and feel her body flow tinglingly away from her" (48). These moments foreshadow her eventual infidelity to Bolton even as they reveal her unmistakably sexual self-awareness.

Jasper Parton, on the other hand, is the ring master come to life, and he, unlike Bolton, exudes a take-charge brand of sexuality. The Oedipal tension between Bolton and Louise Lovehart is reconfigured in Jasper's relationship with his mother, Mrs. Parton, but Jasper is not one to be victimized by maternal control. He asserts himself by calling her "Old Girl," by slapping her on the rump, by marrying against her wishes, and finally by running off to the "circus" of World War II.

Not surprisingly, Bolton has chosen to reenter the world at the very moment it most resembles his attic creations and the tyrannical maternity which was their inspiration. Jasper's enlistment and Bardsville's fervor for war news give added meaning to Bolton's life by granting him a heightened status in the community. Through his stepson's letters, Bolton basks in the reflection cast by Jasper's irrefutable authority as a participant at the European front. Bardsville, newly respectful of the man who before the war had been considered an eccentric at best and a lazy incompetent at worst, now willingly salutes Bolton as an active member of their community. The high point of Bolton's inclusion in the community comes when, upon receiving news of Jasper's death in Italy, he reveals his secret circus and auctions it piecemeal to support the war effort. He privately considers the gift to be an "atonement . . . for the long lie, for all the past" (55–56); the reader recognizes it as an offering to the long lie that *is* the past.

For, like Seth Sykes's and Cash Perkins's "sacrifices," Jasper's death in battle, which Bolton mistakenly perceives as a noble one, conflicts with what the reader knows of that young man's shallow and ignoble personality. Gradually, with the final Allied victory a certainty, Bolton finds his street audiences inattentive and restless. When Mrs. Parton and her army paramour die in a fiery car crash and the end of the war is at hand, Bolton returns grieflessly, automatically, and almost relievedly to his attic and his circus illusions; "finally he had found his way back" (60).

Ultimately, Bolton realizes that the world cannot sustain his circus ideal. In the end, he must retreat to his attic to add to his circus "all the things by which Bardsville had lived, and found life worth living, and died" (62). Jasper is there, as are Simon and Louise Lovehart, the accidental heroes of the Civil War, "and all the heroes who ever died for all their good reasons" (61), reasons which have nothing to do with courage or patriotism or even love but which are founded in "what truth they have to believe to go on being the way they are" (8).

"The Circus in the Attic": The Intertextual Matrix for Warren's Canon

Thematically, "The Circus in the Attic" confronts the myth of southern history while addressing the role art plays in helping the artist achieve self-knowledge and a position in the world beyond that which his art grants him. Confronting these issues with detailed circus personae, while fanciful, is certainly not accidental, nor is it an isolated occurrence in Warren's canon. Indeed, his use of circus personae has much to say about how Warren envisioned himself as an artist and how he defined his own humanity. As critic Joseph Millichap has more recently asserted, Warren's "Circus" is a pivotal point, providing "a controlling metaphor within Warren's diverse artistic achievements."[16]

As I propose to demonstrate in chapters 2, 3, and 4 of this study, the use of the circus image by several artists of the Southern Renaissance establishes it as a southern intertext that conforms with the definition of intertextuality provided by Jay Clayton and Eric Rothstein in their introduction to *Influence and Intertextuality in Literary History* (1991):[17] the image of the circus among writers of the Southern Renaissance is diffuse (rather than "hegemonic") and inclusive (rather than "evaluative") because these writers all relate to the circus as an image to which they have a claim and evince a familiarity regardless of race, gender, or class. On the other hand, the circus intertext also functions as Warren's individual hopeful gesture toward diffuseness and inclusivity within his own canon as the several of his works in which it appears accumulate to gradually define his aesthetic. On occasion, as we will see in chapter 2, the circus intertext will also represent Warren's attempt to understand the feminine other and the racial other, as well as his attempt to discover a balance in his own psyche. Warren's ambivalence for all these tasks of diffuseness and inclusivity—indeed, his ambivalence for the circus image itself—reflects the threat as well as the promise inherent in such an undertaking. To appreciate that ambivalence, however, we must first examine the texts from Warren's canon in which circus images and references appear.

For example, Warren's fascination with the circus acrobat/aerialist metaphor makes an early appearance in a chapter title for *John Brown: The Making of a Martyr* (1929).[18] In "The Tight-Rope Act," John Brown, the historicity of whose political idealism Warren questions, journeys to Kansas not knowing whether to pursue armed conflict there or a compromise over the slavery issue. A few years later, a visiting carnival will provide a prominent setting for one of Warren's early unpublished novels, "The Apple Tree" (1930–32), subsequently retitled "God's Own Time" (1932–33);[19] here, the elopement of protagonist Martha Campbell Miller with a tent-show evangelist reiterates Warren's conflation of spiritual and political fanaticism in *John Brown* and foreshadows Warren's later superimposition of the circus on dramatic religiosity in "The Circus in the Attic."

In *At Heaven's Gate* (1943), Warren's second published novel, circus images make a particularly vivid appearance. Socialite Sue Murdoch has exchanged both the life of moral ease her mogul father provides her and the clownishly staid boyfriend who is her father's protégé for an enlightened, bohemian life style. In a climactic scene, Warren suggests Sue's suspension in time between her recent abortion of a baby fathered by a Marxist labor leader and her murder by Slim Sarrett, a rejected lover. In actions evocative of Mrs. Parton's periodic abandonment of her rigid social control, Sue lies on her bed in a darkened room and drinks heavily from the bottle at her bedside. First, her mind slides "slowly, then swoopingly, off into blackness, and she [does] not feel or think anything." Then, surfacing "like a diver who has gone down deep," she allows herself to slip away once more, "feeling like a trapeze performer who, at the end of a long, wonderful arc, releases her hold on the bar and sails effortlessly, superbly, royally over the lights and faces upturned so far below, the darling of the circus." Slim Sarrett then joins Sue in the darkened room and strangles her as she lies on the bed. After only nominal resistance, Sue's body settles back, "as though she were composing and adjusting herself."[20]

The circus references in Warren's next novel, *All the King's Men* (1946), however, are so similar to those in his later "Circus" novella that one could easily wonder whether the novella is merely a shorter, lesser version of the novel— its bastard child, as Allen Shepherd has previously claimed—or whether the novella is instead an artistically contrived gloss on the novel that preceded it.

As in *At Heaven's Gate,* the girl acrobat provides the most overt circus reference in *All the King's Men,* while the clown and ring master can be inferred from her presence. In one central passage, Jack Burden, on a "dirt-digging" expedition for Willie Stark, seeks out the Scholarly Attorney, the man he believes is his father. Jack finds him attending to a mission project, a man named George who spends his time making sculpted angels from masticated bread dough. George's tragedy, recounted with Jack's characteristic irreverence, is having witnessed the death of his wife, who was the "flying angel," a circus aerialist. George is so traumatized by this experience that he can no longer perform his own high-wire act. More to the point, Jack's failure to equate George's experience with his own symptoms of psychic and moral paralysis is yet another example of his patent lack of self-awareness.[21]

One is reminded of George and his aerialist wife as Jack later reflects on the first summer of his own strangely attenuated and languorous love affair with Anne Stanton. Anne's daring leaps from the hotel high-dive tower become a dominant image of that summer; their Freudian implications grow stronger as Jack's and Anne's desire for one another steadily increases. In language recalling Mrs. Parton's circus identity, Jack watches Anne climb the ladder "rung by rung" then hit the water "as though she had dived through a great circus hoop covered with black silk spangled with silver" (288).

Unlike the clownish Bolton Lovehart, Jack has no need of slotted feet to hold him safely on the rungs of the high-dive ladder; he has no intention of climbing the ladder, much less of flinging himself from it. Social acrobatics are superfluous for Anne, the daughter of the former governor Stanton. Instead, her dives go to the heart of Mrs. Parton's circus identity and bespeak their mutual acceptance of self, sexuality, and mortality, as well as a strangely hopeful idealism—qualities in Anne and potentially in himself that Jack will ultimately reject.

His preference for observation over action, the same character flaw that keeps Bolton Lovehart literally and figuratively secluded in his attic, is the crux of Jack's failed romance. In their unconsummated tryst in his mother's house, Anne allows herself to be undressed "as though she were lifting her arms for a dive" (294). Disconcertingly, she settles herself on Jack's bed in the unmistakable posture, as critic Randolph Runyon has observed, of "a corpse, or a figure carved on a tomb";[22] her thus arranging herself also evokes Sue Murdoch's settling herself into a similar deathlike position. The mortal dimensions of self that Anne willingly acknowledges in her sexuality, however, are the very aspects of his own being from which Jack ignominiously retreats.

Although other circus references can be inferred in Warren's later novels of the1950s, 1960s, and 1970s (even when the clown, the acrobat, and the ring master are not specifically named, their triple dynamic is constantly repeated), such circus references make overt appearances in three revealing poems that appear late in his career. In this sense, the circus literally becomes the matrix of his canon since it leads Warren's creative sensibility inexorably to a resolution of his conflicted relationship with his mother, the protoypical feminine other in Warren's life.[23]

The volume in which these poems appear is *Being Here: Poetry 1977–80* (1980). As its multiple epigraphs indicate, Warren's topic is time examined abstractly through art and experienced concretely in aging bones. Seeming to have more to say about the personal sources for *Being Here,* and yet understandably reluctant to reveal them, Warren includes an "Afterthought" to the poems in which he admits to his reader that their "thematic order . . . is played against . . . a shadowy autobiography, . . . an autobiography [that] represents a fusion of fiction and fact."[24] Clearly Warren struggles with whether to privilege memory or imagination. Both elements, of course, are present in his "October Picnic Long Ago," although certain autobiographical aspects of the poem will later be confirmed by Warren's reminiscence *Portrait of a Father* (1987, 1988).

In many ways *Being Here* could be described as Warren's "portrait of a mother," especially in those parts of the text that examine the intersections of self and death-bound idealism, moments represented here as elsewhere by a feminine mortality linked to circus images. For example, in "October Picnic Long Ago" (381), mingled *shadow and light* like the mingling of memory and imagination, change the familiar faces of mother, father, sister, and baby "*till we looked like a passel of circus freaks crammed tight / On four wheels*" (7, 9–10). Here, Warren claims his circus and its implications, but not without an ambivalence revealed through the poem's several repositionings in narrative perspective. Warren is observer and participant in this family tableau, unwillingly distanced from his parents' unity, "heads together as though in one long conversation / That even now I can't think has had an end" (23–24). All the same, he is joined to the mother he had once resented by a belated adult awareness that the Future, "a hound with a slavering fang," (34) bears a mortality that will be deflected neither by her optimistic song nor by her joy in her gathered family. Older now than his parents had been at the time this poetic recollection is set, Warren realizes that not even his then-youthful mother, whose death in 1931 at age fifty-six was a source of guilty relief for her son, had anticipated the questions he now asks; even if she had, she would still not have the wisdom of his current perspective. At seventy-five, Warren can admit in the Afterthought to *Being Here* that "in life, meaning is . . . more fruitfully found in the question asked than in any answer given" (441). For Warren, nearing the end of his life and necessarily coming to terms with mortality, acknowledging the question must serve.

Warren poses the question again in "Ballad of Your Puzzlement," but unwillingly, as a note attached parenthetically to the title reveals: "*(How not to recognize yourself as what you think you are, when old and reviewing your life before death comes).*"[25] Warren's reluctance to own his certain mortality is again demonstrated by his narrative perspective; the poetic voice addresses a second-person "you" who could be the reader or the self-addressed speaker.[26] In a second remove of perspective, however, that recalls Bolton Lovehart's flirtation with the cinema, the speaker notes that one's recollections of a life past are "Like a movie film gone silent, / With a hero strange to you / And a plot you can't understand" (8–10).

The "hero" Warren observes demonstrates aspects of the three personae already familiar to us through each of the stages of his life. His first identity is as a man who seeks Truth passionately, and who, "clutching his balance-pole, / Looks down at . . . / . . . the crowd swarm like ants, far below" (16–18). As a truth seeker who risks his equilibrium on "the fated / and human high-wire of lies" (19–20), he is uncomfortably aware that the watching crowd will be appalled but gratified by his inevitable fall.

His second identity is comparable to that of the assertive ring master as portrayed by Jasper Parton—carnally responsive and morally numb. He is simultaneously a victim of his own physical desires, "the sweetness of deathly entrapment" (34), and a sexual predator whose phallic blade "slides slick to the woman's heart" (48).

Finally, the praying hero, presented as a "Chaplinesque" clown, yearns for fellowship with the world, which appears to him in the guise of a "loathsome beggar." Even so, the hero "stares at the sores and filth / With slow-rapt kinship" (49–50), but when he reaches out to touch the cancered cheek, he finds himself suddenly transported to a barren Beckett-like landscape and an empty "height of sky" (58).

As interesting as these late appearances of the acrobat, the ring master, and the clown are, they are even more significant because Warren claims each as part of his own identity, even the previously feminized acrobat. Here they function as metaphors for three stages of human life: truth-asserting youth, thrill-seeking young adulthood, and an old age in which he, having lived past both of the former two stages, recognizes and accepts their absurd manifestations and consequences. As Warren concludes,

> Yes, all, all huddle together
> In your Being's squirming nest,
> Or perhaps you are only
>
> A wind-dangled mirror's moment
> That flickers in light-streaked darkness.
> It is hard to choose your dream. (70–75)

In a later poem in the collection, "Aspen Leaf in Windless World,"[27] Warren restates these possibilities when he speculates on the nature of the "unworded revelation" (4) awaiting him at death, the "image—behind blind eyes when the nurse steps back" (25). Would it be the eastern sun and a smiling face? A "great, sky-thrusting menhir" (29)? Or would he see instead a vision from his long-lost childhood that speaks of age and disillusionment, "Tinfoil wrappers of chocolate, popcorn, nut shells, and poorly / Cleared up, the last elephant turd on the lot where the circus had been" (31–32)?

"The Circus in the Attic" and patriarchal influence

Interwoven, however, with the evidences of circus intertextuality that link Warren's novella with his other works is an insistent patriarchal thread of influence, which is, again in Clayton and Rothstein's terminology, evaluative and hegemonic rather than diffuse and inclusive. The title of the single written chapter in Bolton's stillborn history of Carruthers County is "The Coming of the Fathers," in which Bolton parrots the myths of Bardsville's past that have established themselves as the truth that all Bardsvillians have to believe "to go on being the way they are." And even though this written record is soon superceded by Bolton's attention to his alternate narrative, the attic circus, both the written history and the circus miniatures speak to a patriarchal legacies of southern ideology and literary influence.

Warren's Bolton Lovehart reflects the legacies of no fewer than four "fathers." His precursor, as critic Allan Shepherd has suggested, is Jack Burden, who struggles, as the narrator of his own text, with southern ideology, history, and paternity. Bolton's alter ego is Warren's own father, Robert Franklin Warren, whose ambivalent relationship with Warren is figured in "The Circus in the Attic" by the tensions experienced between the clown and the ring master. Because these tensions prove so difficult to reconcile, Warren, Bolton's third father, must, like his creation, ultimately father himself by crafting his art and thus establishing his artistic identity.[28] Finally, however, the father whose literary influence is most meaningfully paralleled with the circus intertext of the novella is Nathaniel Hawthorne.

Robert Penn Warren's "Nathaniel Hawthorne"

Robert Penn Warren's critical interest in Nathaniel Hawthorne is amply illustrated by the variety of his published treatments of his nineteenth-century forebear. As early as 1928, a very youthful Warren wrote a review of a Hawthorne biography that its author Herbert Gorman had interestingly subtitled *A Study in Solitude*. In this review, Warren speaks authoritatively to the issue of "Hawthorne as a recluse" as well as to "the remote, abstract quality of his treatment of character, and the preoccupation with symbol."[29]

Warren's admiration for Hawthorne was manifestly evident when, at a later time and for a different generation, he argued that "Hawthorne *Was Relevant*" in his acceptance speech for the National Medal for Literature, delivered at the Library of Congress in 1970. Warren asserted that Hawthorne demonstrated "the writer's own grounding in his time, the relation of his sensibility to his time, and paradoxically enough, . . . his resistance to his time," all crucial elements of literary relevancy in the critic's eyes.[30]

Three years later, Warren's most lengthy and comprehensive treatment of Hawthorne's life and art appeared with the 1973 publication of the textbook anthology *American Literature: The Makers and the Making.*[31] In his introduction, "Nathaniel Hawthorne," Warren writes not only a perceptive critical analysis of his subject's literary aesthetic but also what could be read as a revealingly subjective narrative of his life. Years later, recalling the pleasures and dilemmas of coediting the anthology with Warren and Cleanth Brooks, R. W. B. Lewis discloses what is already evident in Warren's introduction: Hawthorne was Warren's personal hero.[32] Without a doubt, Warren identified strongly with Hawthorne the man and Hawthorne the artist. Significantly, Warren gives the most space in his introduction to "My Kinsman, Major Molineaux," in which work he cites Saturnalian elements (which we would currently style as carnivalesque) in the midst of a search for a surrogate father, and to *The Scarlet Letter,* whose character dynamic mirrors the very triangularity that dominates "The Circus in the Attic."

The extent to which Hawthorne was a personal hero to Warren is demonstrated as early as the first paragraph of Warren's lengthy introduction to Hawthorne in *American Literature: The Makers and the Making.* In the introduction, the essence of Hawthorne, man and artist, is captured in such a way as to reveal Warren's own artistic and personal empathy with him. R. W. B. Lewis quotes the entire passage in his analysis of "Warren's sense of Hawthorne's creative passion, and the palpable passion of Warren's creative affinity *with* Hawthorne."[33] I can do no less than he to demonstrate how the passage that follows allowed Warren the opportunity to speak insightfully of Hawthorne as well as to speak revealingly of himself:

> He lived in the right ratio—right for the fueling of his genius—
> between an attachment to his region and a detached assessment
> of it; between attraction to the world and contempt for its gifts;
> between a powerful attraction to women and a sexual flinch;
> between a capacity for affection and an innate coldness; between
> aesthetic passion and moral concern; between a fascinated atten-
> tiveness to the realistic texture, forms, and characteristics of nature
> and human nature, and a compulsive flight from that welter of life
> toward abstract ideas; and between, most crucially of all, a deep
> knowledge of himself and an ignorance of himself *instinctively*
> cultivated in a fear of the darker potentialities of self.
>   The drama of such subjective tensions is played out objectively
> in the work. Hawthorne is the first American writer of fiction in
> whose work we can sense the inner relation of life to fiction.[34]

Having brought Warren and Hawthorne into psychic and artistic alignment, it requires but a step further to realize recreated in Bolton Lovehart the artistic qualities Warren recognized in Hawthorne. Initially, Bolton comes to represent the Hawthornesque artist whose inner life is driven by his art, in Bolton's case, a fictional circus. Furthermore, Warren's introduction characterizes the youthful Hawthorne as he had previously characterized Bolton—transfixed by the "contrast between the great past and the meager present" as well as by "the nostalgic appeal of a lost glory and a lost certainty of mission" (433). Warren makes much of his perception of Hawthorne's two conflicting desires: to be, like active men of his acquaintance, "'a man in society,' [learning] 'the deep warm secret' by which other people seemed to live but which somehow eluded him" (434) and to seclude himself, like the attic-bound Bolton, "on the third floor of a house . . . in Salem. . . . [In] the famous 'dismal chamber' under the eaves, where he isolated himself to discover his materials, his style, and his destiny" (435). Finally, like Bolton, Warren's Hawthorne, feeling all too deeply his fatherless state, is mysteriously bound to his mother in a relationship that is "charged in a way which [he] himself did not even suspect until his sudden and overmastering emotion at her death released him . . . for the supreme effort of composing *The Scarlet Letter,* the most moving and deeply human of his works" (434).[35]

Like Hawthorne, Bolton's attic apprenticeship, followed by his mother's death, permits him—in fact, practically demands from him—a more informed and empathetic entry into the world, troubled and temporary though that entry might be. Warren notes that the series of stories Hawthorne composed before *The Scarlet Letter*—"The Snow Image," "The Great Stone Face," and "Ethan Brand"—deal either directly or tangentially with an obsessed hero who, through his preference for cold observation, has "lost his hold of the magnetic chain of humanity" by "converting man and woman to be his puppets" (445). Veering psychically from this Hawthornesque realization, Bolton reenters his community and reclaims his humanity by marrying Mrs. Parton and symbolically fathering the tragic, war-bound boys whom he welcomes into his home; Hawthorne, in his turn, writes *The Scarlet Letter.* Their artistic responses to their mutual fears of becoming alienated from humanity reveal each of them to their respective communities in ways that are unexpected, if not shocking. Witness, in the case of Hawthorne, Warren's report of Emerson's murmur of "Ghastly, ghastly," Sophia Hawthorne's "grievous headache," and Julian Hawthorne's comment that "he found it impossible to reconcile the father he had known with the author of the fiction" after each had read *The Scarlet Letter* (446). Correspondingly, in the case of "The Circus in the Attic," we have Bardsville's belated and bemused realization of Bolton's true attic occupation, the ironic implications of which they would be unlikely to appreciate.

15

But whereas this community response would be deflating enough, it is nothing compared to Hawthorne's and Bolton's mutual realizations of having failed to measure up to the standards of the fathers. Again, Warren cites Emerson's evaluation of Hawthorne at the younger man's death in 1864— an evaluation in which he announced himself "sternly disappointed" in Hawthorne's work (456).[36] Similarly, in "The Circus in the Attic," Bolton's circus creations are clearly only a diminished version of what he imagines as his father's heroic Civil War service, which is later reconfigured in his inflated perception of Jasper's "heroism" in World War II.

In Bolton's case, as in Warren's critical narrative of Hawthorne, the gesture toward joining the world is impossible to sustain, primarily because of the artistic materials each values and requires. As Warren characterizes Hawthorne as a "*writer of romance . . . [who] aims at converting the past into a myth for the present*" (459), we are reminded of Bolton Lovehart, whose circus is inspired by but limited to the myth of southern history. As Warren further notes, Hawthorne's "fiction is . . . a projection of his problem of relating himself to 'reality'" (459) and discovering himself therein. Unfortunately, the possibilities for self-knowledge, while promising, are threatening as well. From this ambivalence, the fearful need to know oneself, arises Hawthorne's artistic commitment to symbol, which Warren passes on to Bolton. This method of relating artistically to the world produces the semblance of a connection with real life which is subverted nonetheless by subconsciously distancing oneself from it. Not that Hawthorne was completely unaware of what his reliance on symbol signified; Warren agrees with Charles Feidelson's assessment that symbolism "at once fascinated and horrified him" (459), probably in much the same way that Bolton is horrified by the prospect of his lonely death beneath the watchful, hateful eyes of his circus creations. Finally, just as Warren's Bolton retreats "almost relievedly" to his attic room and his circus figures, so Warren's Hawthorne retreats more and more within himself until death becomes his triumphant escape from a life too fraught with painful, "hell-fired" ambiguities. He leaves the world nothing of himself but his enigmatic tales and romances. Indeed, Warren muses, "There is something symbolically appropriate, something consistent with the temper of his own work, in the fact that [Hawthorne] died alone, in a hotel room, in the middle of the national tragedy of the [Civil] war" (456).

How are we to read Hawthorne's retreat to a self-imposed alienation, only perfected in death, and Bolton's final retreat to his attic? Are these men to be judged victorious over a shallow, unappreciative world or damned by the very hell-firedness they pursued? Perhaps the answer is found in Warren's refusal to take a morally critical stance against either. Perhaps his failure to do so is founded in his own personal investment in the persona of the artist. At this point, it is important to note Warren's summation of Hawthorne's *The Scarlet Letter,* in which he defends the actions of the three principals and extends the possibility not only of their redemption but also, by extension, of Bolton Lovehart's:

> [M]en must live by the logic of their illusions, as best they can— Dimmesdale by his, Hester by hers, and Chillingworth by his. . . . What compensation is possible in such a world comes from the human capacity for achieving scale and grandeur even in illusion, one might say by insisting on the coherence of the illusion, and from the capacity for giving pity.
> This is the hell-firedness of *The Scarlet Letter.* (453–54)

The Scarlet Letter, in turn, reflects Hawthorne's own coherence of illusion as well as his capacity for giving pity. The novel is his hope for redemption despite the ever-widening gulf Warren's narrative reveals between Hawthorne and common humanity at the end of his life. Correspondingly, Bolton's circus, lovingly crafted through years of isolation in his attic, then broken up and sold to demonstrate his commitment to his community, becomes his redemption, despite his last retreat from the world.

Bolton's resemblance to Hawthorne further explains Warren's tenderly empathetic treatment of him in the face of his ideologically questionable stance on the Lost Cause of the South. Warren's depiction of Hawthorne's stance of racial "gradualism" in the face of the North's growing abolitionism as the Civil War approached reminds his reader of how attuned to Warren's own youthful segregationist views Hawthorne's racial politics had been.[37] Historically, both Warren's and Hawthorne's stances were proven wrong-headed, as Warren had already personally acknowledged by the time of his composition of "Nathaniel Hawthorne." Perhaps Warren's empathy with Hawthorne may explain why he considers Bolton as an artist first and a man second, making art the justification for his ideological faults. To see how Warren characterizes the glory of Hawthorne's art, then, is to realize the four qualities he values in Bolton Lovehart the artist.

First, Hawthorne's art, and, by extension, Bolton Lovehart's circus figures, manage to "distinguish and render images of that infinitely complicated process by which self-knowledge may be approached." Second, "out of the personal struggle, [Hawthorne] manage[s] to create images which, without losing the urgency of the individual (author or character) embodied the relevance of the typical, and which . . . serve as mirrors of haunting revelation to us all" (460). Third, according to Warren, Hawthorne created an American fiction of "deeper psychology" in which "the inward and the outward dramas are intricately intertwined and constitute, in fact, a coherent dialectic." Warren's final critical statement on Hawthorne, however, affirms both this nineteenth-century father and Bolton Lovehart in terms that give ascendancy to their identities as artists. The final glory of Hawthorne's art, Warren asserts, is that "it is art" (461).

"The circus in the Attic" and the Burden of the patriarchy

As deeply felt as Warren's admiration for Hawthorne is, an undercurrent of sadness, of unwilling identification with his subject, runs through Warren's biographical consideration of this literary father. Indeed, all of the paternal relationships revealed through the character of Bolton Lovehart bespeak the same ambivalent admiration and reluctant empathy. I have previously noted the intersections of composition, character, and theme in the novella "The Circus in the Attic" and the novel *All the King's Men* that show how Bolton Lovehart has been fathered by Jack Burden, for example. As surely as Warren's use of circus imagery unmistakably links the novel to the novella and one protagonist to the other, however, his change of narrative focus in the novella points to its veiled purpose: providing an imaginative commentary on the creation of *All the King's Men*. Furthermore, "The Circus in the Attic" was written in 1946, the same year as Warren's final editing of *All the King's Men*[38]—a time when he would naturally find himself reconsidering the themes and purposes of the novel.

In this sense, the novella is a "portrait of the artist," detailing the joys and sorrows attendant to Warren's creation of the novel that remains, to this day, his most highly acclaimed achievement. Indeed, many details point to the autobiographical nature of "Circus" and its protagonist Bolton Lovehart: Bardsville's similarity to Clarksville, Tennessee, a town with considerable meaning and significance for the Warren family; Bolton's real fascination for and preoccupation with history and Warren's own well-documented interest in it; and the real ambivalence that each man experiences with his native region—Warren makes an early physical escape from it but returns imaginatively, while Bolton remains physically and escapes imaginatively.[39]

To posit "The Circus in the Attic" as a portrait of the artist reaffirms the depths in Bolton Lovehart's multilayered identity. Certainly, the youthful

Bolton, "his trousers too short on his bony shanks and his sleeves too short on the wrists" (38), replicates the gawky, young Red Warren. On the other hand, the older, balding, and age-spotted Bolton, whose sacrificial sale of his circus affirms his surrogate paternity to Jasper Parton, evokes Warren's own father, Robert Franklin Warren, a once-hopeful poet who had abandoned the inner creative life to embrace marriage and fatherhood. Warren's loving memoir of this self-sacrificial "man of mystery" is no "portrait of the artist" but instead titled *Portrait of a Father*.[40] Thus, Allan Shepherd's assertion that "The Circus in the Attic" is the bastard child of Warren's canon is further refuted by this fictionalized conflation of Warren's identity with his father's; the novella's compelling legitimacy emerges when, through it, Warren locates his father in himself and himself in his true father.

Yet a final and crucial autobiographical link has to do with what Joseph Millichap has referred to as Bolton's identity as "artist manqué" as well as with the details of Warren's personal life during the creation of *All the King's Men*.[41] Bolton's imaginative involvement with the circus characters becomes so intense that he is most comfortable in the real world only when it conforms to his circus illusion. When he volunteers to auction away his circus figures to further Bardsville's wartime effort, the community, although surprised to learn the nature of what he has actually been creating all these years, accepts his offer. The circus is broken up, parceled out, and never really appreciated for what it has meant to Bolton's survival. Bolton's final return to his attic could very well signify that he has been defeated in his attempt to convert imaginative illusion into a lasting human reality.

Warren may have experienced a similar ironic reversal and some very understandable doubts while he was writing "The Circus in the Attic." He had no way of knowing that *All the King's Men,* which, as Warren later revealed, was completed in an "attic room" in the University of Minnesota library, would bring him professional recognition and acclaim.[42] The fact that it did bring such recognition and acclaim must eventually have weighed heavily against the unhappy reality of his personal life, in which he was witnessing not only the steady dissolution of his long, strained marriage to Cinina Brescia, from whom he was finally divorced in 1951, but also the waning of his ability to write lyric poetry. The seeming inevitability of those two failures was poised in bitter opposition to his success as a novelist. Correspondingly, in the fifty years since the novel's first publication, critics have debated the further inevitability of Jack Burden's personal failures against the possibility of a hopeful dénouement, suggested but never effected in *All the King's Men,* when Jack predicts his eventual emergence with Anne into the "convulsion of the world" and "the awful responsibility of Time" (438). If, as I believe, Warren created Bolton Lovehart as fellow clown, outsider, and observer of history and crafted his character after the example of Jack Burden, then Bolton's eventual retreat to the safe world of artistic illusion may further signify Jack's retreat—and Warren's as well.

Chapter Two

Robert penn warren's clown, Acrobat, and Ring Master
"The circus in the Attic" as personal Myth

> *[The acrobat was] a beautiful little rag doll twirling*
> *far over our heads, charming her faithful, her smile*
> *filled with promise. Though then very young, I*
> *remember her very well, for I had planned to marry*
> *her right after the matinee, but forgot it during the*
> *Wild West show.*
>
> —Robert Lewis Taylor
> *Center Ring*, 1956

The narrative of Nathaniel Hawthorne's life and artistry contained within Robert Penn Warren's "Nathaniel Hawthorne," one of many critical biographies included in the anthology *American Literature: The Makers and the Making*, reveals at every turn the critic's fascination with Oedipal triangulation. This troubled psychological geometry appears first with Warren's analysis of Hawthorne's relationship with his absent seafaring father and his subsequently widowed mother; it reappears as Warren describes how Hawthorne's relationships with his wife Sophia and his friend Ralph Waldo Emerson (that ubiquitous Transcendental father) are redefined as a result of both having bemusedly read *The Scarlet Letter*, which artistically enshrines the triangulated tensions that draw Hester, Dimmesdale, and Chillingworth together emotionally, spiritually, and intellectually. No matter, as Warren hastens to observe, that Hawthorne had been long dead by the time Freud's theories were published, for Freud himself insisted that his theories had already been validated by the intuitive, albeit unscientific, work of thinkers and writers whose lives and careers had predated his own.[1]

James Justus, whose *Achievement of Robert Penn Warren* (1981) remains the definitive study of Warren's canon, describes Warren's disinclination to write jargon-ridden psychological criticism. Despite Warren's avoidance of even the most commonly accepted Freudian language, however, Justus recognizes in his criticism the most common tenets of Freudian investigation: "the psychological intricacies involved in a writer's conversion of autobiography into art."[2] Certainly this aspect of Warren's aesthetic suggests the tenet of traditional Freudian psychology that is currently one of the most criticized.[3]

The Freudianism of Warren's introduction to Nathaniel Hawthorne's works is a case in point; as useful as Warren finds the ordering principle permitted by Oedipal triangulation, he readily admits its limitations for his own critical purposes. In his analysis of the Hawthorne text most often explicated beneath a Freudian template, "My Kinsman, Major Molineaux," Warren registers an immediate qualification to any too-ready adoption of Freud's psychoanalytic perspective:

> This Freudian "meaning" is . . . only one of the several which flow
> into the story . . . and clearly does not account for all the elements
> in it. The Freudian approach deals with a natural process, presumably, but the process occurs in a social, moral, and philosophical
> context and, in fact, has come to exist only in such contexts.[4]

From this point, Warren peels the layers of meaning away from Hawthorne's classic tale of filial rebellion, using not only psychological but also social, historical, and philosophical contexts to do so.

Much the same method can be used to extract meaning from Warren's own nod to the Hawthornesque, "The Circus in the Attic." Admittedly, the novella reflects an insistent Oedipal triangulation; Freud's were, after all, the dominant psychological theories of Warren's time. Nevertheless, the triangular character structures in the novella point also to other possible social, historical, and cultural considerations reiterated in Warren's earlier and later works; these elements encourage his readers to examine possibilities that, like Hawthorne's insights into Freud's theories-to-come, were there to be examined all along but which they are only now empowered to appreciate through the formulations of contemporary literary theories. These formulations include not only Freudian and Lacanian psychology but also René Girard's concept of triangular desire, Eve Kosofsky Sedgwick's concept of male homosocial desire, and Richard King's formulation of the southern family romance. Applying these formulations to "The Circus in the Attic," a unique work in Warren's canon, will demonstrate its role as the matrix from which his reiterated themes, structures, and meanings emanate.

warren and freud: the gendered subject

Several images in "The Circus in the Attic" foreshadow the Freudian triad which is replicated first in the family structure of the Loveharts (Simon, Louise, and Bolton), next in Bolton's circus characters (the ring master, the acrobat, and the clown), and finally in Bolton's late-life family (himself, Mrs. Parton, and his surrogate son, Jasper). One such image is the photographic tableau of the Loveharts moving slowly down their brick walk, Bolton in the middle grasping his parents' hands. The most important of these images, however, becomes apparent as the faint but rhythmic pulse of old-fashioned gospel hymns draws a twelve-year-old Bolton (much as other boys his age were drawn by the circus calliope and its exciting promise) to the creek bank to witness ritual baptisms. For the adolescent Bolton, this unlooked-for religious experience will symbolically confirm his need to navigate the Oedipus complex successfully and establish the role the circus metaphor will play in the rest of his adult life.

Despite the solemnity of the baptismal proceedings, their tone is markedly sexual, further evidence of the Freudian in the novella. The primary actor in this scene is the "tall preacher" whose glittering, creek-soaked clothing creates a spangled, ring master effect. As the conduit through whom his rapt followers seek salvation, he is a person of knowledge and power. His first convert is a young girl whose virginal white dress nonetheless renders her evocatively dancer-like. She is as weak and uncertain as the preacher is strong and convicted, and his baptism of her, accomplished "not too gently," is recounted in terms of sexual domination:

> For an instant she refused to give over, and as he was about to
> place his other hand upon her face to save her from strangulation,
> she seized it desperately in both her own and clasped it to her
> breast. With that, all in one motion, she let herself go, arching her
> back somewhat, in surrender, and letting her head fall back, with
> her eyes wide to the sky. (21)

After having witnessed this baptism and others, Bolton moves quietly yet purposefully to the creek's edge, ensuring that he will also be among those whom the preacher immerses. His willing submission to the preacher bespeaks less a commitment to the heavenly Father (to whom the young girl convert had sent a supplicating look upward before her immersion) than to his single earthly father and multiple cultural fathers as models and guides. Terry Eagleton eloquently describes this very step in the Oedipal process:

> [To the boy-child] his father symbolizes a place, a possibility, which he himself will be able to take up and realize in the future. If he is not a patriarch now, he will be later. The boy makes peace with his father, identifies with him, and is thus introduced into the symbolic role of manhood. He has become a gendered subject, surmounting his Oedipus complex.[5]

As long as he is his father's son in his father's house, Bolton realizes the Oedipal necessity of his maintaining the clown's role in the circus triad. He aspires, however, to the patriarch's role, the role of the ring master, and depends on his father, Simon Lovehart, to instruct him in achieving that role.

Simon, however, whose psychic and perhaps sexual impotence is physically manifested in his limping gait, fails to enact the role that would ultimately liberate his son from his clownish boyhood. Because of his disinclination for personal conflict and his even stronger disinclination for life, Simon acts unwittingly as Louise Lovehart's ally in her campaign to possess Bolton totally and thus block his movement into a patriarchal role. Simon returns her sixteen-year-old son to her after the boy runs away with the circus; later, and even more tragically, he leaves Bolton to her emasculating devices when he weakly surrenders to the fatal effects of his stroke. Consigning Bolton to Louise's will—"Be good—to your mother—son" (29)—Simon dies without ever answering the "thousand questions" Bolton had never thought to ask until he had lost the opportunity. And try as he will after Simon's death, Bolton is continually frustrated by his mother's will when he attempts to assume the role of the ring master; instead, he becomes daily more clownlike, trapped in rather than surmounting his Oedipus complex.

Thus, in Freudian terms, the novella's conflict arises from Bolton's failed struggle to assume the glorified patriarchal role for which he had, willingly and yet of necessity, sacrificed his pre-Oedipal childhood. Ironically, the widowed Louise's assumption of that self-involved and pleasure-seeking pre-Oedipal state demands that Bolton join her there indefinitely, or at least for as long as she lives. Indeed, widowed and bedridden after her heart attack, Louise regresses into girlhood, becoming "almost pretty . . . , young-looking, fresh, and clear-eyed" (30). As the years pass, she is "impervious to time. . . . [Living] as though sustained in the heart of a timeless peace" (44). Louise's unwillingness to acknowledge her movement beyond the Oedipal complex, as evidenced by her emotional attachment to her father's surname (Bolton) and her father's church (Episcopal), and by her consequent "disappointment in the marriage bed" (16), denies Bolton his own psychic movement beyond the Oedipus complex and thus beyond her influence, leaving the young man in social and sexual dormancy. Bolton's several rebellious acts counter Louise's own obsessions: his first act of religious affiliation is for the socially inferior Baptist Church rather than the Episcopal Church; his escape with the circus is marked by his repudiation of his true name for that of "Joe Randall"; finally, his seduction by Sara Darter becomes, for him, both a "victory" over and a "betrayal" of his mother; afterward, he finds the courage for further covert gestures toward selfhood.

Clearly, Simon Lovehart's sin of omission toward his son, his decision to disturb as little as possible "the powerful, vibrating, multitudinous web of life which binds the woman and child together" (17),[6] has a powerful effect on Bolton's life. Regardless of his failings, however, a Freudian reading of the family romance in "The Circus in the Attic" focuses much more emphatically on the castrating effect of Louise Lovehart's sin of commission—her "intensity of egotism" that paradoxically becomes a "selfless and absorbing passion" for her son (16). Louise embodies all that feminist critics have decried as antifeminist in Freudian theory: in denying Bolton his patriarchal sexuality, she effectively preempts it, indulging her own "penis envy" in the process.

Of course, one classic purpose of making a Freudian reading of any literary text is to facilitate locating autobiographical details within the work—to read the writer by interpreting the work. "The Circus in the Attic" seems particularly amenable to such application since, according to other biographical narratives, he had a tense relationship with his own mother. Joseph Blotner, Warren's biographer, dutifully records Warren's reaction to a neighbor's report that his mother was "the most possessive . . . I ever saw"—he called it a "a damned lie"[7]—yet Blotner subsequently and repeatedly describes her in this fashion. For example, he describes how, on one occasion, Anna Ruth Penn Warren stymied her son's plan to make a midyear transfer from the University of California at Berkeley, whose English program he found hopelessly conservative but where he was committed for finishing his work toward a master's degree. Her interference in Warren's scholastic affairs took the form of letters apprising the president of Berkeley and the department head at Yale of Warren's plans to "take French leave" of his commitments at the former school to accept a scholarship at the latter (64). Warren was finally accepted to Yale for the academic year 1927–28 to do doctoral work, but even then his relationship with his mother was hampered by "her possessive love [which] would never alter," even in the face of his growing independence from her (81). In another of Warren's gestures toward personal agency, he secretly married his first wife, Cinina Brescia, but even in that act, Blotner sees a continuation of his mother's possessiveness: "Volatile and emotional, Cinina was obviously different from the quiet, firm Ruth Warren. But Cinina shared one thing with her: she too wanted to dominate" (96). Blotner's description of Warren's frame of mind at his mother's death in 1931 further reveals his difficulties in dealing with Ruth Warren: "[H]is relationship with his mother was his closest one. He loved her . . . but there was ambivalence too. They were both strong-willed. He was ambitious as well as precocious, and she was proud and protective" (120).

According to Blotner, one source of Warren's filial guilt over Ruth Warren's painful final illness and subsequent death was a poem that the son had been working on even as he was receiving medical updates from his father on his mother's condition. In the poem "The Return: An Elegy,"[8] Warren writes in the persona of a man who has been called home to attend his mother's funeral. Grieving?—exulting?—he declares "the old bitch is dead / what have I said!" (36–37). Blotner allows himself only speculation on Warren's authorial intentions with these words, asking, "How much of this poem he regarded as a breakthrough was fiction, as he claimed? Did he harbor a death wish?" (120).[9] Victor Strandberg, another Warren scholar who has written extensively on the early and late poetry, has been adamant, however, that the poem is about Warren's mother.[10] It is true that images of her last moments frequent Warren's fiction, and deathbed scenes in general are practically a commonplace in his fiction. They are especially notable in such works as *All the King's Men* and *A Place to Come To,* the deathbed episodes for which resemble his memories of Anna Ruth Warren's and later Robert Franklin Warren's deaths as their son describes them in *Portrait of a Father* (1988).

warren and Lacan: the unified subject

Recent theorists have, of course, become skeptical of such Freudian formulations as the Oedipal complex, on which many early, classic readings of literary texts depend. Meredith Skura, for example, asks whether, instead of offering the analysand a means to work through his symptoms, Freud's theories have provided him with interpretations that reinforce rather than explain the psychic illnesses of which he hopes to cure himself.[11] Patients' fantasies exist as self-composed narratives whose purposes are to explain violent feelings, or other evidences of psychosis, which they hope to track to their sources and eradicate. In many cases, however, Freud's language is prone to the kind of inexact interpretation that permits the patient to think he is cured of his original fantasy when in reality he has merely substituted another in its place. The inclination to avoid looking at the real sources of one's psychic illnesses by creating or accepting other fantasies is demonstrated, Skura tells us, by "the oedipal child, upset by his own violent feelings, [who] makes up a story blaming everything on somebody else ('I didn't know it was wrong!' or 'My mother seduced *me*!')" (23).

Consequently, Skura recognizes in Freud's own writings a desire to structure a "scientific psychology," a desire made suspect by his conflicting roles as "biographer, mythographer, historian, and philosopher" (19). When Warren attributes psychological vision to the fictions of Nathaniel Hawthorne, he confirms what Freud himself was fond of pointing out: "The poets and philosophers discovered the unconscious before I did" (qtd. in Skura 1). And yet, Skura insists that the unconscious is not so easily isolated or explained; psychoanalysts are themselves as much in the thrall of their metapsychological language as are the patients they hope to cure.

This movement away from narrative and toward the building blocks that structure it—language—is one of the tenets of Lacanian psychology. As Terry Eagleton explains, Jacques Lacan improves upon the Freudian view of how a child integrates himself psychically into a family structure as well as into society by adding the dimension of how a child relates to its language.[12] Such an approach is also invaluable to a reading of "The Circus in the Attic" because it takes into consideration not only Bolton's identity as an artist who simultaneously creates a self and its world with his art but also his conflicted artistic role among signifiers and signifieds, reality and the imaginary.

Lacan's mirror stage is often used to define a child's movement from the infantile world of the "imaginary" into the "symbolic order" in which he apprehends and accepts the role he is expected to play sexually and socially, both in the family and in society.[13] Thus Lacan's mirror stage can be applied to the same baptism episode examined earlier beneath the lens of Freud's Oedipus complex with interestingly disparate results. Most important, Bolton's Oedipal fears, accepted and succumbed to in a Freudian reading of this passage, are less apparent in a Lacanian reading; the delay in Bolton's entry into the symbolic order is attributed not to his mother's castrating fixation on him but on his own inability to see himself as a unified subject.

Lacan's mirror stage is itself, in effect, a metaphor for how an infant begins to develop its sense of self. The delightful phenomenon of a baby's discovery of self in its mirror image is familiar to most adults, but the mirror represents any process in which the child finds its identity reflected. Such reflections, as in the eyes and through the responses of people interacting with the child, are

at first partial but eventually accumulate to form a complex self of many integrated parts.

Yet, as Anthony Wilden puts it, the limitation of the mirror stage is that it
is "a vision of harmony by a being in discord," which Lacan terms the "*corps
morcelé.*"[14] Terry Eagleton explains that as long as this split, unintegrated reflection of self remains in the "sealed circuit" of the mirror reflection, the child
experiences plenitude, "with no lacks or exclusions of any kind: standing before
the mirror, the 'signifier' (the child) finds a 'fullness', a whole and unblemished
identity, in the signified of its reflections" (166). When the child sees itself
reflected in the eyes of others, however, its understanding of the "symbolic
order" begins to develop, and with it the child's sense that the self it had
encountered in the mirror had been incomplete and is now insufficient to meet
social and familial expectations. Nevertheless, the lure of that first perfect image
is difficult to abandon, as Bolton Lovehart discovers.

In "The Circus in the Attic," Bolton encounters at every turn the eyes that
convict him of his role in Lacan's symbolic order. Primary among them are his
mother's eyes. Louise Lovehart has a firm understanding of what Bolton's role
in the family should be: he will perpetuate the aristocratic ideals established by
her family, the Boltons, and his father's family, the Loveharts. When faced with
Bolton's inevitable rebellions, Louise has only to fix her eyes on him to assert
her will and ensure that he will fulfill the role she and their community of
Bardsville have defined for him.

Bolton is uncomfortably aware of those eyes as he wanders aimlessly
toward the revival meeting whose rhythmic hymns draw him to Cadman's
Creek. An old bitch hound with mournful, searching eyes follows him "like
guilt" in spite of the stones and harsh words he pitches her way. Her insistent
presence fills him with anger. Suddenly, "with the eyes upon him, he felt . . .
lost, bewildered, and friendless. He felt that he had no place to go in the wide
world, that nobody knew his name" (20). Bolton's reaction is confusing for the
reader who knows that everyone in Bardsville knows his name and the social
responsibilities it confers. He has been marked by the Lacanian "Name of the
Father," doubly so since his name is composed of not one but two honorable
patronymics, and he will receive through it the knowledge of the phallus that
should enable him to join the symbolic order. And yet Bolton desires another
name, an identity that will mark him not as his father's or mother's son but as
the perfect, integrated self he envisions himself to be. Psychically, Bolton still
abides in the mirror stage.

Thus, guiltily, Bolton retreats from the demands of the symbolic order
reflected in the bitch's eyes. As he approaches the religious faithful awaiting

their baptisms, the narrator reflects that "if one pair of eyes had truly fixed upon him, he would have gone away" (20). Instead, Bolton hovers on the edges of the proceedings, more observer than observed. His baptism is less a spiritual rebirth than a return to the womb. As he lies smugly in bed days later, recovering from a chill and his parents' anger at his refusal of their expectations of him, his thoughts dwell again on the womblike comfort he has sought in the baptismal ritual: "he wanted to lie here forever, lapped in the long, soft rhythm of day and night, like a tide." His parents belatedly plan his confirmation at St. Luke's, the Episcopal church of his father and his grandfather, but one Bardsville old-timer proclaims him "jist as Baptist as air-y mud cat" (23).

In the long years that follow his father's death, Bolton manages to elude his mother's eyes, the expectant eyes of Bardsville, and his inclusion into the symbolic order by escaping to his attic to create his circus figures. The circus figures, through and in which he seeks a self-defined identity, reinforce the fragmented quality of that identity; they are, in essence, who he desires to be and who, albeit only in his attic, he can be. Their figures, as his is over the years, are crafted and recrafted both through time and his gradually more skillful artistry—always changing externally and yet still the same inwardly in purpose and intent. They people the imaginary world of self in which he manages to escape the symbolic order.

Significantly, the circus figures' eyes, particularly those of the girl acrobat, which are habitually cast downward, pose no threat to him. Instead, by not focusing on him, they reaffirm the Lacanian imaginary and support Bolton's illusion that his identity is his own to construct. Not until his mother's solitary death does he feel the weight of the circus figures' eyes upon him, realizing that "the hateful, painted eyes of the creatures he had made" (45) would be the only ones to witness his own lonely death in the seclusion of his attic. Furthermore, his mother, convenient, as Meredith Skura would note, as the Freudian scapegoat to whom he could attribute his seclusion from the world, can no longer "prevent" his entry into the symbolic order. If Bolton remains in the attic to die there, he can hold only himself responsible.

Thus, at the age of fifty-nine, Bolton ends his childlike sojourn in the Lacanian imaginary and accepts his role in the symbolic order. His satisfaction at being there is demonstrated in part by the pleasure he takes in Janie Murphy, who, as his step-daughter-in-law, fixes him with "a nice, direct look . . . out of her gray eyes" (49). Now, it is a look he welcomes rather than avoids.

Bolton's move from his attic to the streets of Bardsville accomplishes the primary task necessary for the move from the imaginary to the symbolic order: the acquisition of language. Bolton's years in his attic are preoccupied with symbolic representations of selfhood, but his entry into the symbolic order and his acceptance of his roles as Mrs. Parton's husband and her son Jasper's surrogate father give him the literal power of speech. As the situation in Europe becomes an issue of concern even for Bardsvillians, Bolton educates himself through newspapers, magazines, and books, until he is recognized as the town authority on the subject. When war is declared and Jasper goes off to fight, Bolton reads bits and pieces of his letters from the front to the men he encounters on the street. The reader has already discovered in Jasper a master of the self-aggrandizing narrative as he shamelessly plans how best to tell the tales of his brief honeymoon with Janie to his army buddies; predictably, his letters from the front, probably written in much the same vein, reinforce the authoritative role Bolton has accepted in the symbolic order. Happier than he had ever thought he could be, Bolton must constantly remind himself, "It was all real. It was real" (51).

Nevertheless, Bolton is unaware of the inevitable slippage that occurs between sign and signified, language and reality. Bolton consistently misrecognizes his circus figures in the configuration of his new family, and he also fails to recognize repeated in his new family dynamic the very same relationships that shaped his childhood family. For example, even though Mrs. Parton shares characteristics with the girl acrobat—the one that makes her most attractive to Bolton is her downcast, innocent blue eyes—her most significant quality, though hidden from him, is her familiarity with every step of the social ladder and her delicate balancing act between public propriety and private sensuality. In a narrative in which patronymics are the bases of individual power struggles, Bolton's wife desires not him but his name. For Bolton, this lapse in his ability to assert the Name of the Father through his legitimate offspring bespeaks the rift not only between the imaginary and the symbolic order but also between language and reality, thus creating the lack that produces his desire for his "son" Jasper. Furthermore, it bespeaks the emptiness of his conjugal relationship: like Louise Lovehart, Mrs. Parton's disappointment in the marriage bed is the cause and effect of her parallel desire to control her son.

Conversely, without Mrs. Parton, Jasper Parton, the surrogate foundation on whom Bolton bases his claim to the phallic, the patriarchy, and the paternal, could not exist. Jasper Parton and his letters from the front permit Bolton to claim him before all of Bardsville as "my boy Jasper"—"my son." In a way, Jasper's letters satisfy the needs of the little boy who is left behind with "a thousand unanswered questions" when Simon Lovehart dies. When young Bolton, soon to be bereft of his father, thinks in desperation of the "thousand questions" to be left unanswered, he already mourns the loss of the narrative that will prove his paternity (the identity of his father) and ensure his place in the symbolic order (his ability to be a father). As Christine van Boheemen claims, in Western culture "the role of the mother in originating the child is natural, biological, and self-evident, [but] the father's participation needs the proof of language, of story."[15] Jasper's is the valued yet unreliable narrative of patriarchy that "fathers" Bolton—that is, gives him a father and makes him a father—in a much more complete sense than Bolton fathers Jasper or than Jasper needs him to. This paradox of Lacanian psychoanalysis discounts Freudian narrative but confirms the use of language to construct the validating patriarchal narrative.

warren and girard: triangular desire

Whether "The Circus in the Attic" is read as a Freudian narrative that validates paternal primacy or as a Lacanian narrative of language and its confirmation of the Name of the Father, it clearly relies upon an unbalanced triangular character structure that privileges male over female, father over mother. Warren also notes the similar privilege granted to the masculine in his 1973 analysis of Nathaniel Hawthorne and his novel *The Scarlet Letter,* written for the anthology *American Literature: The Makers and the Making.* In this analysis, Warren acknowledges that Hester is edged aside as the two men who had engaged her mind and heart—Chillingworth and Dimmesdale, respectively—become locked in a mutually destructive relationship. Warren's critical voice is remarkably untinged with ironic awareness as he concludes that "[i]n the end the two men are more important to each other than Hester is to either; theirs is the truest 'marriage'" (451). The fact that this "marriage" is driven by secrecy and suspicion might also suggest that Dimmesdale and Chillingworth's strange relationship is a dynamic of careful repression and enforced revelation worthy of that of any patient and psychotherapist—or literary text and critic.

Warren's triangular character structure in "The Circus in the Attic" and his observations of a similar structure in Hawthorne are resonant of the patterns of triangular desire mapped out by René Girard in his study *Deceit, Desire, and the Novel: Self and Other in Literary Structure.* As Girard observes, his concept of triangular desire "allude[s] to the mystery, transparent yet opaque, of human relations."[16] On this level, "human relations" translate to romantic gender relationships, and Girard quotes Marcel Proust to illustrate this basic level of triangulation: "It would fall to our lot, were we better able to analyze our loves, to see that often women rise in our estimation only because of the dead weight of men with whom we have to compete for them. . . . [T]he counterpoise removed, the charm of the woman declines."[17] On a deeper level, however,

Girard sees in the mere convenience of the relationship triangle, which he admits is structurally similar to yet essentially different from the Oedipal triangle, a system for the creation of desire. A subject, usually male, looks to a mediator, another male who becomes both model and rival, to determine what is or could be the object of the mediator's desire. The desire for the female object that the subject detects, or imagines he detects, in the mediator is the desire that the subject will imitate since, for reasons of youth or general naïveté, he does not possess the resources from which to draw original desires. Thus, the desire that the subject thinks he feels for the female object of his rivalry with the mediator is only a delusion; the subject's desire, ostensibly for the mutually admired object, is in reality for the rival mediator.

Applying the theory of triangular desire to "The Circus in the Attic" reveals how readily the Oedipal triangle informs Girard's structural patterns of internal and external mediation even though the dynamic of desire is male-male rather than male-female. In the case of "Circus," the mother and wife, Louise Bolton and later Mrs. Parton, fulfill just as passive a role in Girard's narrative as in Freud's. The difference in Girard's pattern, however, is that the female "object of desire" is doubly negated, as events in "The Circus in the Attic" illustrate: Bolton's real desire is not for the female object but for his rival and model, embodied first by his father, Simon Lovehart, and later by Jasper Parton.[18]

Bolton's desire for the mediator is most consistently expressed in his desire to "be" the ring master, despite his more obvious and consistent resemblance to the circus clown. Try as Bolton might to achieve the look and style of the "impresario," however, he can never quite carry the role off—either because he lacks or imagines he lacks some aspect or another of it. Furthermore, as Girard points out, the subject imitates the desire of the mediator based not necessarily upon actual knowledge of his character or personality but upon who the subject imagines the mediator to be. To better understand his father Simon Lovehart, who is almost pathologically private, Bolton must garner what clues and relics he can to help him formulate the desires of his model: a tattered regimental flag and a cavalry saber. Bolton imagines that the relics speak silently to Simon's heroism in the war; the reader, however, suspects they represent the more grim epiphanies Simon encountered during his wartime experiences. Lacking this crucial information and the actual wartime circumstances that would permit him to bear a flag or a saber in his turn, however, Bolton unconsciously pursues a debased version of the war: the circus.

In fact, the less Bolton actually knows about his father, the more he desires his rival and model; at Simon's death, Bolton is overcome by "a sense of discovery, the discovery of the man on the bed" (28). His "discovery" of what he will never know about the dying man is a simultaneous discovery that Simon is now his son's to create and, in creating, to imitate. In Freudian terms, Bolton should achieve two varieties of Oedipal victory through Simon's death: the first, the displacement of the father that bequeaths the mother to the son, and the second, the removal of the father that confers to his heir the father's role in all other cultural and social matters. In Girardian terms, however, Simon's death serves only to increase Bolton's desire for his model and rival as well as Bolton's sense that, lacking the qualities his father had possessed, he could acquire them by imitation.

This first pattern of triangular desire foreshadows the next, accomplished when Bolton marries Mrs. Parton and welcomes her nineteen-year-old son into his home. In fact, Mrs. Parton fills Bolton's house with "sons" when she invites young soldiers from the army post to parties on "Rusty-Butt Hill." Tellingly, Bolton is delighted rather than dismayed by Jasper's cavalier treatment of his mother, and the single conjugal exchange that the reader witnesses between Bolton and Mrs. Parton involves her son. Jasper's death, like Simon's, is a pivotal moment for Bolton, while Mrs. Parton's death occurs almost as a narrative afterthought, with no record of Bolton's reaction to the news of it; in point of fact, Bolton has already returned to his secret attic occupation before Mrs. Parton's death. Obviously Bolton's desire is for Jasper, the recapitulation of his former Girardian model and rival, rather than for his wife, who in a Freudian narrative would have assumed the role of the traditional object of Oedipal struggle between the two men.

The pattern of triangular desire demonstrated in "The Circus in the Attic" is confirmed through its reiteration in Warren's other works as well. For example, his 1943 novel *At Heaven's Gate* features the young and idealistic country boy Jerry Calhoun, whose admiration for his mentor and father-figure, Bogan Murdoch, leads him into an ill-conceived affair with Murdoch's daughter Sue. Even though Sue ends the affair when she realizes Jerry's blindness to her father's failings, Jerry's faithfulness to this surrogate father endures, with disastrous results for the younger man. Jerry is downcast when Sue breaks off with him, but he is shattered by the revelation of Bogan Murdoch's personal and professional duplicity.

In Warren's *All the King's Men,* Jack Burden's desire for his mentor, Willie Stark, is complicated by their mutual involvement with Anne Stanton. One of the most significant moments of that novel, especially in terms of its demonstration of triangular desire, occurs when Jack confronts Anne, with whom he has had a conflicted albeit asexual love affair, with his knowledge of her sexual relationship with Stark, to whom Jack has made a near-filial commitment. As he arrives at Anne's door to confront her about the affair, the ordinarily glib Jack cannot find his voice: he can merely look his question—correspondingly, Anne only nods her answer. The nature of the unspoken question, however, remains tantalizingly beyond the reader's reach: would Jack have charged Willie with Anne's seduction or Anne with Willie's? In other words, is Jack's debilitating grief over this unexpected turn of events a reflection of his desire for Anne or for Willie?

Perhaps the most striking example of triangular desire in Warren's canon occurs in his 1950 novel *World Enough and Time,* the fictionalized account of a sensational nineteenth-century murder case in western Kentucky.[19] Young Jeremiah Beaumont gratefully affixes his desire for a mentor/father surrogate to Cassius Fort, whose honorable instincts and successful business practices epitomize all that Jerry hopes to become. When Jerry discovers that Fort has fathered an illegitimate child with Rachel Jordan, an unfortunate young woman who has no one to redeem her reputation, he seeks her out, courts her determinedly, and lives imaginatively for the "moment when he should strike Fort and the moment when he would at last take her into his arms[.] . . . [T]he two acts became one act, the secret of life" (138). Consequently, the description of Fort's murder is profoundly sexual, indicating the true direction of Jerry's desire:

> The blade sank deep into Fort's chest above the heart, with shocking ease. . . . Then, as the blade lifted again, Fort breathed deep, with a kind of gasp, and said, "Ah, Jerry—so you had—to come."
> "And come again!" Jeremiah exclaimed, and struck again with all his force. (240)

A pattern of triangular desire persists in Warren's final novel, *A Place to Come To,* published in 1977.[20] Jed Tewksbury's life, like the lives of so many Warren protagonists, is shaped by his desire for his absent father, distanced from Jed not only by death but by a drunkenly ignominious and fatal action that shames the boy his entire life. Jed's flight from his small southern hometown is prompted by his eagerness to escape being labeled as his father's son; if he had wished to return, however, his unresolved tensions with his mother would have discouraged him. For that reason, Jed's climactic reconciliation with his father's memory is effected not through the ministrations of his proudly sacrificial mother but by the second husband she leaves behind after her own death—Perk Simms, who, as a surrogate father, welcomes Jed "home" in her place.

Finally, insofar as Bolton Lovehart's biography can be construed as Warren's autobiography, Bolton's desire to know and to be his father parallels Warren's own loving regard, expressed in the memoir *Portrait of a Father,* for "the man of mystery" who was his father, Robert Franklin Warren.[21] Warren's lifelong preoccupation with the identity of the man who had fathered him gives an added dimension to Bolton's desire to know and emulate his father.

For an author whose canon is steeped in an awareness of history, Robert Penn Warren voices an amazing ignorance of his own father's history in *Portrait of a Father,* even just the "personal history from which that man emerged" (7). Joseph Blotner dates Warren's literary fascination with the search for the father from his first published novel, *Night Rider* (1936). Yet in his perhaps ironically and certainly ambivalently titled memoir of Robert Franklin Warren, Robert Penn Warren writes of a lifelong search for his father's identity—a search that unearths several suggestive clues but no real answers. When Blotner explains the importance of such a search for Warren the artist, a greater understanding of Warren the man emerges as well: "The quest for self-knowledge—and sometimes the seeming effort to avoid it—would recur. And one aspect of that self-knowledge would involve the search for the father."[22]

Not surprisingly, therefore, the now-familiar pattern of triangular desire is apparent even in *Portrait of a Father.* As Warren informs us, the marriage between Robert Franklin Warren and Anna Ruth Penn, by all accounts a love match, was nevertheless one of his father's few hasty actions, since the couple married before the senior Warren considered himself properly "established" to do so. This failure to ensure that he was economically grounded for marriage may have come back to haunt Warren's father in his later years; it is certain that it haunted his son. The father's failure as a bankrupt businessman in the 1930s was something that the younger Warren felt deeply and sought to shield his father and himself from in the decades that followed.

More disturbing, however, was the scant evidence that Warren was able to gather over his lifetime that his father had been a failed poet. In *Portrait of a Father,* a title that evokes Joyce's *Portrait of an Artist,* Warren describes his childhood discovery of a great marvel: a large volume of poetry containing several written by Robert Franklin Warren long before he had married and fathered children. The father's reaction when his curious son confronts him with the vanity press publication is to bear it silently away—possibly, the boy thought at the time, to destroy it, but definitely never again to speak of it.[23] Warren had always known his father to aspire to intellectual pursuits; yet from this silent encounter with an unexpected artistic element of his father's personality, and one that Warren would in time share, came the conviction that poetry was an ambition that Robert Franklin Warren had "laid aside . . . in favor of another aspiration" (50): marriage and fatherhood. For this reason, when in later years Warren's father quietly asserted to his son that the "first thing a man should do is learn to deny himself," Warren assumed that the vanished book of poetry was the reference point for that remark and intuited that his father "was speaking of his whole life" (71).

Understandably, this moment of revelation had the effect of convicting the younger Warren of "all past indulgence," of which his poetry, no doubt, was preeminent. Warren's irrational guilt over his father's failures becomes a theme of his own adult years. Blotner describes Warren's "strange sense of guilt, as a successful poet, for having somehow appropriated the vocation his father had vainly cherished,"[24] his feeling that he had "usurped his father's career" (416), and his guilt for having "somehow stolen the poetic career his father had wanted" (493). In Freudian terms, Warren had indeed displaced his father to assume his role as poet; in Lacanian terms, Warren had found in poetry the text containing his own self-confirming narrative, the Name of the Father. In Girardian terms, he had successfully wrested poetry, the object of their mutual desire, from his father. To do so without guilt, Warren would have had to know that what his father had gained in giving up that desire—a wife and a family—had been of equal value to the sacrifice. To complicate matters, Warren's need to know stems from his identity as both son and rival.

Yet his father's words of expiation are always just beyond Warren's reach, as *Portrait of a Father*'s (auto)biographical formulation of triangular desire reveals. Time and again, Robert Penn Warren depicts himself in *Portrait* as an observant but obviously excluded third party to the love story of Robert Franklin Warren and Anna Ruth Penn as they "seemed to be engaged in a continuing private conversation" (55). These moments might occur as they sat by the fireplace on a winter evening with the children tucked in bed or wandered into the woods, hands clasped and heads together, after a family picnic (55). Later in the memoir, Warren returns, almost compulsively, to that "characteristic image" of his parents, "heads . . . slightly bowed as though they were trapped in an interminable conversation never finished, and always there waiting to be resumed" (68–69). Warren would never know the substance or tenor of the conversation; indeed, what seems to concern him most are the simple facts of his exclusion and his lifelong ignorance. Ironically, those facts never change, for even after Anna Ruth's death in 1931, Robert Franklin Warren remained a man of secrecy and self-control. Near the time of his father's death in 1955, as if to reinforce his inability ever to know his father as completely as he would wish, Warren would once more witness, again at a distance, the familiar posture as his father and Warren's wife Eleanor Clark sat together, "heads leaning a little forward in a close and uninterrupted conversation" (77).

Inevitably, this curious image had already found its way into Warren's poetry in "October Picnic Long Ago," from *Being Here: Poetry 1977–1980* (1980),[25] confirming in one stroke the autobiographical nature of this particular poem and the weight of personal myth that the image of the circus carried for Warren. In the "Afterthought" to *Being Here,* Warren affirms some of the poems as "shadowy autobiography,"[26] and "October Picnic Long Ago" certainly acquires more autobiographical substance when read in the light of *Portrait of a Father.*[27] Not only does Warren describe his parents and their children as "*a passel of circus freaks crammed tight / On four wheels*" (9–10) as they head out of town and into the woods for a family picnic, but here too we find the "characteristic image" Warren recalled in *Portrait:*

. . . Father and Mother gone, hand in hand,
Heads together as though in one long conversation
That even now I can't think has had an end—
But where? Perhaps in some high, cloud-floating, and sunlit land. (22–25)

Death has irrevocably removed Warren's father from him, but, in doing so, has hardly rendered him less knowable or the expiation he could have offered less attainable. Warren remains the desiring outsider in the triangle.

warren and richard king: the southern family romance

Eve Kosofsky Sedgwick's study of gender asymmetry and erotic triangles, *Between Men: English Literature and Male Homosocial Desire* (1985), updates René Girard's structure of triangular desire and adapts it to reflect a feminist perspective.[28] According to Sedgwick, male homosocial desire—a structure that includes "men-loving-men," "men-promoting-the-interests-of-men," or a combination of both—perpetuates the kind of patriarchy Heidi Hartmann defines as "relations between men that have a material base, and which, though hierarchical, establish or create interdependence and solidarity among men that enable them to dominate women."[29]

Viewed in terms of the male domination of women, the five examples of Girardian triangular desire in Warren's canon cited above can also serve as examples of male homosocial desire, as defined by Sedgwick. The "victor" in men's struggles for power is ultimately determined by his possession of a woman, the ostensible source of their mutual "desire," but their struggle relegates the woman to the various roles of object and commodity; metaphorically speaking, her presence—although the mere idea of her is all that is required—is the "cement" which bonds one man with another. For Warren, whose limited development of his women characters has made him notorious with the critics, the concept of male homosocial desire, as applied to several of his novels, explains much about the patriarchal structure that he knew and undoubtedly privileged.

A further interesting detail in Sedgwick's explanation of male homosocial desire is her positing classical Greece as an early successful blending of male homosexuality and male homosocial bonding, untroubled by contemporary Western homophobia. In that culture, male homoeroticism was an accepted element of a system of mentorship; adolescent Greek boys entered into sexual and political apprenticeships with older male citizens, which in turn determined the apprentices' later adult success and their subsequent desirability as adult mentors. A specific outcome for the young apprentices was their initiation into the rights and privileges they would ultimately possess when they came of age: namely, "the power to command the labor of slaves of both sexes, and of women of any class including their own" (465). Sedgwick quotes Hannah Arendt's *Human Condition* to show that an awareness of not only gender but also class fed the privileged Greek male's view of himself: his male and female slaves and even free women existed to perform the work that the privileged male considered beneath him since his "[c]ontempt for laboring [. . . arose] out of a passionate striving for freedom from necessity and no less passionate impatience with every effort that left no trace, no monument, no great work worthy to remembrance" (465).

While Sedgwick's inclusion of this cultural model of classical Greece is intended to show the distance that Western culture has created between male homosocial and male homosexual behaviors, what is most striking about the model to a student of southern literature is its similarity, in homosocial if not in homosexual terms, to another cultural model—that of the southern antebellum plantation system. The antebellum plantation system seems a *locus classicus* for male homosocial bonding in Western culture since the model often included an absent male plantation owner, who tended to seek the company of men like himself in a variety of social, political, and intellectual settings. For these reasons, he would leave the daily workings of the plantation to his wife and his male and female slaves.

Thus the early Greek homosocial model parallels in several ways the southern antebellum plantation structure. In its turn, the plantation structure provides the basis for Richard King's reformulation of the Freudian family romance into the southern family romance, which he details in *A Southern*

Renaissance: The Cultural Awakening of the American South, 1939–1955
(1980); inevitably, King's analyses return full circle to the original Freudian triangle with which this chapter began.

As with Warren's southern family romance in "The Circus in the Attic,"
King's southern family romance is comprised of three interrelated triangular
structures. King's first triangular structure, like Warren's symbolic images of the
ring master, the acrobat, and the clown, asserts the southern family romance as
cultural construct. As King explains, the plantation legend evolved, from the
first, as a "cultural compensation" for the letdown experienced nationally after
the heroic Revolutionary age had ended and the crass Jacksonian age had
begun.[30] Despite alterations in the legend, it persisted during the Civil War, during Reconstruction, and even through World War I and the Depression, and is
parleyed romantically in such novels as *Gone with the Wind,* tragically in
Faulkner's *Absalom, Absalom!* and (in an application we are now prepared to
make) ironically in "The Circus in the Attic." Without a doubt, Bolton seeks the
circus as a compensation for a heroic way of life no longer available to him.

The second triangular structure is made up of the aristocratic southern
white family. In King, the members of that triangle are the father/grandfather,
the mother, and the son, recognizable in Warren's novella as Simon and Louise
Lovehart and their son Bolton. Simon satisfies both of the qualities King
attributes to the two paternal figures: a genuine "war hero" like the southern
grandfathers, he is at the same time a disappointingly "prosaic" father to his
son. To Bolton, Simon simultaneously embodies the glory of the Old South as
well as its lamented decline. On the other hand, Louise Lovehart would be
included among the desexed southern ladies who, according to King, can
assume diverse forms: from the impossibly pure "queen[s] of the home" to
"neurasthenic women, castrating bitches, spiky but asexual older aunts and
grandmothers," or completely absent mothers (35–36).

Then King posits a third family structure, in which "the white father and
mother assumed dominant positions, [but] blacks occupied the role of permanently delegitimized and often literally illegitimate children" (36). As King
notes, this formulation was fraught with peril for the psychic equilibrium of
the South: on one hand, to admit black slaves into the white family romance
risked investing it not only with new versions of incest taboo but also with
racial taboos. For this reason, the plantation family welcomed the black men
and women it had enslaved into its structure, but only as long as they could
be conveniently infantilized.

Locating this third family structure of the white father, the white mother,
and the black "child" in "The Circus in the Attic" requires that we examine

what critic Forrest Robinson identifies as Warren's "conspicuous omission" of considerations of black slavery—indeed, of racial issues in general—from his fiction and poetry.[31] Robinson claims that, like his characters, Warren betrays an "ambition to have things both ways, the competing urges to tell and to remain silent, to see and be blind" (524), especially as "telling" and "seeing" would mean admitting guilt for or complicity in black slavery in the South. Even though Richard King detects "[l]ittle nostalgia in Warren's work for the culture of the family romance" (234), such a conclusion would offer small comfort to Robinson, who sees in Warren's persistent thematic search for personal identity a moral "evasion" of the issue of slavery.

Following Robinson's lead, then, becomes an exercise in locating racial subtexts in the form of characters who appear to be struggling to emerge from Warren's texts as the black "child" in the southern family romance. Robinson's observation that race is conspicuously omitted from Warren's work is based specifically on a critique of *All the King's Men* but could apply to "The Circus in the Attic" as well.[32] The novella, whose historical context includes events of the Civil War—indeed, Simon Lovehart can trace his incapacitating physical wounding, as well as his psychic wound, to his participation in the conflict over slavery—touches not at all on the war's ideological bases. In this regard, King and Robinson are agreed that Warren's theme of the search for the father in order to effect personal identity forestalls (or does it simply preclude?) his dealing effectively with race. Both critics agree that for a southerner, racial considerations are part and parcel of individual and collective identity—or, as Robinson pointedly indicates with a quotation from Warren himself, "You can't be a Southerner and not have the whole race question on your mind in one way or another. It's bound to be there" (511).

The "one way or another" that the race question emerges in "The Circus in the Attic" could be through the character of Jasper, whose metaphoric presence in the novella as Bolton's surrogate son is complicated by his corresponding identity as the illegitimate black child from King's southern family romance. Jasper is an extension of the ring master, a role established originally in the Baptist preacher, perpetuated by Simon Lovehart, and fruitlessly aspired to by Bolton Lovehart. Basic to Jasper's characterization are his confident sexuality and his equally confident approach to war and his participation in it. Yet Jasper has his clownish aspects as well, as if to remind the reader of Bolton's persistent early misrecognition of himself as the ring master, and perhaps reminding the reader as well of the two male components of the Girardian triangle, who are more "married" to each other than either is to the female for whom they vie. And significantly, Jasper has even closer ties to Bolton than either knows: the narrator reveals that if she had wished to do so, Mrs. Parton might have traced her ancestry to Lem Lovehart, the same founding father of Bardsville to whom Bolton traces his privileged position on Rusty-Butt Hill. Where Bolton is the recognized heir to Lovehart privilege, however, Mrs. Parton's veins boast only "the secret blood"—her claim to Lovehart ancestry, certainly, but possibly a suggestion of mixed blood resulting from the sexual encounters forced upon enslaved black women by their white masters, acts that are the shameful, hidden legacy of the South.

No wonder, therefore, that the description of Jasper in "The Circus in the Attic" is notably similar to the broadly stereotypical depictions of African Americans that were popularized by minstrel shows:

> [Jasper] had curly brown hair, a wide heavy mouth, full of good teeth which he showed often in an expectant smile when he looked around after he had made some remark. He laughed readily, and most readily at his own words. He would say something and roll his large brown eyes like a comic stallion, and then laugh. He had the habit of rubbing his hands together, or pulling at his fingers to crack the knuckles. He called his mother "Old Girl," or "My Little Chickadee," and was accustomed to slap her on the rump in playful good spirits. He soon got the habit of slapping Bolton Lovehart on the shoulder, and calling him "Pop," or "Pop, Old Boy." (49)

This allusion to minstrelsy is particularly apt since the minstrel show grew in popularity in nineteenth-century America alongside the circus. Minstrel characters (the interlocutor, the endman, and female impersonators) correspond interestingly to circus performers (the ring master, the clown, and the woman acrobat), and minstrel blackface, like clown whiteface, is a version of theatrical mask. Along these lines, cultural analyst Robert C. Toll suggests that the "blackface mask allowed [white] performers and their patrons, to cast off their inhibitions and play out fantasies of themselves in the stereotypes of blacks."[33]

Whether Warren has an authorial awareness of this extra dimension to Jasper's character and his putative identity as the illegitimate black son in the southern family romance is a matter for debate. Robinson would deny it by pointing out that Warren's bad faith on the issue of race has simply been subconsciously overcome by his guilty knowledge of the South's racial sins, which "will out" in unplanned and unexpected ways in his texts. All the same, one should be mindful of Warren's essay submission to *I'll Take My Stand* (1930), "The Briar Patch," in which, according to Michael Kreyling, Warren resisted the Agrarian "party line," to some extent by deliberately interjecting the issue of race, a topic that Donald Davidson had insisted that the essayists avoid.[34] Furthermore, as out-of-date and even racist as Warren's "Briar Patch" views sound today, Kreyling credits him for having found "some intellectually, culturally significant role for African-Americans in the (white) southern agenda" as a counterbalance to the "strident racism" of some of his fellow essayists, Davidson among them (177).

At any rate, Warren's portrayal of Jasper Parton in "Circus in the Attic" is an ambiguous one, an attitude further revealed in the narrator's consigning him, "valorously" dead but not forgotten, to Bolton's circus in the attic. Jasper belongs there with all the other illusions that have been cherished by Lovehearts and Bardsvillians alike. Notable among them is "the sinister ring master" (62), who once again calls to mind Bolton's vision of the preacher and his childish expectations of his father, but is especially evocative of Jasper Parton. Warren's word "sinister," used in conjunction with the ring master only in the final paragraph of the novella, is rich with meaning. On one hand, Warren allows his characters their illusions even as he recognizes the potential harm in them—ominously, inevitably, Bardsville's illusions are "the truth they have to believe to go on being the way they are." On the other hand, the word "sinister" owes a debt of meaning to the "bar sinistre," the heraldic denotation of bastardy. Thus, the "sinister" ring master is an incarnation of the illegitimate results of those stubbornly held illusions, the ideology that allows southern culture to perpetuate its most dearly held beliefs in denial of racial realities. In Warren's South, seen in the microcosmic Bardsville of his novella, these illusions permit Bolton and his community to define the Civil War as a struggle over honor rather than race, to glorify their warriors as heroes rather than oppressors, and to affirm African Americans as adoptees into the southern family romance rather than as "blood kin."

The roles Bolton, Mrs. Parton, and Jasper play in this third variation of King's southern family romance are reincarnated in several of Warren's later fictions. One of the most bizarre examples of the triangle is played out in *Flood: A Romance of Our Time* (1963), in which writer Brad Tolliver returns home to Fiddlersburg, Tennessee, to document what remains of his small corner of the South before it is obliterated, under government mandate, by flood waters impounded by the area's newly built dam.[35] His hometown, however, is already more vital in his memory than in present-day actuality, as the Seven Dwarfs Motel, a modern (or perhaps postmodern) addition to Fiddlersburg's landscape, will attest. Ironically, Brad seeks sexual oblivion there with the virginal Leontine Purtle, whose physical blindness seems to promise him (as the girl acrobat's downcast eyes seemed to promise Bolton) a view of himself unobstructed by the assessments of others. With Leontine, "[Brad] knew where he was. And who he was" (302).

Brad's fantasy that he will find redemption through Leontine's purity dies when his seduction of her reveals her considerable sexual expertise, a fact later confirmed by the clownishly dressed Jingle Bells, the black attendant and porter at the Seven Dwarfs Motel. During Brad's previous patronizing encounters with Jingle Bells, he had ignored the parodic foreshadowing of the motel's signage, on which "the bloated, minstrel-show-white lips of a benignly grinning black face" offered "BREAKFAST SERVED IN COTTAGE / TENNESSEE SMOKED HAM AND RED GRAVY / YASSUH, BOSS!" (10). Jingle Bells, a college student from Chicago who has taken the summer job at the Seven Dwarfs Motel "to know what it felt like to be a Negro in the South" (307), momentarily abandons his obsequious postures and his practiced "expression of idiotic innocence" (14) as Leontine and Brad emerge from their cottage. He contemptuously assures Brad that "everyone knows Miss Purtle" and effortlessly knocks the older man down when Brad automatically attempts a gesture of "Southern chivalry" (306).

Brad Tolliver's misreading of Leontine Purtle and Jingle Bells reflects the author's reassessment of the character triangle initiated in "The Circus in the Attic"; in *Flood,* these characters emerge even more clearly as a triangulation of the southern white male, the feminine other, and the racial other. Warren's next novel, *Meet Me in the Green Glen* (1971), is a continued reassessment of the triangle in which Warren more forcefully suggests that the perception of agency cherished by the southern white male is only illusory.[36] In this novel, Warren textually marginalizes the southern white male "protagonist" and focuses instead on the relationship between his wife and a darkly ethnic young Sicilian immigrant.

In *Meet Me in the Green Glen,* the youthful and inexperienced Cassie Killigrew is called to care for her dying aunt and kept on after the funeral to marry her now-widowed uncle, Sunderland Spottwood. Sunder, a privileged white southern man who pursues every appetite with a single-minded self-absorption, little realizes the toll that seclusion and hard work take on Cassie. After several years of marriage, Cassie finally liberates herself from Sunder's passions and vagaries when she learns he has fathered a child with the wife of his black tenant farmer. Sunder's subsequent paralysis from a stroke is a further reprieve for Cassie, although it binds her to him in a different way, as his caretaker for the next twelve years.

Cassie hires Angelo Passetto, a transient with a questionable past and an uncertain future, to repair Sunder's home, the rotting legacy of his southern heritage. She keeps Angelo on when she realizes her passion for him and recognizes that he, like she, understands what it is like "to be locked up and lying in the dark" (149). Strangely, Cassie and Angelo's is an emotional plight shared physically by Sunder, a similarity that Warren emphasizes when Cassie takes Angelo to her husband's sickroom to help him understand the desperation of her life before she had met him. There, gazing at Angelo over the body of her paralyzed but not totally unaware husband, she declares her love for the younger man, a love that demands that she release him, nonetheless, when he eventually falls in love with Sunder's daughter Charlene, who lives with her mother in the tenant shack at the back of the Spottwood property. In a tragic ending reminiscent of those of Faulkner's *Absalom, Absalom!* and *The Sound and the Fury* in its failure to affirm either the Old South or the New, Angelo is executed for Sunder's murder, Cassie goes mad in the midst of her hopeful delusion that Angelo has escaped with Charlene, and Charlene, taking refuge in Chattanooga with her mother, drifts into drug addiction.

Warren's most ambitious element in *Meet Me in the Green Glen* is his willingness to shift the center of the novel away from the white southern male; that willingness does not carry over into his next novel, *A Place to Come To* (1977), although the triangular geometry of the white southern male, the feminine other, and the racial other recurs. In this, Warren's final work of fiction, Jed Tewksbury pursues an ill-fated romance with Rozelle Hardcastle, who draws Jed into a triangular dynamic with her and a series of other men. Jed hardly knows if he fulfills the clown's or ring master's role in any of these structures, but when he finally makes a permanent break with Rozelle, she becomes the lover of a man their group knows simply as "the swami." The swami is reminiscent of *Flood*'s Jingle Bells, for he too is a black man who adopts a persona, although in the reverse of the earlier character; rather than downplay his education by relying on stereotypical assumptions of how an African American in the South should act, the swami obscures his southern background by learning to speak Hindi, Italian, and Oxford English. Notwithstanding the one-upsmanship due her as the lover Jed has scorned, Rozelle's pleasure in revealing to him the success of her marriage to "the swami" reminds the reader of Richard King's conclusions on the cultural message sent by liaisons between black men and white women: "To the former [were] denied power; to the latter, sexuality. Hence, as we shall see, the ultimate challenge to the [southern] family romance was the sexual relationship of black men and white women."[37]

———

Robert Penn Warren's use of triangularity, whether applied socially, historically, culturally, or psychologically, compels a reader's appreciation for its symbolic as well as narrative applications. As a literary critic, Warren demonstrates his attraction to the triangular pattern through his analysis of Hawthorne's Dimmesdale, Hester, and Chillingworth in *The Scarlet Letter;* as an artist, he affirms it in his own works. Imitating Hawthorne's character structure offers Warren compelling symbolic possibilities, as in the triangulation of the clown, the ring master, and the acrobat. Additionally, it provides the psychological tension necessary to multiple reworkings of narrative, all within the scope of a single text, "The Circus in the Attic," Warren's re-vision of and tribute to Hawthorne's themes and characters.

The richness of Warren's text—indeed, what justifies calling it the matrix for his other works—is verified by the numerous critical approaches/psychological narratives through which it proves accessible. Certainly "The Circus in the Attic" is an inward drama of self that recalls Freud's narrative of the Oedipal complex or Jacques Lacan's narrative of the mirror stage. But the novella is an outward drama of the self interacting with the other as well, reflecting gendered narratives by René Girard and Eve Kosofsky Sedgwick and Richard King's racial narrative. As it reveals and absorbs all these approaches, we can only ask ourselves what further readings of it await us.

Chapter Three

"pure and impure poetry"
The circuses of Thomas wolfe and robert penn warren

Poetry wants to be pure, but poems do not. . . . They mar
themselves with cacophonies, jagged rhythms, ugly words
and ugly thoughts, colloquialisms, clichés, sterile technical
terms, headwork and argument, self-contradictions, clev-
ernesses, irony, realism—all things which call us back to
the world of prose and imperfection.

Sometimes a poet will reflect on this state of affairs
and grieve.

—Robert Penn Warren
"Pure and Impure Poetry," 1943

[Y]ou can't go home again. . . . I found that out
through exile, through storm and stress, perplexity and
dark confusion. I found it out with blood and sweat
and agony, and for a long time I grieved.

—Thomas Wolfe to his mother, 1938

By 1935, Robert Penn Warren had established himself as a biographer, a fiction writer, a poet, and a literary critic. His *John Brown: The Making of a Martyr* (1929), several individual short stories,[1] and *Thirty-Six Poems* (1935) were the works on which the first three of his literary identities were based. His subsequent cofounding, with Cleanth Brooks, of the *Southern Review* in 1935 gave him a forum from which to validate many other fine writers of the period and to define the literary tastes of his generation. Warren was becoming a literary force to be reckoned with, and his judgments as an editor and critic would, in the decade to follow, prove very helpful to the careers of such authors as Katherine Anne Porter, Eudora Welty, and William Faulkner. Porter's and Welty's works were steadily solicited during the late thirties and early forties for the pages of the *Southern Review;* furthermore, Warren's favorable review of and insightful observations on *The Portable Faulkner* (1946) helped establish Faulkner as the premier American author of the twentieth century.

Also by 1935, Warren's evolving stance on modernism, the predominant literary movement of the time, had helped him redefine his own unique artistic goals. As a student at Vanderbilt University during the early 1920s, he had been introduced to modernism by his friend and fellow student Allen Tate. Warren took up the modernist torch eagerly, but as he matured as a poet, he recognized his need to differentiate his work from that of his earliest poetic influence, T. S. Eliot. Moreover, Warren had by 1935 reconsidered some of the fundamental principles of modernism, such as its claim that poetry should be difficult to understand, its emphasis on image or effect rather than on meaning, and its exclusion of the reader through the use of intensely personal references.

Not surprisingly, Warren's individualistic refinements of literary modernism manifested themselves in his poetry and his fiction. One striking fictional result is the novella "The Circus in the Attic," in which an artist who yearns for modernist distance from the world is drawn back into it, thus affording him an opportunity to fulfill and enrich his artistry. What makes the novella even more striking is its use of the circus trope, which is also one of Thomas Wolfe's favorite images. Warren's and Wolfe's uses of that trope reveal similarities in and distinctions between the responses each has to literary modernism. What Warren observes about modernism through his fiction, however, he had already observed critically in a 1935 review of Thomas Wolfe's novel *Of Time and the River.*[2]

Warren clearly had conflicting editorial and critical responses to the fiction of Thomas Wolfe. As editor, he recognized the advisability of including an author of Wolfe's stature in the pages of the *Southern Review;* he even requested a piece by Wolfe for its inaugural issue.[3] Yet these negotiations between editor and potential contributor had a critical subtext the two parties could not have ignored. As literary analyst, he had already gone on record as one of Wolfe's most exacting and, as it would evolve, most quoted critics in "A Note on the Hamlet of Thomas Wolfe," his review of the prodigious writer's second novel *Of Time and the River.*

In this review, Warren voices both praise and disapproval for the "enormous talent" of his fellow southerner. Wolfe's genius had produced, according to Warren, "fine fragments, . . . brilliant pieces of portraiture, and . . . sharp observations on men and nature."[4] On the other hand, Warren finds *Look Homeward, Angel* and *Of Time and the River* too willingly autobiographical; he objects that "the pretense of fiction is so thin and slovenly that Mr. Wolfe in referring to the hero writes indifferently 'Eugene Gant' or 'I' and 'me'" (206).[5] This propensity for self-reference, combined with Wolfe's overzealous attempts to communicate "the visionary moment" only to wreak "some indignity on the chastity of the vision" is among his greatest failings in Warren's eyes. The poet in Wolfe, whom the poet Warren wants to admire, cannot come to satisfactory terms with his prosaic materials. As Warren states the case,

> [Wolfe] attempts to bolster, or as it were, to prove, the mystical
> and poetic vision by fusing it with a body of everyday experience
> of which the novelist ordinarily treats. But there is scarcely a fusion
> or a correlation; rather, an oscillation. (214)

According to Warren, it is possible to write of the "mystical and poetic vision" and blend it with "everyday experience"; unfortunately, in his view, these two modes of writing never complement each other or even coexist in a convincing artistic way in Wolfe's novels. In Warren's judgment, Wolfe tries to express character development poetically before the character's experience has rendered that development possible or believable. In the process, Wolfe grants his characters, especially Eugene Gant, possession of an unearned, intangible "visionary truth" that has never been tested in reality or even questioned by irony. Warren implies that Wolfe is not only a writer who has allowed himself to be mastered by his own poetic yearnings but also that his commitment to this pure but unproven artistic vision renders his art inaccessible to "the ordinary citizens of the Republic" (214) who cannot read Eugene's story without finding themselves excluded from it as part of the insensitive, prosaic world against which he struggles. The title of Warren's review, "A Note on the Hamlet of Thomas Wolfe," initially directs the reader to Wolfe's difficulty with integrating vision with reality. When, as his final word on the topic, Warren reminds his reader that "Shakespeare merely wrote *Hamlet;* he was *not* Hamlet" (216),[6] it becomes clear that, as far as Warren is concerned, Wolfe's unreflective biographical impulse and his commitment to the unearned poetic vision are prime targets for the ironic tendencies of his readers—not to mention the more than ironic standards of literary critics.[7]

Warren comes at this same problem—the unearned vision that is tested by a more experientially minded readership—from a slightly different critical direction a few years later in the essay "Pure and Impure Poetry," which he originally delivered in 1942 as the Mesures Lecture at Princeton University.[8] Here Warren's explicit topic is poetry, but it becomes clear in this essay, as in his later essay "Democracy and Poetry" (1975),[9] that the term "poetry" is an inclusive one:

> For poetry—in the broadest sense, the work of the "makers"—is a dynamic affirmation of, as well as the image of, the concept of the self. . . . "[M]ade things" may, of course, belong to any of various orders of art.[10]

In literature, Warren considers a poem, fiction, or drama generically poetic. Thus, regardless of the art form, the weakness of the pure poem, or in the purely poetic approach, lies in its fixation on the single narrow poetic effect that disallows experience. As Warren puts it, the "pure poem tries to be pure by excluding, more or less rigidly, certain elements which might qualify or contradict its original impulse. . . . [For] . . . pure poems want to be, and desperately, all of a piece."[11] The weakness of pure poetry is ultimately its inability to withstand the realistic application of human experience as a test of whether its vision has been earned or merely assumed by the poet.

As one of several practical demonstrations of "Pure and Impure Poetry," Warren uses a Shakespearian model. Romeo, for example, standing in blissful isolation beneath Juliet's balcony, is the poet of the perfectly pure, with whom nature "conspires" to create the single, shimmering moment justly celebrated as the paradigm for first love. Warren quotes Romeo's worshipful words about the invisible Juliet: "But soft! what light through yonder window breaks? / It is the east . . ." But, as Warren quickly inserts, just outside the garden wall lurks Romeo's friend Mercutio, ready to spoil the pure moment with a bawdy joke or a clever riposte. Such elements and more—"[r]ealism, wit, intellectual complication" (6)—force impure poetry upon poor Romeo, and when Juliet herself appears, pure poetry dissolves into a welter of practicality as she admonishes the poet/lover for his rhetorical carelessness in pledging his love by the "inconstant moon." Her logical frame of mind demands a more exact metaphor for his love ritual; inevitably, she "injects the impurity of an intellectual style into Romeo's pure poem."[12]

Warren contends that pure poetry, lacking the "dross" of the impure, is naked, vulnerable to the "recalcitrant and contradictory context" in which it must eventually find itself. It must either invite the participation of the nay-saying context or risk its destructive ridicule (7). Shakespeare's appreciation for this fact of poetic life qualifies him for greatness, for, as Warren claims, not only is "nothing that is available to human experience . . . to be legislated out of poetry" but "the greatness of a poet depends upon the extent of the area of experience which he can master poetically" (24). Warren might also have added, apropos of his previous advice to Thomas Wolfe, that Shakespeare merely spoke pure poetry through Romeo's voice; he did *not* aspire to be Romeo.

For this reason, and others developed within the essay, Warren is as wary of poets who privilege the purity of the moment over the impurity of experience as he is of "attempts to legislate literature into becoming a simple, unqualified, 'pure' statement of faith and ideals" (27). Instead, he defends the "condemned" artists of the impure such as Proust, Eliot, Dreiser, and Faulkner from critical minds that are "hot for certainties," and praises them

> because they have tried . . . to remain faithful to the complexities of the problems with which they are dealing, because they have refused to take the easy statement as solution, because they have tried to define the context in which, and the terms by which, faith and ideals may be earned. (27)

pure and impure poetry in warren's "circus in the attic"

Warren's engaged, colloquial tone in the essay "Pure and Impure Poetry" demonstrates that this is no coolly distanced critic speaking over an insurmountable divide that separates him from artists and their readers alike. He, too, is an artist and a reader who, on the one hand, seeks to measure up artistically to his own critical judgments and, on the other hand, expects to discover moral and social as well as aesthetic applications in what he reads.

Indeed, advocates of the purely poetic ideal figure prominently among the protagonists in Warren's fiction: Percy Munn in *Night Rider* (1939), Jerry Calhoun in *At Heaven's Gate* (1943), Jeremiah Beaumont in *World Enough and Time* (1950), and Brad Tolliver in *Flood: A Romance of Our Time* (1964) all seek to assert pure ideals which they have not earned the right to claim. Each, in his own way, is called from the brink of the purely poetic moment of blind idealism by what Jack Burden finally recognizes in *All the King's Men* as "the awful responsibility of Time."[13] All are forced to abandon the purely poetic moment for a realistic, often harshly ironic, glimpse of self; in retrospect, each would willingly have sacrificed the purely poetic in order to join the world and become more fully human.[14]

The novella "The Circus in the Attic," one of the least characteristic of Warren's fictions, seems to speak even more directly to his earlier conviction that the best artistic expressions contain both pure and impure elements. Written a scant four years after the essay "Pure and Impure Poetry," the novella demonstrates one poet's instinctive struggle first to express himself ideally in his art and then to incorporate the impure into it. Bolton Lovehart's "poetry" is textualized in the painted wooden forms of circus characters that represent his limited notion of the world beyond his attic. Bolton seeks to inform his art with a broad range of human experience by participating in an outdoor Baptist revival meeting, by running away with the circus, a classic gesture of childhood rebellion, and even by advocating the advent of a daring new art form—silent films—in Bardsville. When these expediencies fail to deliver him from his enforced adolescence, Bolton uses what is available to him—an idealized view of the circus and an understanding of human relationships bounded by auto-biographical constraints—to construct the "pure poetry" that becomes his only recourse under his restricted circumstances.

As regards his own composition of the novella, Warren formally acknowl-edges its source as a bit of local color from his home state of Kentucky, leaving it to his critics to uncover its imaginative impurities by using their own "special strategies" of "the psychological, the moralistic, the formalistic, [and] the his-torical."[15] Joy Bale Boone and Will Fridy have each noted that Warren first learned the history of John Wesley Venable some time in the 1930s, when he, Ford Madox Ford, Katherine Anne Porter, and Allen Tate visited Warren's for-mer student, the Rev. Frank Qualls Cayce, in Louisville, Kentucky.[16] Cayce recalled their conversation for a 1978 interview with Fridy: "[W]e were just sit-ting around and just telling stories about characters we knew and I got to talk-ing about . . . John Venable in Hopkinsville who had a circus in his attic and sort of an eccentric life" (72). From what both Warren and Cayce insisted was "scarcely more than a few sentences" outlining Venable's idiosyncratic hobby, Warren projected a remarkably accurate account of the Hopkinsville native's life—and one that, according to one source, caused some local consternation when the novella was first published in *Cosmopolitan* in 1947.[17]

Despite Warren's avowed ignorance of the details of John Wesley Venable's life, the similarities between Venable and Warren's protagonist Bolton Lovehart are, nonetheless, remarkable. As Boone reports, Fanny Moore Venable was evi-dently just as "fiercely possessive" of her son as Bolton's mother was of him, choosing to think of Venable as "a writer in the ivory tower of the attic, [and] preferring that aura to any employment that she considered beneath his level of aristocracy" (11). Venable, who never said a harsh word about his mother, was described by his Hopkinsville neighbors as "an impeccable gentleman of the old school and his mother's 'escort.'" According to Fridy, Venable was completely devoted to Fanny and married only after she had been dead for three years, when he himself was fifty-four (73). Notably unlike Bolton's circus, however, which is sold and scattered among the children in his community, Venable's circus, in its entirety, found a home after his death in 1976 in the Pennyroyal Area Museum in Hopkinsville, Kentucky.

As a museum piece, Venable's circus, which Warren evidently never saw, is singularly unprepossessing. Some of the figures are no more than magazine and newspaper cutouts mounted on pasteboard. One cigar box circus wagon has bottle top wheels, and the calliope is made from old lipstick tubes. Even though Venable's circus is not accessible to every reader of "The Circus in the Attic," its shabby reality lends, for those who do know of it, a greater poignancy to Bolton Lovehart's wood and paint figures, the devotion he expends on them, and the gradually cooling attitudes of Bardsvillians toward Bolton after he presents his creation to the town as a combination tribute to his dead stepson Jasper and contribution to the war effort. As "pure poetry," the result of a lifetime of seclusion from the real world, the circus figures have little meaning to Bardsville other than as playthings for the town's children. But for Bolton, this once lavishly assembled circus is "used and broken" as a "kind of atonement . . . for the long lie, for all the past"[18]—not merely his lifetime lie to his mother and the past he has devoted to pure poetry, but also his acceptance of a limited concept of history that made Bolton's circus sufficient to his needs for so many years. This is the concept Bolton has steadily protected against the impure elements of time and irony. As Warren cautions his reader in "Pure and Impure Poetry," the theory of purity "will forget that the hand-me-down faith, the hand-me-down ideals, no matter what the professed content, is in the end not only meaningless, but vicious" (28). Perhaps this discovery, that history must be tempered with irony, is what Bolton carries back with him to his attic.

For when, at the war's end, Bolton returns to his attic to begin his circus anew, he takes with him many impure poetic elements found only in the world of experience. For one thing, Mrs. Parton and Jasper have acted the logical Juliet and ribald Mercutio to his romantic Romeo, calling him back from the rarified air of pure poetry. Thanks to them, he is no longer limited to the clown, the acrobat, and the ring master, pure poetic symbols that have been purged, as Warren the critic notes in his essay, of "all complexities and all ironies and all self-criticism" (27–28). Newly self-discovered as a potential poet of the pure *and* the impure, Bolton returns to his attic to join not only the clown, the acrobat, and the ring master, who are the three romanticized figures of his original circus, but also their more humanly realized prototypes:

. . . Seth Sykes and drunken Cash Perkins and all the heroes who
ever died for all their good reasons, and old Lem Lovehart, who
laid himself down amid birdsong at dusk and was scalped by a
Chickasaw, and Simon Lovehart with the wound and the prayer
book as his truth, and Louise Bolton Lovehart with her dear,
treacherous heart in her bosom.[19]

"Jasper will be at home there," Warren's narrator concludes. Whether Bolton
Lovehart will prove his mettle there as a poet of the pure and impure remains
to be seen.

Thomas Wolfe's Pure and Impure Circuses

To Wolfe's credit, he used the occasion of Warren's perceptive analysis of his
literary faults in "A Note on the Hamlet of Thomas Wolfe" as an opportunity
somewhat to alter his approach to his materials; he even admitted at a dinner
party he attended with Warren at the 1935 Writers' Conference in Boulder,
Colorado, that he had learned more from Warren's review of *Of Time and the
River* than from any other he had read. Warren and Wolfe enjoyed several
friendly encounters after that meeting; decades later, a few years before his
death in 1989, Warren would recall the remarkable generosity of Wolfe's comment.[20] Vastly divergent in approach and style, Warren and Wolfe nevertheless
shared many elements of a common culture, including their fascination for an
image common among writers of the Southern Renaissance—the circus.
Throughout Warren's canon, but especially in "The Circus in the Attic," the
circus is the symbol in which the dichotomy of pure and impure poetry must
be resolved. Similarly, in Wolfe's canon, the circus demonstrates at first the
youthful artistic exuberance sometimes associated with pure poetry and later
the development of impure elements in his art. Two works best reveal, through
his use of the circus trope, Wolfe's yearning toward pure poetry. The first is
"Circus at Dawn," which is included in *From Death to Morning* (1935), the
only short fiction collection Wolfe published during his lifetime. The second
is a lengthy dream sequence from *The Web and the Rock* (1939), the first of
Wolfe's posthumous novels edited by Edward Aswell and published by
Scribner's.

According to David Herbert Donald, Wolfe's biographer, *From Death to
Morning* was the last work composed in his "opulent manner" (345); after 1936,
Wolfe's works reflect his response to the critics (Warren, no doubt, among them)
who quibbled over his verbosity, rhetorical extravagance, and romantic expan-
siveness. The short piece "Circus at Dawn," included in this collection, is char-

acteristic of Wolfe's writing before he schooled himself to the critics' responses and tried to develop greater control over his materials.[21] Moreover, "Circus at Dawn" is a fine example of the early Wolfian voice, colored by wonder and singularly lacking in the ironic tones that the older, more satiric Wolfe would later develop. The circus, especially early on in his canon, was one subject on which Wolfe would find it difficult to take an ironic stance; as key passages reveal, the circus bore close ties to his devotion to his romanticized image of his father, to his idealized concept of the monumental immutability of nature, and to his own desire to create a body of work that was equally romantic and monumental. Most important, "Circus at Dawn" is a prime example of what Warren would call "pure poetry," first in the respect that it embraces a single rarified and unreflective moment of effect and second in its achievement of purity through the exclusion of the "realism, wit, [and] intellectual complication" to which we have seen Warren refer. Unlike Warren's preferred practitioners of impure poetry—Proust, Eliot, Dreiser, and Faulkner—Wolfe asserts "faith and ideals" to his readers as a fait accompli without first defining the context in which these qualities are earned.

The distinction between pure and impure poetry as they apply to Wolfe's circus work is, in fact, supported by the theories of anthropologist Yoram Carmeli and the study he has made of nonfiction books about the circus in the first half of the twentieth century. According to Carmeli, nonfiction books about the circus whose explicit intentions are to reveal the performers' private lives—to tell the "inside story" about these individuals—function instead as literary extensions of actual circus performance and have the effect of reinforcing the roles of the performers as objects of display. The result, Carmeli concludes, is society's recovery of what it feels it has lost through modernity; in other words, "[t]hrough the performed apartness of the circus traveler, spectators in modern, fragmented society experientially conjure up a totality they have lost."[22] In literary terms, the "performed apartness" that is initially achieved in the actual circus spectacle is reiterated in books about circus performers that purport to offer a behind-the-scenes view but actually seek to preserve what Warren would call the "pure poetry" of the performance beyond the performance itself. In this way, the public's appreciation for the pure, separate, and rarified moment is extended and the comments of sensible Juliets and jesting Mercutios from outside the circus tent are ignored.

When applied to Wolfe's "Circus at Dawn," Carmeli's theory of performed apartness and Warren's definitions of the pure and impure in poetry complement each other in interesting ways. For one thing, while Wolfe's "Circus at Dawn" is technically a fictional treatment of a boy's encounter with the circus, the voice of the first-person narrator and his mention of actual historical circuses—"the Ringling Brothers, Robinson's, and Barnum and Bailey shows" (205)—lend a documentary quality to the story not unlike the nonfiction works about the circus on which Carmeli focuses. Given Wolfe's practice of including biographical elements in his fiction, it is very likely that this story is an idealized compilation of actual childhood memories. While revealing his familiarity with these several circuses, however, Wolfe also universalizes his experience as typical of the mornings when "the circus" arrived in town. As Carmeli notes, the general public's tendency to refer to "a" circus as "the" circus is yet another method of enforcing apartness and objectifying circus performers. When the narrator's reference is to "the circus," each individual circus unites with every other in a set of cultural expectations that endows all circuses with common, generic qualities.

Furthermore, the narrator's experience of the circus in Wolfe's text inhabits a single wonderful moment when nature conspires with him to effect the timelessness characteristic of pure poetry. Racing to his goal through the "glorious sculptural stillness" of the first dawn, the narrator sees the moment reinforced by the town's "sculptural still square" and, even more humbly, by his father's "shabby little marble shop" (205). The narrator's anticipation of what he will see at the circus's temporary camp site affects as well his response to nature, community, and family, including them, temporarily, in the timeless moment of perfection. The mention of his father is significant because Wolfe will associate the circus with a later protagonist's desire for a more meaningful relationship with his father.[23]

Finally, in Wolfe's account, as in Carmeli's analysis, the arrival of the circus and its daylong preparations for the evening show are clearly as much a spectacle as the actual performance, which is never mentioned in "Circus at Dawn." From a respectful distance, the narrator and his brother watch the elephants drink from and wallow in the nearby river, the drivers "curse and talk their special language," circus tents appear as if by magic, and "circus toughs" drive the stakes to secure them with the speed and accuracy of "a human riveting machine." Although this particular image in Wolfe's short story reminds the narrator of "accelerated figures in a motion picture," it is an even more fitting example of the "magic, order, and violence" (207) that is the mystical province not of modernity and its technological advances but of the circus.[24]

The impromptu circus "show" continues in the stage-like food tent, "a huge canvas top without concealing sides" (208) where the gargantuan appetites of the circus performers are subject to equally close observation by the narrator and his brother. Even menial workers display their circus skills as the cook flips wheatcakes in the air "with the skill of a juggler" and a waitress bears "loaded trays held high and balanced marvellously on the fingers of a brawny hand" (209).

In the circus created by Warren's Bolton Lovehart, the figures of the clown, the acrobat, and the ring master that line his attic walls are consistent over the decades of his creation, offering Bolton the comfort of predictability and continuity that the outside world cannot offer. This is pure art, the perfection that only timelessness can produce. Similarly, Carmeli notes the public's perception "that circuses are conservative, that circuses never change, and that they are all the same"[25]—in other words, that they repeat the identical creative moment with every show—and posits this public misconception of the circus as evidence of society's need to minimize the cultural fragmentation brought on by modernity. Warren's and Carmeli's conclusions are borne out by Wolfe's narrator, who muses on the "splendid and romantic creatures, whose lives were so different from our own, and whom we seemed to know with such familiar and affectionate intimacy" (211):

> [T]he circus men and women themselves . . . were such fine-looking people, strong and handsome, yet speaking and moving with an almost stern dignity and decorum. . . . There was never anything loose, rowdy, or tough in their comportment, nor did the circus women look like painted whores, or behave indecently with the men.
>
> Rather, these people in an astonishing way seemed to have created an established community which lived an ordered existence on wheels, and to observe with a stern fidelity unknown in towns and cities the decencies of family life. (209–10)

As "Circus at Dawn" concludes, the narrator and his brother leave the circus grounds with a ravenous hunger; because they literally cannot wait to get home to satisfy their appetites, they stop in town to gorge themselves at a lunch counter. Symbolically, the hunger they carry with them is for the ordered, purposeful lives led by the romanticized members of the circus community. Paradoxically, however, it is their hopeful construction of the everyday life of the circus community in a "performed apartness"—as pure poetry—that momentarily satisfies their hunger, permitting them to accept the imperfections of their own lives and eventually turn homeward.

Circus life is similarly romanticized in Wolfe's next lengthy treatment of it in *The Web and the Rock* (1939).[26] As Wolfe's fictive alter ego George Webber stands looking at a circus newly arrived in Libya Hill, he has a vision—another of those moments sought through pure poetry—in which two images appear to him "with an instant and a magical congruence": they are the circus and "his father's earth" (87). In this passage, George envisions a reunion with his father that is made possible when he joins a circus and serves as its provisioner. Not surprisingly, the descriptions of the circus here recapitulate the earlier descriptions in "Circus at Dawn." For example, the skill that qualifies George for membership in this elite community is neither acrobatic nor equestrian, but has instead to do with his understanding of how great needs must be nurtured and supplied. This understanding, in Wolfe's canon, is again uniquely patriarchal, especially as we consider, for example, the gargantuan appetites experienced and appeased at the table of another father, W. O. Gant in *Look Homeward, Angel.* Possessed as he is of a massive symbolic hunger, George Webber, Gant-like, embraces the task of procuring hearty foodstuffs for the circus community, whose opulent meals are described in much the same language as Wolfe uses in "Circus at Dawn." Here, too, are the precise stake-drivers, the huge animals making their way to the river, and the larger-than-life wanderers whose everyday life is a "performed apartness." Including himself in this performed apartness confers upon George a measure of stability and monumental purpose that will be confirmed when he discovers "his father's earth," the Pennsylvania farmland where he seeks knowledge of a self as yet undiscovered.

These circus people further suggest the wandering children of Israel; the primary difference, however, is that they find the land of milk and honey everywhere they stop across the broad expanse of America. Wolfe's allusion to epic Old Testament wandering is soon transformed into New Testament parable as George realizes that despite his happiness with the circus, he is still overcome by "the pain of loneliness and the fierce hungers of desire" (90). He yearns, in his loneliness and desire, for his father, and the circus serves the purpose of returning him, in prodigal son style, to his father's land in the North, which he apprehends amid "the attentive and vital silence of the earth" in "the moment just before dawn" (89).

Obviously, Wolfe shared with other southerners the common perception that the American circus was run by Yankees.[27] This perception becomes a personal conviction for George, who has come to associate the circus not only with his Pennsylvania-born father but also with his personal need to leave the South to pursue his artistic identity in the North. In the conclusion to his vision, George is welcomed home by his father and his brothers and fed from their teeming abundance. Thus, through the timeless image of the circus, George dreams his escape from his mother's family, who are "time-haunted" and "time triumphant" and realizes his goal to leap "all barriers of the here and now, and [travel] northward, [where] gleaming brightly there beyond the hills, he saw a vision of the golden future in new lands" (91).

The vision was Thomas Wolfe's, of course, before it was George Webber's, and George's eventual disillusionment with achieving his goal of a northern sojourn reflects Wolfe's own. George Webber resumes his pursuit of art and self when he reappears as the protagonist in *You Can't Go Home Again* (1940).[28] In this, Wolfe's final novel (and the second published posthumously), George has satisfied his need to live in the North and discover himself artistically, but his loneliness and desire remain still unsatisfied. A lengthy section from *You Can't Go Home Again* details a lavish party at the home of Esther and Theodore Jack and remains Wolfe's most artistically balanced use of the circus because of its inclusion of contrasting pure and impure elements. Certainly, it is one most readily traced to his own experience since for this sequence Wolfe has fictionalized his recollections of the evening of January 3, 1930, when he attended a party at the home of his mistress Aline Bernstein and observed firsthand one of the many documented performances of Alexander Calder's "Circus."[29]

"The Party at Jack's," as this section has become known, is Wolfe's final, lengthy treatment of the circus trope; the section hearkens to his previous circus treatments, but in doing so it reflects his changing attitudes about his role as an artist of pure poetry. For one thing, "The Party at Jack's" reveals Wolfe's growing awareness that even the best of his work lacks social relevance. To redress what he has come to understand as a weakness in his art, Wolfe crafts this section to deal thematically with the Great Depression, the impending economic catastrophe that will overtake the effete guests at Esther's party. Then, to reinforce his new socially conscious artistic goals, Wolfe claims identity with and then turns aside from the circus sculptor Piggy Logan, the character he creates from his actual encounter with the modernist artist Alexander Calder.[30]

In their introduction to the most recent version of "The Party at Jack's," Suzanne Stutman and John Idol take pains to posit Piggy Logan as Wolfe's literary incarnation of everything that is superficial and trivial about modernism, a movement for which Wolfe admittedly had little sympathy. During his graduate school years at Harvard, Wolfe spoke and wrote dismissively about T. S. Eliot and the Lost Generation, as well as about "Cocteau, Gide, Morand and Proust."[31] Even though Wolfe himself frequently claimed the influence of that paramount modernist, James Joyce, George Webber is as dismissive of the moderns in *You Can't Go Home Again* as the youthful Wolfe had once been:

Not to be able to discuss [Logan] and his little dolls intelligently was, in smart circles, akin to never having heard of Jean Cocteau or Surréalism; it was like being completely at a loss when such names as Picasso and Brancusi and Utrillo and Gertrude Stein were mentioned. Mr. Piggy Logan and his art were spoken of with the same animated reverence. (175)

Yet Wolfe's narrative contempt in *You Can't Go Home Again* is reserved not for the hapless Piggy Logan but for those members of the intellectual elite who spout the meaningless jargon of "the cognoscenti—those happy pioneers who had got in at the very start of Mr. Piggy Logan's vogue" (175):

. . . Mr. Piggy Logan's fame was certainly blazing now, and an entire literature in the higher aesthetics had been created about him and his puppets. Critical reputations had been made or ruined by them. The last criterion of fashionable knowingness that year was an expert familiarity with Mr. Logan and his dolls. If one had it, his connoisseurship in the arts was definitely established and his eligibility for any society of the higher sensibilities was instantly confirmed. (176)

Wolfe's narrator is markedly neutral about Piggy Logan as an individual and even speaks impersonally of Piggy Logan the artist as a Cause, a Force, an *It* with seemingly little to do with the intellectual furor at whose center he finds himself. Lionized by the world of modernity, Logan has also been commodified and dehumanized by it. Yet in the midst of the tumult he has created with his circus, Piggy Logan conducts himself, to the narrator's eye, "calmly, quietly, modestly, prosaically, and matter-of-factly," and no more so than as he prepares for his circus by removing his own trousers and putting on a pair of canvas pants (178)—by Wolfe's implication, no more or less remarkably than any other man. Piggy Logan's primary concern is for the circus that gives him real personal enjoyment. He is childishly pleased with the results of his creative energies and seems unaware of his critical reputation. In this manner, he resembles Wolfe himself, whose reluctant attendance at Aline Bernstein's original party, where he witnessed the Calder circus, was only possible—as well he knew—because of his status as her lover and as the author of *Look Homeward, Angel,* which had been published just months before on October 8, 1929.

Other significant similarities between Wolfe and his Piggy Logan character surface throughout this section of the novel. The reader's first glimpse of Piggy Logan finds him encumbered with his circus creation, "two enormous black suitcases" bulging with the weight of the evening's performance (173). The parallel with Wolfe's similarly burdened state as a writer is striking: his biographer reveals that the size alone of his *O Lost!* manuscript discouraged all but the most courageous of the publishers to whom Wolfe submitted it in two suitcases.[32] Even after the novel's publication, Wolfe was never without huge pine boxes into which he tossed drafts and fragments—anything he thought might later be publishable. It was probably this practice that prompted him in 1938 to observe to his mother that "[t]his business of being a vagabond writer with two tons of manuscript is not an easy one."[33]

Furthermore, Piggy Logan is as grotesque in appearance as Wolfe's first surrogate identity, Eugene Gant, and his present one, George Webber. In reaction to critics who were too ready to note the resemblances between the youthful, lanky Eugene and his creator, Wolfe attempted to make George less obviously the image of himself, describing him as being of normal height but "simian" in appearance: low-browed with short black hair and long-armed with hands held palm backward. Logan, similarly striking in Wolfe's earlier manuscripts, is

> a thickset, rather burly looking young man of about thirty years,
> with bushy eyebrows of coarse black, a round and heavy face
> smudged darkly with the shaven grain of a heavy beard, a low
> corrugated forehead and close cropped hair of stiff black bristles.[34]

Piggy Logan is thick-fingered, ham-handed, and, in the context of his miniature circus, of gigantic proportions. His ironic nickname emphasizes not only his unpoetic appearance but also Wolfe's perception of the extracultural lengths to which Esther Jack, who is Jewish, will go to trump "all of those 'rich' Long Island and Park Avenue people" for whom she feels "a patronizing scorn."[35] Her desire to have Piggy Logan perform his circus is no more informed by a real appreciation for it than is the desire of "the smart society crowd" who also claim it; in this ironic shuffle of one-upsmanship, the artist and his creation are alternately ignored and ridiculed. The only person who is genuinely pleased by the spectacle is Logan himself, who is oblivious to his audience's lagging enthusiasm for his lengthy circus performance.

For finally, Piggy Logan's presentation of his circus emulates Thomas Wolfe's own idiosyncratically constructed texts and recalls some of the sternest rebukes leveled at them by critics of Wolfe's style and materials. For one thing, Logan's circus characters are surprisingly humble and inelegant in form and execution; comprised of wire, bits of cloth, scrap metal, and painted wood, they are the "found objects" that modern artists prized and of which Thomas Wolfe's autobiographical pool of characters is the literary counterpart.[36] Furthermore, Logan's grand procession of the animals and performers, accomplished as he walks each individual wire figure into the circus ring by hand, is interminable, possibly in self-parody of Wolfe's own fondness for great numbers of named characters even in some of his shorter works, the present text included. Finally, in *You Can't Go Home Again,* despite Piggy Logan's obvious engagement with his performers and their acts, his audience are often puzzled about what each wire figure is meant to be and do, and they grow restive when these artistic devices fail; the audience's failure at times to "get" what Logan is after casts doubt upon the artist's skill and execution:

> [W]hen the act did begin, it was unconscionably long because Mr. Logan was not able to make it work. . . . Again and again the little wire figure soared through the air, caught at the outstretched hands of the other doll—and missed ingloriously. . . . But Mr. Logan was not embarrassed. . . . [W]hen it became obvious that nothing was going to happen, Mr. Logan settled the whole matter himself by taking one little figure firmly between two fat fingers, conveying it to the other, and carefully hooking it onto the other's arms. (219)

Piggy Logan's example condemns the artist who, like Wolfe, is too readily evident in his art. The magic evaporates with the intrusion of this self-appointed *deus ex machina* who makes no effort to conceal himself from his audience— a circumstance universally recognized by his critics as Thomas Wolfe's own greatest artistic flaw.

Eagerly anticipated by Esther's guests, Piggy Logan's circus finally becomes "painful" to the assemblage, but surely no more to them than to Thomas Wolfe, who in the guise of George Webber, remains convinced that his scowling artistic presence is similarly endured by Esther Jack's guests out of their friendship to her. At the core of Wolfe's noncommittal portrayal of Piggy Logan lies the fear that art might never reflect more than personal obsession or literary fetish, thus dooming his creative efforts to what Robert Penn Warren would dismiss as "pure poetry."

For these reasons, Wolfe cannot disclaim his resemblance to an artist like Piggy Logan, but he can set higher artistic goals for himself. A turning point in *You Can't Go Home Again* occurs when George Webber plans to accomplish those goals, first by divorcing himself from his dependence on Esther Jack and the attractions of her world and second by committing himself to an art for which (in a seeming paraphrase of Bernard DeVoto's earlier critique) "love is not enough" (243)—not Esther's love for him, not Piggy Logan's love for his self-indulgent circus, and not his own love for the pure artistic vision. Thomas Wolfe, of course, is like his alter ego in this resolve, but finally, the choice comes down to whether Wolfe will continue to indulge himself with pure poetry or accept the challenge of impure poetry. He characterizes this very choice in a passage from a 1938 letter, in the context of which he foreshadows the title of the novel that will document George Webber's similar resolve:

> I have found out something which is, I think, the most important
> discovery of my whole life, and that is this: you can't go home
> again, back to your childhood, back to your town, your people,
> back to the father you have lost, and back to the solacements of
> time and memory. I found that out through exile, through storm
> and stress, perplexity and dark confusion. I found it out with
> blood and sweat and agony, and for a long time I grieved.[37]

With this statement, Wolfe voices his commitment to impure poetry by acknowledging his willingness to turn his back on pure poetry and to take the personal and creative step Robert Penn Warren had prescribed: to "define the context in which, and the terms by which, [artistic] faith and ideals may be earned."

As if to prove that Piggy Logan is not the only artist in command of a circus at Esther Jack's home that night, Wolfe acts upon his commitment to impure poetry by presenting an alternate circus. Alexander Calder, recalling for his autobiography the sequence of events that led to the infamous Bernstein performance, describes how Aline Bernstein offered to let him hold the circus in her home, joking "it is often a circus here, anyhow."[38] No doubt she intended this metaphor as a modest appraisal of her skills as a host; on the other hand, the comparison of her social world to the circus is serious literary business to Thomas Wolfe, whose presentation of the colorful assemblage at Esther Jack's party is a flamboyant, carnivalesque overture to Piggy Logan's self-indulgent, small-scale, and subsequently unsatisfactory spectacle.[39]

As we see from the text of *You Can't Go Home Again*, Wolfe's descriptions of the partygoers who gather at the Jacks' home establish the circus quality of the proceedings long before Piggy Logan sets up his performance. In fact, when one guest discontentedly describes Logan's circus as "some puny sort of decadence" (221), his disappointment clearly stems from its not having exceeded the exemplars of modern decadence who had earlier gathered in Esther's drawing room. Verging upon the carnivalesque, the behaviors of Esther's guests seem deliberately chosen by Wolfe as foils to the idealistic sketches of humanity that fill his paean to pure poetry, "Circus at Dawn."

One character, for example, the notorious Amy Carleton, contrasts with the earlier circus women, who neither look like "painted whores" nor "behave indecently with the men." As Wolfe's catalogue of Amy's steady moral downfall becomes lengthier and more detailed, she proves a tragic, decadent contrast to the chaste women of the circus, marked as she is by a "look of lost innocence" and a pack of men trailing her as after "a bitch in heat" (204). Wolfe's earlier vision of the circus women praises them as marvels of stability in a transient community, but Amy is the child of modernity whose distinctively fragmented speech patterns—"I *mean*! . . . You *know*!" (193)—represent her meaningless path through life. She is characterized in language more commonly reserved for descriptions of circus daring: "Her life expressed itself in terms of speed, sensational change and violent movement, in a feverish tempo that never drew from its own energies exhaustion or surcease, but mounted constantly to insane excess" (196).

Next, Wolfe draws a scathing portrait of a homosexual, a popular member of the Jacks' set whom he pillories as "a cross between a lapdog and a clown." George Webber bitterly deplores "the spirit of the times that [has] let the homosexual usurp the place and privilege of a hunchback jester" and has granted him the same noble language once spoken by the "ancient clowns" (203). And in the final "act" of the carnival that precedes Piggy Logan's display, the "dignity, . . . decorum [and] stern fidelity" to "the decencies of family life" that Wolfe had noted earlier among the three members of the trapeze team in "Circus at Dawn" are markedly absent in the demeanor of another threesome: Esther Jack's childhood friend Margaret Ettinger, her philandering husband, and his current mistress, whose collective presence produces first scorn and then self-recognition in George Webber.[40]

Their effect on Webber is to implicate him in the carnivalesque life-style in which Esther revels and to remind him that, at one time, theirs was the society to which he had aspired. To give George Webber (and Thomas Wolfe) credit, he is not so blind or foolish that he thinks he will dissociate himself completely from Esther's carnivalesque friends:

> It was not so much what they did, for in this there was no appreciable difference between themselves and him. It was their attitude of acceptance, the things they thought and felt about what they did, their complaisance about themselves and about their life, their loss of faith in anything better. (204)

Realizing the insufficiencies of pure poetry as it is displayed in Piggy Logan's circus, Thomas Wolfe, in the guise of his alter ego George Webber, is nonetheless ill prepared for the stringencies of impure poetry.

Even Robert Penn Warren, however, admits the inadvisability of turning poetry completely over to the carn(iv)ally minded Mercutio. For this reason, he offers a solution to the pure poet's dilemma:

> [T]he poet should have made early peace with Mercutio, and appealed to his better nature. For Mercutio seems to be glad to co-operate with a poet. But he must be invited; otherwise, he is apt to show a streak of merry vindictiveness about the finished product. Poems are vulnerable enough at best. . . . [T]hey need all the friends they can get, and Mercutio . . . is a good friend to have.[41]

Wolfe's George Webber and Warren's Bolton Lovehart have sought out their respective Mercutios and invited impure poetry into their art—George Webber by admitting his bond to people he has scorned and who have scorned him and Bolton Lovehart by his willingness to share what he treasures most with a world that can never fully comprehend it. But, as Warren cautions, discovering the terms for peace between the pure poet and his own personal Mercutio is more complicated, for it involves not merely his commitment to write poetry but also his commitment to write what he knows about living into the poetry. The only acceptable peace between pure and impure poetry must begin with the poet himself who, only by inviting the cold and skeptical world into his poem, will be able to prove "that his vision has been earned, that it can survive reference to the complexities and contradictions of experience."[42] This is the goal Warren sets for his art, and this is his prescription for the pure poetry of Thomas Wolfe.

Chapter Four

The Circus as Southern Intertext
The Myth of History and Initiation into Time

> *And at last, sure enough, all the circus men could do,*
> *the horse broke loose, and away he went like the very*
> *nation, round and round the ring, with that sot laying*
> *down on him and hanging to his neck . . . and the*
> *people just crazy. It warn't funny to me, though; I was*
> *all of a tremble to see his danger.*

> —Mark Twain
> *Adventures of Huckleberry Finn,* 1885

Cultural historians note that America's circus heyday lasted roughly during the final three decades of the nineteenth century through the second decade of the twentieth century.[1] The surge in popularity of the circus as a form of mass entertainment may well explain the abundance of circus references in the works of American authors who came of age during that period. Robert Penn Warren, of course, was one of those American authors, and his 1947 novella "The Circus in the Attic," as I have discussed in previous chapters of this study, reflects both the cultural distinctions of the circus during the early decades of the twentieth century as well as the literary and autobiographical significance for Warren of its most visible performers: the clown, the acrobat, and the ring master.

Warren is also a figure included among the several writers of the Southern Renaissance whose selected works focus on the image of the circus. Explaining the attraction the circus held for these writers is a complex task. Certainly the circus is a fitting modernist trope that proved useful to these authors for its low culture flouting of traditional art forms. More significantly, southern writers may have recognized the history of their own post–Civil War region in the image of the circus; both the circus and the South have traditionally been forced to a status of otherness and yet both have been honored all the more by their constituents for the contradictory qualities that alienated them from the mainstream American culture of the North. Key to the South's alienation from the North is its resolute pursuit of the myth of southern history, complicated, in many cases, by northerners' own eager acceptance of that myth. This cultural myth of the South posits certain class, gender, and racial assumptions on which the antebellum South was founded and which the postbellum South has sought to prolong. The image of the circus in the literature of the Southern Renaissance both supports and negates those assumptions, elevating the myth of southern history even as it educates its "spectators" about its flaws.

The educational role played by the circus in southern literature is in keeping with such circus stories and novels as *Toby Tyler* by James Otis Kaler and *Chad Hanna* by Walter D. Edmonds, which traditionally involve the initiation experience of an adolescent character. Correspondingly, semiotician Paul Bouissac notes that the fright and even trauma experienced by young children at the circus speaks to an ultimate appreciation for the spectacle that must be the "result of education rather than a spontaneous phenomenon."[2] Adults typically delude themselves with the thought that the circus is an art form created for the benefit and natural enjoyment of children; in reality, an adult status born of certain rites of initiation is a prerequisite to the full appreciation of its cultural codes. Children must learn, as adults have learned, to transform the fear they feel watching death-defying aerial acts into pleasure and to translate the pity they feel watching clown acts into laughter. Moreover, they learn to internalize the social, racial, and gender assumptions promoted by the circus.

This paradox of the common perception of the circus as a simple and natural enjoyment versus the circus as the staging ground for a mature appreciation of cultural subtleties is exemplified in the works of southern writers who grew up or achieved adulthood during the heyday of the twentieth-century circus. Robert Penn Warren's literary response to the cultural influence of the circus has already been examined in the previous chapters of this study. A portion of that literary response, however, might be attributed to circus images and references encountered in the works of four additional writers of the Southern Renaissance whom Warren read deeply, critically, and appreciatively: Katherine Anne Porter (1890–1980), Caroline Gordon (1895–1981), William Faulkner (1897–1962), and Eudora Welty (1909–2001). In works that place the initiation process in a circus context to explore the realities of southern culture, each of these authors has used the circus to project the South's childlike predilection for timeless historical myth as well as the inevitability of the South's initiation into time and adult awareness.

κatherine anne porter

Robert Penn Warren first met Katherine Anne Porter in New York in the summer of 1927 during his visit there with former Vanderbilt classmate Allen Tate and Tate's wife Caroline Gordon. Not only was the twenty-two-year-old Warren struck by Porter's social activism (she had come to New York by way of Boston, where she had been arrested protesting the executions of Sacco and Vanzetti), but he became increasingly aware that he could learn as much from her about writing fiction as he had learned from the Fugitives at Vanderbilt about writing poetry. Warren later recalled that as of that summer and his first meeting with Porter, "I began to have a sense of the inside of fiction . . . and began to get interested in fiction as an art form."[3] These sentiments would later find critical expression in Warren's essay on Porter titled "Irony with a Center," and the two writers remained lifelong friends and literary confidantes.[4]

From that summer, Warren became an ardent admirer of Porter's short stories, numbering hers among the greatest of the genre.[5] Porter, on the other hand, preferred Warren's poetry to his fiction, claiming to own every book of poetry he had published and voicing exasperation with characters like Warren's Jack Burden, whom she called types of the "ubiquitous hero-heel" who "by doing nothing . . . assists all evil."[6] Nevertheless, their admiration for each other's work took very practical forms. For example, Porter provided Warren with the source materials that would become one of his most critically successful novels, *World Enough and Time* (1950). Correspondingly, Warren and Cleanth Brooks included her "Noon Wine" in their textbook anthology *Understanding Fiction,* and Warren elsewhere wrote critically important analyses of her other achievements in the short story genre.[7] Additionally, in 1935 in the *Southern Review,* Brooks and Warren published her short story "The Circus," which was subsequently included with a group of other stories in the significantly titled short story sequence "The Old Order" and later published in *The Leaning Tower and Other Stories* (1944). This story features Porter's recurring semiautobiographical character Miranda, through whose consciousness the reader comes to appreciate a disquieting struggle between illusion and reality, the myth of southern history and the initiatory force of real time.

Katherine Anne Porter began her examination of a modern consciousness by seeking in "The Old Order" to "deny the past's impingement on the present, to deny all confirming priorities";[8] the themes that occupied her there would find fruition in "Old Mortality" and "Pale Horse, Pale Rider," two works which appeared in the spring and summer 1938 issues of the *Southern Review,* respectively. Of these loosely but significantly connected works, Robert Penn Warren would write that their protagonist Miranda finds "a truth that will not be translatable, or, finally, communicable. But it will be the only truth she can win, and for better or worse she will have to live by it. She must live her own myth. But she must earn her myth in the process of living."[9] In a feminist critique of "Old Mortality," Suzanne Jones states the issue more bluntly: unlike Miranda, who accomplishes a gradual and finally less perfected "reading" of the family stories and legends that will shape her expectations of life, Porter's readers question from the outset the particularized myth of southern history that Miranda's family has claimed and by which it functions: "the myth of the Southern belle, [and] the [patriarchal] politics of its use."[10]

In "The Circus," the myth of southern history so dominates Miranda's family that even a setting as potentially transgressive as the circus becomes a site for the affirmation of its values. Collectively and conservatively, Miranda's family seizes the opportunity of the circus to foreground her unsuitability to fulfill the role of a proper southern woman. In fact, one of the cruelest ironies of Miranda's ejection from the circus is its fulfillment of the prophecy of her traditionally minded grandmother, who pronounces an afternoon at the circus an inappropriate activity for one so young. The entire afternoon evolves as a patriarchal conspiracy, in which Miranda's youth and inexperience are remarked upon and confirmed. Against her will, Miranda becomes a part of "the show" by demonstrating her potential for realizing the same kind of powerful, self-fulfilling family legend used in "Old Mortality" to categorize her Aunt Amy as a belle and her Cousin Eva as a repressed feminist. Even the grotesque circus clowns, one of whom gives her a disconcertingly "true grown-up look,"[11] are allowed their contributions to the familial judgment of her cultural inadequacy and social naïveté. This inversion of roles in which Miranda becomes the spectacle and the clowns the spectators makes the situation all the more humiliating for Porter's young protagonist and all the more ominous to the reader.

Miranda's frightened response to the acrobatic clown's performance hearkens to Paul Bouissac's comment, noted above, that a person's acknowledgment of the artfulness of circus spectacle is the "result of education rather than a spontaneous phenomenon." Bouissac further reveals that "circus performers usually loathe audiences which are primarily made up of children because they cannot 'appreciate' the skill of their feats and the complexity of their act as a whole and 'react indiscriminately' to whatever happens in the ring" (144).

This observation makes Miranda's perception that the acrobatic clown and the dwarf feel displeasure and antipathy for her a realistic element of one of the thematic layers of Porter's novella: Miranda's ingenuous acceptance—indeed, at this moment, her preference—for the illusions that serve the myth of southern history.

With this same point in mind, critic Janis Stout develops a convincing link between Porter's "Circus" and the circus episode from Mark Twain's *Adventures of Huckleberry Finn*.[12] Yet unlike Huck, who overcomes his initial fearful response to an inebriated backwoodsman's claim to equestrian prowess and finds humor in having been duped by the performer's disguise, Miranda is unable to resolve the clownish appearance of the high-wire performer with his acrobatic skill.[13] Thus, the most characteristically childlike of Miranda's initial responses to the clown's performance is her assumption that he is neither human nor bound by the physical laws humans must obey. Miranda is perfectly at ease with the idea that this "creature" might be "walking on air, or flying" (23); such a thought is consistent with the romantic notions of life that support her family's various roles in the myth they have made of southern history. When the acrobat is revealed merely as "a man on [a] wire" (24), however, Miranda shrieks in terror and real pain. She has come to a sudden and unpleasant appreciation for what Paul Bouissac terms the intrusion of "linear time[, which] upsets dramatically the presentation of an act in the form of an accident. In those conditions, [spectators] move from the circus to the drama of real life" (147).[14] Miranda's sudden realization of the proximity of the one to the other proves too much for her to bear, and she becomes the primary incongruity in a circus performance brimming with what are to Miranda unimaginable challenges to reality.[15]

Furthermore, as Bouissac points out, clown acts always have at least two participants, each of whose roles determine the other's. For this reason, the physical appearance of the white-faced acrobat clown declares the purposefulness of Miranda's inclusion in his high-wire act. In the recognized hierarchy of clowns, a white-faced clown, like the beruffled acrobat, is the "epitome of culture" who wears an elaborate costume and dancer's shoes and is knowing and authoritative. He acts as a foil for the clown proper, who is also called an auguste or ugly clown, and he exists primarily to demonstrate the ugly clown's comic potential.[16] Miranda's assumption of the ugly clown's bumbling, socially inept role is reinforced as she is led by Dicey toward the tent-flap exit. There a costumed dwarf imitates her clownlike, "distorted face with its open mouth and glistening tears" before his face unexpectedly assumes an adult look of "haughty, remote displeasure" (25). Miranda's role as the ugly clown extends even after the circus is over, when her cousins' enjoyment of it is enhanced by their knowledge of what she, through her fear and inexperience, has missed. Their initial reluctance at Miranda's inclusion in the family's circus outing earns unexpected dividends when her consequent exclusion allows them to compare their superior level of sophistication to hers.

For the reader, of course, Miranda's plight is peripherally comic but basically tragic; Porter clearly intends that we identify with her, the filtering consciousness of the story. Porter's intention for the character Dicey is not so well defined. Dicey's expulsion from the circus mimics Miranda's in a way that diminishes the relevance of the black servant's circus experience and thereby encourages the reader's more amused reaction to it. Miranda's banishment necessitates Dicey's, and all the more undeservedly since Dicey is plainly knowledgeable of the circus behaviors in the ring as well as those even more suspect behaviors in and under the trestled plank seats. Her metaphorical references to the circus performers as "monkeys right here in the show" (23) reminds the reader of a similar reference in "The Old Order" wherein the same metaphor is used derogatorily of a black slave;[17] this reference foregrounds the potentially transgressive social circumstances of Dicey's role as a circus spectator. She is quickly reminded, however, that she is not present to enjoy herself or to consider herself socially superior to the performers in the spectacle but to see to Miranda's needs and, by extension, to the needs of Miranda's father and grandmother. Dicey's ostensibly proper, ladylike disapproval of the outing, so like that of the Grandmother, changes to a plainly voiced disappointment when she must accompany Miranda home. Equally comically, she projects her anger over her exclusion from the circus and from the corresponding opportunities to engage in social commentary on it to the least effectual member of that society who nonetheless has more potential for autonomy than she: Miranda. Even though Miranda begins in "The Circus" the process of escaping "the bondage of the dead past to enter the freedom of the unconnected present,"[18] a process she will complete in "The Grave" and then reassert in "Old Mortality" and "Pale Horse, Pale Rider," Dicey and black characters like her are less assured of finding a comparable freedom in the unconnected present.

caroline gordon

Robert Penn Warren's relationship with the literary couple Allen Tate and Caroline Gordon was longstanding and complex. Warren always named Tate, along with John Crowe Ransom, as one of his earliest mentors in writing poetry. When Warren had to leave Vanderbilt briefly after a failed, youthful attempt at suicide, it was to Tate he turned when seeking someone supportive to join him during a summer sojourn in his small Kentucky hometown. Gordon, a newspaper reporter and aspiring novelist, was visiting her parents in Trenton, Kentucky, at the time; knowing the three young people's collective aspirations to become writers, her mother and Warren's mother arranged for them all to meet, and thus began the most volatile, albeit productive, literary romance of the Southern Renaissance.[19] After almost three stormy decades of marriage, interrupted in the mid 1940s by a brief divorce and an almost immediate remarriage, the Tates decided to divorce again, not for lack of love but because of their relationship's hurtful intensity. Describing their marriage in a letter to her husband, Gordon invoked a circus image fashioned by yet another Fugitive/Agrarian, John Crowe Ransom. "We are not ordinary lovers," Gordon wrote. "We are Equilibrists, like the lovers in John's poem."[20] Indeed, as Ransom writes:

> At length I saw these lovers fully were come
> Into their torture of equilibrium;
> Dreadfully had forsworn each other, and yet
> They were bound to each, and they did not forget. (25–28)[21]

Like Katherine Anne Porter, Caroline Gordon was one of the first practitioners of fiction to convince Robert Penn Warren of the genre's literary value. He was particularly struck by her speaking of her fiction with the "same excitement, [the] same sense of [its] being a complicated, rich thing inside" as poets used speaking of their poetry.[22] Warren also wrote an important critical essay on Caroline Gordon's short fiction, the introduction to her *Collected Stories of Caroline Gordon* (1981), in which he notes the agrarian means by which "cousinly marriages" are made in Gordon's fiction to facilitate the preservation of the land, intact and unparceled, among her southern families.[23] This phenomenon is especially well observed in Gordon's short story "The Petrified Woman," which was published in *Mademoiselle* in September 1947, the same month and year Warren published "The Circus in the Attic" in *Cosmopolitan*. Further evidence of the use of the circus as a southern intertext lies in Nancylee Jonza's observation that Gordon's story, dedicated to Eudora Welty, was written in response to Welty's own circus-based short story "Petrified Man,"[24] a discussion of which appears later in this chapter.

Much of Gordon's work deals with the people, places, and occurrences from her childhood in her native Kentucky, in an area of Todd County very near the Guthrie, Kentucky, of Warren's birth. "The Petrified Woman" is particularly evocative of this place, Gordon's convoluted southern family relationships and rituals, and the child Gordon herself had been. For better and for worse,

Gordon reveals the enduring qualities of the Old South in a circus context. Insofar as some of those enduring qualities continue to reinforce more conservative gender expectations, Gordon reveals herself as deeply ambivalent about what constitutes modern yet womanly behavior in New South settings that nevertheless reflect Agrarian tendencies. As a result, critics continue to struggle with their estimations of Gordon's commitment to a feminist agenda.[25]

The narrator of "The Petrified Woman," Sally Maury, is as much Caroline Gordon's fictionalized self as Miranda is Katherine Anne Porter's; Sally, in her turn, experiences cultural initiation in a circus setting: the annual Fayerlee reunion at Arthur's Cave. Similarly, gender roles in the Old South lie at the crux of Gordon's story, just as in Porter's Miranda stories. Sally, visiting at her Uncle Tom's home, the Fork, views these conflicts from several different perspectives: on the verge of adolescence, she has a romanticized view of her family, all literally "kissing cousins," that is tempered by the presence of her new Aunt Eleanor, who resists the unexamined communal urges toward a shared past and future felt by the rest of the Fayerlees. The admiring but naïve Sally is in awe of lovely Eleanor even though others among the family may find her less attractive; as Sally childishly and unironically observes, "My grandmother said that she didn't like her mouth" (4). Oblivious to the double meaning of "mouth" in the country vernacular, Sally is only dimly aware that Eleanor's less than submissive disapproval of some members of the family—and of her husband Tom's persistent drunkenness in particular—has obviously not been silenced in spite of the dictum voiced by even the youngest among the clan: "She better get used to it. . . . All the Fayerlee men drink" (12). An Agrarian dimension to the story, common to Gordon's works, further complicates the relationship between Tom and Eleanor. She who was once the Birmingham city golf champion for several years running considers herself "an outdoor girl" (13), but Tom's relationship with the land is more elemental; as a planter he values instead the hard work of his farm hands that results in getting his crops "laid by." The tension in Tom and Eleanor's marriage colors Sally's memory of the family reunion and prepares the ground for this subtle, retrospective reevaluation of her role among her southern family as well as in her southern community.

The other perspective from which Sally can appreciate the scene of the reunion involves the degree to which she can be identified as a pure Fayerlee. All of the Fayerlees are doubly connected by blood and marriage. Sally knows herself "connected" because her mother was a Fayerlee; she knows herself "not connected" because her father, Professor Aleck Maury, was not a Fayerlee but only married one. Sally's father attends the reunion because, as Sally observes, "I reckon he didn't want to stay home by himself and, besides, he likes to watch them making fools of themselves" (6). He keeps an emotional distance from it, nonetheless, asserting his acquired familiarity with the ritualized goings-on with anthropological pride as he offers to show an uninitiated Fayerlee "the ropes" at the barbecue. Sally speculates that her father's lack of family connection as well as his insistence that she take her lessons "with the boys" at the school he runs makes her "peculiar." And, indeed, she is peculiarly positioned to accept or reject the lesson in gender dynamics taught by what she witnesses among the gathered Fayerlee clan.

One lesson she learns is enhanced and a further lesson subsidized, appropriately enough, by Cousin Tom, with whom Sally has a repressed sexual fascination. Bored with the barbecue, she and two other young cousins wander over to the traveling carnival, another self-contained family unit made up of father, mother, and daughter, which is encamped beyond the Fayerlee picnic. Tom is already there, and, perhaps as cover for his own desire to see the show, he makes the avuncular gesture of giving the cousins fifty cents apiece, rewarding them for being "three sweet, pretty little girls" (9). Along with Tom and cousin Giles Allard, a true Fayerlee even though he is "not quite right in the head" (8), the three young girls are admitted to observe "the world's greatest attraction": Stella, the Petrified Woman, "Sweet Sixteen a Hundred Years Ago / And Sweet Sixteen Today!" (9). As Sally describes Stella, she unwittingly focus on the qualities that tradition demands of southern women: Stella is virginal—yet seductive—passive, and silent, her eyes colorless and veiled. Tom's assessment of this spectacle, naturally of some importance to the impressionable Sally, reinforces these few essential "womanly" qualities as he pronounces, "'I don't know when I've seen a prettier woman . . . lies quiet, too'" (10).

The troubling complications inherent in defining a woman's role in southern culture achieve final expression as Sally juxtaposes her last sight of Cousin Eleanor with Tom's image of Stella the Petrified Woman. Eleanor, vividly stylish in a black evening gown, challenges the drunken Tom, in the presence of their dinner guests, to define the qualities that establish a woman's "real charm." As if to chastise her for the demanding intensity of her cold, blue-violet gaze upon him, Tom shouts that women should "look sweet. . . . Hell, they ain't got anything else to do!" (14). Sally's tale moves to a quick resolution that proffers this ugly confrontation as the catalyst for Tom and Eleanor's divorce that very year. Two lingering images, however, bespeak Sally's youthful irresolution over the roles played by men and women in the South: Cousin Tom, lying on the floor, drunken and bleeding, the picture of ineffectual passion, and Cousin Eleanor, virginal, cool, and moonlit, in a long white dress.

william faulkner

Joseph Blotner, the biographer of both William Faulkner and Robert Penn Warren, notes that the two writers met only once during their lifetimes although they had a longstanding awareness of each other as artists and southerners.[26] Unfortunately, Faulkner's most quoted words of admiration for Warren take the form of a backhanded compliment for the younger writer's new novel *All the King's Men*. As Faulkner wrote in a July 25, 1946, letter to Lambert Davis, "The Cass Mastern story is a beautiful and moving piece. That was [Warren's] novel. The rest of it I would throw away."[27] Warren, on the other hand, had occasion to be a closer and more thoughtful reader of Faulkner's work. His review of Malcolm Cowley's *Portable Faulkner* (1946), published in two parts for the *New Republic* (August 12 and 16, 1946) is generally considered to have helped regenerate public and critical interest in Faulkner's works. As preparation for writing this review, Warren was obviously both rereading and rethinking his Faulkner, and at a crucial time in his own career: when he was engaged in the final editing of his soon-to-be-published *All the King's Men* and in writing "The Circus in the Attic."[28] And for an artist like Warren, who had himself a demonstrated appreciation for the tropic possibilities of the circus, Faulkner's canon would offer several satisfying examples of the southern circus intertext.

One example, however, Warren was unlikely to have seen. Chance has provided Faulkner scholars with two intriguing versions of an author's introduction to *The Sound and the Fury* (1929), which Faulkner wrote to be included in a limited edition of the novel planned in 1933 by Random House but then never published.[29] Nevertheless, the contents of one of these draft introductions, discovered by James Meriwether in 1957, supports my assertion of the role the circus plays as a southern intertext and links Warren's and Faulkner's mutual artistic preoccupations with the myth of southern history and initiation into time.

Despite having confided to Ben Wasson that he had worked on the introduction to *The Sound and the Fury* "a good deal, like on a poem almost,"[30] by late May 1946, Faulkner's desperation to have it returned to him extended even to his volunteering to return the five-hundred-dollar advance Random House had paid him for the short piece eleven years earlier. As Faulkner indicated in a postscript to his 1946 letter to Robert N. Liscott, an editor at Random House, after the document's return, "I'm certainly glad to have it back. I knew all the time. I had no business writing an introduction, writing anything just for money. Now I am convinced of it and cured."[31] André

Bleikasten speculates that Faulkner's "strong sense of privacy" prompted his anxiety to have the piece destroyed, adding that the "introduction to *The Sound and the Fury* is one of the rare texts in which [Faulkner] reveals something about the hidden springs of his creation, and this is precisely what makes it so valuable to us."[32]

This draft, dated "19 August, 1933," was made public almost forty years after its original composition; what it reveals is an intertextual bond uniting *The Sound and the Fury,* Faulkner's own meditative and retrospective introduction to it, Robert Penn Warren's "Circus in the Attic," and every other Southern Renaissance text that recognizes the link between the circus trope and artistic process. Beginning with the observation that "[a]rt is no part of southern life,"[33] Faulkner proceeds to describe the difficult task of the southern artist, speaking in terms that Warren's Bolton Lovehart would understand and using the same circus trope that he had previously implemented in the final two sections of *The Sound and the Fury:*

> [I]n the South art, to become visible at all, must become a ceremony, a spectacle; something between a gypsy encampment and a church bazaar given by a handful of alien mummers who must waste themselves in protest and active self-defense until there is nothing left with which to speak—a single week, say, of furious endeavor for a show to be held on Friday night and then struck and vanished. . . . Yet this art, which has no place in southern life, is almost the sum total of the Southern artist. It is his breath, blood, flesh, all. . . . Because it is himself that the Southerner is writing about . . . who has, figuratively speaking, taken the artist in him in one hand and his milieu in the other and thrust the one into the other like a clawing and spitting cat into a croker sack. . . . We need to talk, to tell. . . . [T]o try in the simple furious breathing (or writing) span of the individual to draw a savage indictment of the contemporary scene or to escape from it into a make-believe region of swords and magnolias and mockingbirds which perhaps never existed anywhere. (411–12)

Here Faulkner's circus allusions reveal his personal struggle with the myth of southern history and initiation into time. In a further revelation, Faulkner admits attempting both the courses available to him as a southern writer: "I have tried to escape and I have tried to indict. . . . [I]n [*The Sound and the Fury*] I did both at one time."[34] Circus allusions are certainly a part of Faulkner's indictment of the South and essential as well to his characters' escape from its mythic bonds, not only in *The Sound and the Fury* but also in such works as *Light in August* (1932) and "Barn Burning" (1939), in which the Compsons, Joe Christmas, and Sarty Snopes have curious links to the circus that project the entrapment of each in the myth of southern history. Ultimately, to the accompaniment of circus subtexts, Jason Compson's niece Quentin, Joe Christmas's mother, and Sarty Snopes must escape their myth-mired families to enter a world of adult knowledge—and adult regrets.

The climactic Easter weekend with which *The Sound and the Fury* ends is replete with references to "the show" that has pitched its tent in Jefferson for a Friday through Saturday run. And even though he has nothing but disdain for the circus on which poverty-stricken hill farmers spend their hard-earned quarters, Jason Compson finds his own use of circus images and language as inescapable as the sounds of the band that lures the spectacle-hungry Jeffersonians to a Friday matinee. The show proves no temptation, however, for Jason; as he bitterly complains with a consciously adult sense of fiscal responsibility, he already has his own "side show and six niggers to feed."[35] Not surprisingly, Jason seeks to establish himself the ring master of the Compson household.

Clearly, the Jason section of *The Sound and the Fury* describes a struggle for identity within a circuslike hierarchy. Jason is intensely resentful of the elusive itinerant pitchman, a rival figure of the ring master, complete with red tie, who squires Quentin around Jefferson while the show is in town. Jason is not unaware that the man with the red tie is "pitching woo" with Quentin and further blackening her already questionable reputation. What disturbs him most, however, is not his suspicion of the pitchman's sexual designs on his niece but the idea that Quentin, and not her putative lover, is the driving force behind a plot to diminish Jason's hard-won economic and familial stature: "If he could just believe it was the man who robbed him" (191), then Jason could maintain his image of himself as ring master and as the head of the Compson household, two identities he has worked so hard to assert.

Jason's life centers on wreaking vengeance against his siblings Caddy and Quentin and his parents Mr. and Mrs. Compson by verbally denigrating and physically threatening his niece Quentin. In the Compson family circus, Jason assigns Quentin the function of comic relief, spitefully remarking that "her face [was] painted up like a dam clown's" (145) and that "her nose looked like a porcelain insulator" (161). Nevertheless, try as he will to relegate Quentin to an ineffectual clownlike status, the role of the clown becomes more and more identified with Jason himself. As Fred Chappell notes, Jason becomes the comic relief in *The Sound and the Fury* in spite of his best efforts to maintain the dominant role in his family.[36] Furthermore, Jason is consistent with Henri

Bergson's delineation of comic character "as that which acts mechanically, predictably, single-mindedly, no matter what changes occur in the outer circumstances."[37] The quality of not being able to learn from experience, a marked flaw in Jason Compson's character, is further asserted as clownlike behavior by S. Tarachow, who observes certain behaviors as common to the group:

> The clown does incredibly stupid things and never seems to learn.
> . . . He engages in endless bickering or problems with another
> clown, problems and quarrels that could be settled in a moment if
> either clown showed an ounce of intelligence. Other clowns act out
> the most fantastic childish indulgences. . . . There is a good deal of
> aggression as well as masochism. They strike each other, quarrel,
> fall, trip.[38]

Quentin, on the other hand, transforms from circus clown to acrobat in a dramatic reversal frequently observed in circus performances and similar to the aforementioned passage from Mark Twain's *Adventures of Huckleberry Finn.* Emerging as the unexpectedly daring heroine of the piece, she abandons the role of the circus clown and claims instead the role of the circus aerialist with her bold descent into life from her second-story bedroom window. In his study of the semiotics of the circus, Paul Bouissac describes just such an embellishment on the basic acrobatic performance: a clown enters the ring comically announcing himself to the doubting audience as the most talented acrobat in the world. Miraculously, after a series of near-disasters, which the clown seems to survive by mere chance, he flings aside his clownish garb, reveals acrobatic tights, and steals the show by successfully performing the most difficult stunts of all. Quentin's reversal of fortune is just as dramatic, even to the detail of the carelessly flung clothing her family discovers discarded in her otherwise empty bedroom. Not only does she "steal the show" but she reclaims her birthright in the form of the money Jason has extorted over many years from his sister, Quentin's mother Caddy. Bouissac further notes that such "transformation by inversion" is common in folktales;[39] we might note that this device is appropriate as well to the myth-centered fiction of a southern writer like William Faulkner.

Another such "transformation by inversion" occurs in the Dilsey section of *The Sound and the Fury,* and it too is accompanied by circus aerialist references. The Easter morning service at Dilsey's church is to be preached by the Reverend Shegog, who has been summoned from St. Louis for that purpose. Because of his impressive advance billing, the congregation expects to see an imposing and commanding figure; instead, Shegog's monkeylike, "undersized" and "wizened" stature draws from them a collective sigh of "astonishment and disappointment" (182), only compounded when they note that his voice is "like a white man['s]. . . . [L]evel and cold" (183).

Like Bouissac's hero clown, however, whose seemingly ludicrous claim to authority is unexpectedly affirmed by a perfect acrobatic performance, Shegog's voice compels his listeners' stunned recognition of his preaching ability:

> They began to watch him as they would a man on a tight rope.
> They even forgot his insignificant appearance in the virtuosity with
> which he ran and poised and swooped upon the cold inflectionless
> wire of his voice, so that at last, when with a sort of swooping glide
> he came to rest . . . his monkey body as reft of all motion as a
> mummy or an emptied vessel, the congregation sighed as if it
> waked from a collective dream and moved a little in its seats. (183)

That this "performance" occurs on the same Sunday morning as Quentin's transformation by inversion—that is, the evolution of her role as Jason's clownish stooge to a role as his acrobatic nemesis—unites Quentin and Shegog in a gendered and racial challenge to the myths of the white patriarchs of the Old South. Nevertheless, this hopeful challenge is only ambiguously realized when examined in the context of Faulkner's other works.

Quentin's actions, of course, mirror those of her mother Caddy, whose climb to the top of the pear tree to view Damuddy's funeral alternately thrills and dismays her clownish audience, the most annoyingly vocal of whom is the child Jason. Most importantly, it permits Quentin a knowledge of life and death denied her "audience" by their lack of courage. Such knowledge will certainly be part of the reward garnered as well as the price paid for Quentin's privilege of duping her uncle Jason. The knowledge of life and death is traditionally the Freudian perquisite of the circus aerialist, whose imitation of flight (we should note that in circus jargon aerialists are called "fliers") becomes a trope for sexuality. Quentin's and Caddy's assertions of their sexuality become an integral part of their feminist challenge to the myth of southern womanhood and the first step toward their individual initiations into time.

Similarly, Reverend Shegog, who claims the knowledge of spiritual life and death, has himself escaped the bonds of southern history by physically removing himself from the South. His ability to leave and reenter the South at will, suggested by his facile switch from "white" to "negroid" intonations, voices a racial challenge to the myth of southern history and a critique of the white patriarchal South. Faulkner's portrayals of Quentin's feminist and Shegog's racial challenges to historic southern hegemony are, however, double-edged. Quentin disappears from Jefferson and from the text of *The Sound and the*

Fury without a trace, engulfed by the modern world of which she has no real understanding. Her destiny is figured in the ambiguity of Caddy's own. Shegog finds his experience mirrored in other African American characters from Faulkner's works who manage to leave the South in triumph only to return to it in infamy or through death. Obviously, in Faulkner's universe, merely challenging the structure of the old world has not proven an effective means of creating a new one. In her article relating the Great Migration of 1915–28 to the events in *The Sound and the Fury*, critic Cheryl Lester suggests that Faulkner was among the many white southerners who refused to acknowledge that the mass northern migration of a million blacks during that period spoke to their ability to "participate in the historical process, act in protest against their lot in the South, and change their destiny."[40] Furthermore, Caddy and, by implication, her daughter Quentin, perform as figures for "displaced feelings provoked by black migration." Lester asserts that "when [Caddy] ceases to play the Southern belle, she effectively disrupts the Southern dialectic of gendered relations, just as black migration disturbed a dialectic of racialized relations" (140).

Indeed, as the fates of Quentin and Reverend Shegog illustrate, escape from the myth of the South does not always guarantee ascendancy over it. We see this Faulknerian truism demonstrated by Joe Christmas, the likely product of a racially "suspect" circus pitchman and a young white woman whose relationship with him challenges the cultural mores and religious teachings of her culture. Despite his parents' social rebellion, Joe Christmas remains bound to the myth of southern history—perhaps even more fatally bound than most southerners. We see the same fatality of southern heritage in Faulkner's story "Barn Burning" as Sarty Snopes gazes at "a tattered last year's circus poster . . . at the scarlet horses, the incredible poisings and convolutions of tulle and tights and the painted leers of comedians."[41] This is the moment when Sarty begins to acknowledge what he has already long suspected: his father, never noble, was more horse thief than staunch Confederate during the Civil War. Given the choice between his sense of justice and his sense of loyalty, his adolescent appreciation for the noble myth of the Old South and his charter membership of blood in the New South, Sarty tells himself, "*I could run on and on and never look back, never need to see his face again. Only I can't. I can't*" (21). Sadly, not even a physical escape from these irresolvable forces can prevent his reliving this painful initiatory epiphany "twenty years later."

Finally, we see the inescapability of the myth of southern history demonstrated in Faulkner's own compulsive return to the classist dilemma between the Old and the New South by way of his many fictive residents of Yoknapatawpha

County. Jason Compson's fate is to become part of the "sideshow" he scorns. One critic notes that Jason's posture, helplessly hunched in pain as he is driven home from Mottson, mimics Benjy's as he is paraded daily into Jefferson by T. P. (an inversion of P. T. Barnum?) to circle the statue of the Confederate soldier on the square.[42] Jason's bitterness results not only when he discovers the degree to which he has deceived himself—for, in reality, he has not accepted the requirements of living in the present—but also when he discovers that the myth of southern history (which for him includes patriarchal privilege, the attitude of noblesse oblige that accompanies it, and the sexual favors appropriated by it) no longer exists for him to claim. Doomed to tradesman status, he is saddled, instead, with the pitiful leftovers of a system he claims superiority to and yet yearns for nonetheless. As John Sykes notes, this is the truth behind the myth of southern history—that the noble and honorable men who supposedly represented the glory of the South were in reality so many Jason Compsons, Thomas Sutpens, and W. C. Falkners, "ruthless innocents" who aspired to the culture that actively worked to exclude them.[43] To some extent, all these figures, even Jason Compson, reflect Faulkner himself, caught and held in his own myth of southern history.

Eudora Welty

As with his relationship with Katherine Anne Porter, Warren's early professional admiration of Eudora Welty developed into a friendship, first through the correspondence that resulted when she submitted some of her earliest stories to the *Southern Review* and later through personal meetings. Upon reading some of these stories in the *Review,* Katherine Anne Porter took up the promotion of the youthful Welty, for whose first volume of short stories, *A Curtain of Green and Other Stories* (1941), she wrote an admiring and amiable introduction. Of the seventeen stories in that collection, seven had already been published in the *Southern Review* by coeditors Cleanth Brooks and Robert Penn Warren.[44] Welty was mindful of her debt to the two Louisiana State University professors, who had begun in the late 1930s to make a name for themselves and their quarterly: Brooks and Warren are prominent among those whom Welty names in the Preface of her *Collected Stories* (1980). Warren, however, was not unmindful of the editors' equal indebtedness to such authors as Welty and Porter, who allowed much of their best work to appear in the pages of the *Southern Review.* Welty would later have her works published in more popular magazines (with wider readerships) that paid tidy sums for the privilege. Warren read Welty as deeply and appreciatively as he did Porter, and he responded critically to her work, most notably in the essay "The Love and the Separateness in Miss Welty."[45]

Eudora Welty's *One Writer's Beginnings* (1983) provides a retrospective self-analysis of the circus imagery she had used in earlier short stories and novels. These early works suggest the necessity of becoming initiated out of the timelessness of childhood into time-bound adult awareness. Interestingly, her earliest memories of the circus parallel her memories of afternoons spent at the movies with her brother, just as Bolton Lovehart's circus yearnings emerge in his brief escape as ticket taker/ring master at the local movie theater. In a darkened theater, Welty and her brother Edward greeted the antics of movie clowns Buster Keaton, Charlie Chaplin, Ben Blue, and the Keystone Kops with delighted laughter. Even darker offerings such as *The Cabinet of Dr. Caligari* prompted the two Welty children and an audience made up entirely of other unchaperoned children to "scream with laughter, laughing at what terrified us, exactly as if it were funny."[46]

The children's enactment of Bouissac's above-mentioned observation that appreciation for spectacle is a learned rather than a natural response seems especially appropriate in the context of Welty's literary memoir. She moves quickly from this early experience of a socializing initiation into adult awareness to a particular memory of the circus's arrival in her hometown of Jackson, Mississippi. The author recalls that that year, a little neighbor boy, too incapacitated to attend an actual performance, was given the distinction of having the circus parade routed right past his sickroom window. This unheard-of treat of course drew the envy of the youthful Welty and her friends as they imagined his privileged viewing of "the ponderous elephants, the plumes, the spangles, the acrobats, the clowns, the caged lion, the band playing, the steam calliope, the whole thing!" When afterward the little boy died of "what had given him his special privilege," even the youthful Welty knew enough to realize that "he had been tricked, not celebrated, by the parade's brazen marching . . . and [she] had somehow been tricked by envying him—betrayed into it." Recognition of this betrayal resulted in a very personal semiotics of the circus, and Welty directly links this incident with her subsequent artistic awareness that "an ominous feeling often attaches itself to a procession."[47] Correspondingly, critiques of her work note Welty's singular thematic and stylistic blend of the comic with the ominous, the childlike with the adult, and the illusory with the real—all elements, by the way, of any successful circus production.

Critic Jan Nordby Gretlund dates Eudora Welty's professional interest in the circus and similar arts from her assignment with the Works Progress Administration in 1931–36. In this, Welty's first full-time job, she "traveled by bus and car all over the state of Mississippi, writing newspaper copy and taking photographs of various 'projects,'" including those at circuses, traveling freak shows, and county fairs.[48] Speaking to interviewers in 1989 about her WPA experiences, Welty shares her personal version of an American classic, "the day the circus came to town":

> I always did love the fair and circuses. Once or twice to photograph them, I got up early before daylight and went down to see them arrive, watch them set up the tents and the rides down at the fairgrounds. And I remember once happening to eat breakfast with some of the carnival people in the bus station. *That* was getting close to life![49]

Not surprisingly, Welty's childhood memories of the circus as well as her adult experiences with the WPA informed her later fiction in meaningful ways. Many of Welty's early unpublished stories and those later included in 1941 in *A Curtain of Green and Other Stories,* her first published volume, contain circus and sideshow references.[50]

For example, "Retreat" (1937) is about a young boy named Norris whose enjoyment of the circus is marred by the frightening bestiality of the trained animal acts and the daring sensuality of the girl high-wire performer. In another story, the mentally retarded title character of "Lily Daws and the Three Ladies" (1937) escapes the best intentions of her sober country mentors, who think her fit only for the local home for the "feeble-minded," when she runs off to marry a xylophone player with the traveling tent show. The disgruntlement of the three ladies over Lily's bold defection parallels that in "Petrified Man" (1939) of the small-town beautician Leota and the pregnant customer with whom she shares the details of her brief friendship with the exotic New Orleans native, Mrs. Pike. Through the machinations of the sharp-eyed and clever Mrs. Pike, a woman who is privy to the worldly mysteries of the circus sideshow, Welty reveals just how unremittingly bound by their gender roles—figured by their preoccupations with pregnancies, children, and childlike men—the two country women are.

Welty's early fascination with the circus and its thematic possibilities is also revealed in the short story "Keela, the Outcast Indian Maiden" (1940).[51] In it, the circus becomes a site for examining southern racial attitudes. Welty details the gruesome duties of Keela, the former circus "geek" whose act had included biting off the heads of live chickens, sucking their blood, and eating their raw flesh. Yet, as we learn from the agonized confessions of Steve, the young midway barker who had announced the hourly shows, Keela is in reality a clubfooted black man cruelly shanghaied into the act by the show's owners. Two years after the geek's rescue and release from the circus, Steve is so tormented by the role he has played in the persecution of Keela—in reality, Little Lee Roy from Cane Springs, Mississippi—that he tracks the black man to his quiet and secluded house in the woods. Helping Steve is Max, a genial but puzzled white man from town; his soothing, placatory tone as he addresses the younger man reveals his conviction that Steve is mentally unbalanced.

And, for that matter, as the story progresses, Steve's real purpose in finding Little Lee Roy becomes less admirable. Faced at last with the putative object of his search, he neither looks at nor speaks directly to the deformed black man; as he tells the story of the unsuspecting role he claims he played in Keela's dehumanization, Steve refers to the geek neither as "he" nor even "she" but as "it." Finally, the reader understands that what Steve desires most is not Keela's forgiveness but the understanding of Max, the white man; what Steve fears most is not that the older man would consider him socially depraved but that his own youthful ignorance would reveal him as a man who couldn't "tell a man from a woman and an Indian from a nigger." When Max voices that very accusation, Steve knocks him to the ground in a strange moment of white male bonding, explaining afterward, "First you didn't believe me, and then it didn't bother you." Little Lee Roy, who goes "as still and dark as a statue" at this unexpected development now knows himself completely excluded from the spectacle he is witnessing from his own front doorway.[52]

What might have been a story of Steve's absolution for Keela's ill treatment or of his newfound empathy for the racial, and perhaps even for the gendered, other has become transformed instead into the story of a white man's self-doubt, caused by his having been unaware of the circumstances of Little Lee Roy's abasement and his role, as dictated by the patriarchal Old South, in achieving it. The value of the circus as a trope for the patriarchal southern society in which Steve is just beginning to define his place and the extent to which African Americans continue to be silenced are emphasized when even Little Lee Roy's own children refuse to hear him tell about "de ole times." Significantly, these are remembered times much like the old times of slavery referred to in sentimental tones in such works as James Pendleton Kennedy's *Swallow Barn,* or even in ironic tones in Charles Chestnutt's Uncle Julius stories. These are, in Little Lee Roy's words, the old times "when I use to be wid de circus" (45). As the dubious star of a carney act, Little Lee Roy's connection with the more socially acceptable circus is peripheral at best, yet it is a claim that memory and the inevitable passage of time allow him to make with pride.

"Acrobats in a Park," another Welty short story with a circus context, is a curiosity of her 1930s period. This story was steadily refused publication, even by the coeditors of the *Southern Review,* who had up to that time proven themselves committed to publishing Welty's work. Cleanth Brooks's rejection of "Acrobats in a Park" for publication came in a July 1, 1940, letter to Welty, and thus the piece has appeared in print only relatively recently, to be read purely for scholarly purposes.[53] Welty readily admitted that the short story failed because of her fascination with materials beyond her sphere of knowledge: "I was writing about Europeans, acrobats, adultery, and the Roman Catholic Church . . . in all of which I was equally ignorant."[54] Her characters, members of the acrobatic Zorro family, are famous for their pièce de résistance, the Zorro Wall, an interlocking structure made of their own bodies. The story begins the day after the Zorro Wall, composed of mother, father, sons, daughter, and daughter-in-law, collapses during a performance, the weakness of a single member having caused the failure of the entire unit. Even from the perspective of almost fifty years after the story's composition, Welty has defended the story's significance to her canon: "Writing about the family act, I was writing about the family itself, its strength as a unit, testing its frailty under stress. . . . I've been writing about the structure of the family in stories and novels ever since."[55]

Indeed, in her first novel, Welty drew upon a circus image to demonstrate the fragile yet interdependent structure of family. One scene from *Delta Wedding,* published in 1946 (the same year as Warren's *All the King's Men*), provides an interesting intersection of two qualities that Welty herself has observed in her work: first, the sense of the "ominous procession" derived from her youthful ambivalence toward the circus parade and second, the organizing principle of family structure and dynamics. A third quality has been discussed throughout this chapter: the equation of the circus with the customs, practices, and general culture of the patriarchal South. In the nearly tragic trestle-walking incident from *Delta Wedding,* George Fairchild and the Fairchild cousins seem to balance between the New South and the mythic Old South with the same equilibrist care shown by the Depression-era circus acrobats Welty photographed for the WPA.

In their efforts to affirm the universal themes of the novel, critics Ruth Vande Kieft and Michael Kreyling discount critical efforts "to place within the story the definite and incontestably 'real South' of economics and politics."[56] Nevertheless, Welty's artistic skill has produced a novel irresistibly evocative of its moment—the Mississippi Delta of 1923, a time and place rich with cultural and historical significance. To deny that significance would be to ignore, perhaps, the cultural moment that thematically informs the novel. According to Joseph Millichap, the physical and geographical details of the Delta landscape which Welty includes in her novel are fictionally recreated with respect to Shellmound and its neighboring plantations but accurate with respect to the Yazoo River's course through it and the railroad's introduction of outside elements to it.[57] The Fairchilds' near fall from the railroad tracks at the approach of the oncoming Yazoo Delta, nicknamed the "Yellow Dog," foreshadows their forced entry into modern time from the myth of history. The Fairchild family's impending "coming of age"—and here we should note their infantilized patronymic—through circumstances that later develop from this circus-based incident comes through a collective initiation experience that will include them as well as other members of their Delta region.

Thus, Robert Penn Warren was hardly unique in his literary response to the cultural phenomenon of the early-twentieth-century American circus. No less surprising than the pervasiveness of the circus trope in the literature of the Southern Renaissance, however, is the remarkable consistency with which it is used to show the overwhelming need among Southern Renaissance writers to respond to their region, to explore its cultural strengths and possibilities, and, at the same time, to recognize that some of its cultural assumptions and practices were catastrophically outmoded. Southerners, like their circus counterparts, are admittedly (s)o(u)ther(n); yet, within the confines of their seemingly transgressive milieu, hegemony is disputed only at great risk in the face of a prevailing patriarchal tradition.

Chapter Five

Ralph Ellison and Toni Morrison
African American writers and the southern circus intertext

It's a Barnum and Bailey world,
Just as phony as it can be,
But it wouldn't be make believe,
If you believed in me.
—Rose, Harburg, and Arlen
"It's Only a Paper Moon," 1933

Ella Fitzgerald's recording of the 1933 hit "It's Only a Paper Moon" was released in 1938. With its reference through Billy Rose and E. Y. Harburg's lyrics to Barnum and Bailey's circus, this popular song demonstrates that the circus was, indeed, a dominant cultural image during the early decades of the twentieth century. Viewed from another perspective, however, Fitzgerald's recording, like the other African American rerecordings of the primarily white musical standards of the day, lends additional levels of meaning and thus greater cultural significance to the lyrics simply by virtue of their being sung by a black voice rather than a white one. When the white voice sings, "It's a Barnum and Bailey world," it is with the awareness of having had a dominant role in creating the cultural structure of that world, which, for all its transgressive assertions, still references the codes of the primary culture. On the other hand, when the black voice adds "Just as phony as it can be," listeners become even more aware of the lyrics' potential to affirm racialized hierarchic power even in such traditionally transgressive images as the circus; listeners may also become aware of the singer's implicit rejection of these enforced hegemonies. Two African American authors, Ralph Ellison, a full-fledged participant in the

Southern Renaissance, and Toni Morrison, an heir to many of its most recognizable themes and images, similarly demonstrate the profound white patriarchalism, comparable to the celebration of what Mikhail Bakhtin terms "official feasts," at work within the southern circus intertext.

ralph ellison

Robert Penn Warren and Ralph Ellison first met at a publication party for *Invisible Man* in 1952 and further developed their friendship in the fall of 1956 as residents at the American Academy in Rome. There, as Ellison recalls it, "[Warren] became the companion with whom I enjoyed an extended period of discussing literature, writing, history, politics—you name it—exploring the city, exchanging folk tales, joking, lying, eating and drinking."[1] Their meeting was more than likely inevitable, as Albert Erskine was their mutual friend and editor, and, as artists, each had cast the same character type in his first major novel. Both Warren's Jack Burden and Ellison's Invisible Man find themselves, at the end of the novels in which they are narrators, on the verge of entering the world and claiming a place in it, and both tell their stories from the vantage point of a timeless narrative moment that precedes the possibility of their claiming action from passivity, life from art. Warren and Ellison, however, had already unwittingly crossed intertextual paths some five or more years before their first meeting. Warren's publication of "The Circus in the Attic" in 1947, as we noted earlier in this study, codified many years of his increasingly developed references to the circus and the emblematic circus figures in his prose works. Also in 1947, Ralph Ellison acquiesced to a request by the editor of the British magazine *Horizon* to include a chapter of his as-yet-uncompleted novel in an issue showcasing American literary art.[2] That chapter, titled "Battle Royal," would become the first chapter of *Invisible Man*, published in its entirety in 1952, and it, like Warren's novella, bespeaks its author's cultural interest in the circus and a literary appreciation for its possibilities in his fiction.

Even without consideration of his novels and short stories, Ralph Ellison makes more direct references to the circus than any of the other Southern Renaissance authors previously examined. As Ellison clearly demonstrates in several of his essays, the circus, along with the accompanying figure of the clown, plays a major role in his concept of what constitutes American identity. Even more significantly, however, Ellison's hopeful portrayal of this circus aesthetic and his centering this aesthetic in the figures of some of his most admired white American heroes is distinctly at odds with the ironized use to which he puts the circus image in his best-known fiction, clearly demonstrating his ambivalence about those roles permitted to and those aspired to by African Americans. Thus, at the same time that Ellison's use of the circus in his essays confirms his belief in a single, unified American culture, his use of the circus in his fiction deconstructs that hopeful vision by linking the circus with the lingering cultural beliefs associated with the Old South.

One of Ralph Ellison's earliest associations with the circus is his realization that its unwritten laws of inclusion and exclusion are based on more broadly defined cultural terms than mere race. Ellison, as it turns out, was one of those thousands of young boys who every year played hooky from school to help set up the Ringling Bros. Circus—in his case, in his hometown of Oklahoma City. Ellison's fond memories of the experience include his becoming the source of entertainment for the circus workers, who sent him on a "fool's errand" to find a tent wrench, a patently nonexistent item. According to Ellison, the greatest lesson he learned from this initiation was its nonracial application: every young worker, white or black, is inducted into service through this or a similar ritual.[3] This account of a personal circus experience, among other factors, enables Ellison to voice a later theory of American rites and rituals that will structure his belief that the clown is intrinsic to a collective American identity.

Admittedly, Ellison will also use the term "clown" in a negative sense, as when he writes in *Shadow and Act* that he, recognizing the white pillars of society as "crooks, clowns, hypocrites," turned to black jazzmen to find the heroes of his youth.[4] On the other hand, in the essay "Change the Joke and Slip the Yoke," which includes a more positive interpretation of the clown's cultural role, Ellison designates the role of the clown to one of those very jazzmen:

> [Louis] Armstrong's clownish license and intoxicating powers are almost Elizabethan; he takes liberties with kings, queens and presidents; emphasizes the physicality of his music with sweat, spittle and facial contortions [and] performs the magical feat of making romantic melody issue from a throat of gravel.[5]

Ellison is careful in this essay to make the case that the role of the clown follows no strict racial delineation but is, rather, an element of Yeatsian mask. To support his claim, he cites Robert Penn Warren's assertion of "the 'intentional' character of our national beginnings" (53); such intentionality was first demonstrated by British colonists who adopted the name "American" with the full expectation that they would subsequently be required to invent the national characteristics needed to comprise that self-proclaimed identity.

Furthermore, as Ellison notes in his essay, all Americans are clowns in the sense that each is an *eiron,* "the smart man playing dumb," a role that he recognizes is often assigned to a black trickster figure but which he describes as "more 'Yankee' than anything else. . . . [B]asically, the strategy grows out of our awareness of the joke at the center of American identity" (54). For this reason, Ellison dismisses the significance of the black trickster figure to American identity, first because the trickster in general is too archetypally ubiquitous and second because it belongs more properly to African folklore than to the folklore of the American Negro to which white thinking has affixed it (46–47). Thus Ellison traces American tricksterism not to black rebellion against white stereotypical thinking but to the American colonials' rebellion against the intransigent British "fathers." Frequently, the joke reveals an awareness of one's having asserted a hopeful identity without having first achieved it or of one's using a clownish persona to placate an anxious anti-intellectual public. Ellison's illustrations of this strategy reveal a few of his own most admired "clowns": Benjamin Franklin as Rousseau's Natural Man, Abraham Lincoln as a simple country lawyer, Ernest Hemingway as a nonliterary sportsman, and William Faulkner as a southern farmer. Had he thought to, Ellison might also have included Robert Penn Warren in this list since readers familiar with the intellectual depth of Warren's works were often surprised by his rural demeanor and sometimes incomprehensible Kentucky accent. Warren's essay "Democracy and Poetry" (1972), in its balance of the colloquial with a sophisticated philosophy of art, is comparable to the knowing cultivation of the clown's role by the American *eirons* Ellison lists.

Finally, the role of the *eiron,* as Ellison points out here, "makes brothers of us all. America is the land of masking jokers." Ellison's reminder, however, that "we wear the mask for purposes of aggression as well as for defense; when we are projecting the future and preserving the past" (55) reveals his lack of sentimentality even as he regarded these four figures for whom he had such great admiration: Franklin had been a slaveholder, Lincoln married a woman who had been one, and Hemingway and Faulkner were the heirs to the racist mindsets of their own century. Robert Penn Warren, it should be noted, had penned the segregationist essay "The Briar Patch" very early in his career and, despite his later regret over writing it, was never to escape the notoriety that had resulted from it. Nevertheless, Ellison warns that failure to recognize the brotherhood of the clown denies what brings white and black Americans together in a "dual culture." As Ellison states elsewhere, the "Negro is a member of an American-bound cultural group" that at the same time possesses "its own idiom [. . . and] its own psychology, growing out of its preoccupations with certain problems for hundreds of years, out of all its history."[6]

In the essay "The Little Man at Chehaw Station," Ellison provides his reader with a pointed example of the results of ignoring the "dual culture" he has posited and follows this example with a comical description of what a dual culture might entail, illustrated with a circus trope. Ellison's voiced resistance to what he calls racial mysticism and black nationalism clearly places this essay in a social context that precedes such cultural advances as the African American studies movement in American colleges and universities, and his consequent purpose is to assert his theory of blacks and whites united in a dual culture rather than to pursue greater knowledge of individual cultures. Thus, he derides claims to ethnic and genetic insularity; this attitude, he claims, has merely "helped give our streets and campuses a rowdy, All Fool's Day, carnival atmosphere."[7] Such demonstrations of insularity, he asserts, accomplish the opposite of their intended effect and serve merely as "a call to cultural and aesthetic chaos" (22). In this passage, Ellison's conjunction of the carnivalesque with the chaotic gives added significance to his subsequent alignment of the circus with the type of order that at its best affirms the dual culture and at its worst mirrors Bakhtin's "official feasts" by confirming gender and racial hierarchy.

Ellison's tone changes as he abandons his trope of the carnivalesque to describe a circuslike scene that makes a case for the dual culture with which he identifies himself. In a distinctly comic tone, he describes his encounter with a young man who bursts into his field of vision "with something of that magical cornucopian combustion by which a dozen circus clowns are exploded from [a] . . . miniaturized automobile." The young man is "[l]ight-skinned, blue-eyed, Afro-American-featured . . . [and] . . . Afro-coiffed"; he is dressed in riding boots, English riding breeches, a dashiki, and a Homberg hat. Pulling a Japanese camera from a Volkswagen Beetle unexpectedly "decked out with a gleaming Rolls-Royce radiator," the young man takes a series of self-shots as he poses "in various fanciful attitudes . . . against the George Washington Bridge" (22–23).

In this "willful juxtaposition of modes," Ellison apprehends something essentially American—what he calls "an integrative, vernacular note" that twenty-first-century cultural observers will recognize in the current attitudes of some bi- and multiracial Americans who resist the demand that they allow themselves to be limited to a single racial identity. This integrative, vernacular note is the

> American compulsion to improvise upon the given. His garments were, literally and figuratively, of many colors and cultures, his racial identity interwoven of many strands. Whatever his politics, sources of income, hierarchal status . . . he revealed his essential

"Americanness" in his freewheeling assault upon traditional forms of the Western aesthetic. Whatever the identity he presumed to project, he was exercising an American freedom and was a product of the melting pot and the conscious or unconscious comedy it brews. Culturally, he was an American joker . . . [playing] irreverently upon the symbolism of status, property, and authority, and [suggesting] new possibilities of perfection. More than expressing protest, these symbols ask the old, abiding American questions: Who am I? What about me? (24)

Ellison counters the hopeful possibilities in this philosophical use of the circus, however, with a more doubtful voicing of the ability of white Americans to recognize the dual culture of which he speaks. From Ellison's perspective of the black experience in the 1960s, a period when the necessity for institutionalizing African American studies was still challenged, the myth of southern history is complicated by the fact that the true history of the black experience, as far as any history can be true, had yet to be written.

In 1968, Ellison joined fellow panel members William Styron, C. Vann Woodward, and Robert Penn Warren at a meeting of the Southern Historical Association to debate the viability of attacks by black activists upon the historical reliability of Styron's recently published novel, *The Confessions of Nat Turner.* As Ellison has aptly noted:

Much of [my story] is not in the history textbooks. Certain historians and untrained observers did their jobs, often very faithfully, but many of them have been forgotten except by scholars and historians, and the story they recorded was altered to justify racial attitudes and practices. But somehow, through our Negro American oral tradition . . . these reminders of the past as *Negroes* recalled it found existence and were passed along.[8]

According to Ellison, this oral record is the source of the values by which African Americans have continued to live despite the contradictory messages of "official history" to which they have ostensibly accommodated themselves. Nonetheless, "the result has imposed upon Negroes a high sensitivity to the ironies of historical writing and created a profound skepticism concerning the validity of most reports of what the past was like." The value of fiction—and especially, Ellison purports, the fiction of southern writers—is that it addresses what the historians will not: "that part of the human truth which we could not accept or face up to in much historical writing because of social, racial and political considerations" (154). Here, as elsewhere, Ellison posits William Faulkner, whom he had previously listed among his most admired American clowns, as the best example of a southern writer who will "face up" to the human truth of history.

Additionally, we recognize Faulkner, and also perhaps Warren, in yet another of Ellison's essays, "The Myth of the Flawed White Southerner." In this essay, Ellison identifies an "old slave-born myth of the Negroes" that compounds the myth of history propagated by the dominant white culture:

> [N]ot the myth of the "good white man," nor that of the "great white father," but the myth, secret and questioning, of the flawed white Southerner who while true to his Southern roots has confronted the injustices of the past and been redeemed. Such a man, the myth holds, will do the right thing however great the cost, whether he likes Negroes or not, and will move with tragic vulnerability toward the broader ideals of American democracy.[9]

His personal adherence to this Negro myth (for, as Ellison remarks, he "must be true to the hopes, dreams, and myths of [his] people") in the face of the persistent myths of "official" white history must inevitably manifest itself in the artistic ambivalence with which Ellison participates in the southern circus intertext. As we have seen in Ellison's essay "The Little Man at Chehaw Station," he uses the circus to predict society's inevitable acceptance of the American dual culture. In his fiction, however, Ellison uses the circus deconstructively to replicate instead the patterns of the hierarchic barriers which must be overcome before recognition of the dual culture can become a reality.

One early short story, "King of the Bingo Game," first published in 1944 and later appearing in his collection *Flying Home,* demonstrates how the circus trope in Ellison's fiction works to reaffirm not his essayist's vision of a dual American culture but rather his awareness of intractable Old South ideologies.[10] The unnamed black protagonist of this story, penniless in the face of unemployment and family illness, turns desperately to a game of chance similar to those found in circus sideshows. As long as he can prolong the game by keeping the bingo wheel turning under his control, the sense of displacement and anonymity produced in him by his relocation from the South to the North is replaced by hope and a sense of life's possibilities in the timelessness of the unconnected present. Ultimately, however, his control of the bingo wheel is revealed as only an illusion when the white masters of ceremony violently reassert their control by beating him to the stage and stopping the wheel. Instead of achieving the direction of his own life, he finds himself merely a "mark" in a rigged carny game that leaves him more desperate than when he began. Even though he had had nothing to begin with, his prize is double nothing, the double zero on which the wheel stops; even worse, his official identity as a nonperson, symbolized by his missing birth certificate, devolves into his loss of individual identity when he forgets his own name in the excitement of the game. Forced to clownish status, his reward is not the identity to which an American *eiron* might aspire but an even more greatly diminished status than he had already possessed.

In yet another Ellison short story from the same collection, the circus becomes an image toward which a young boy seeking to transcend his childhood yearningly turns for adult order and validation. Appearing first in 1956, Ellison's "A Coupla Scalped Indians" is a short story with circus implications similar to "King of the Bingo Game," and it presents just as ambiguous an awareness of the unconnected present, the identity it promises, and the risks inherent in asserting the possibilities of self-awareness. Two boys, the unnamed eleven-year-old narrator and his slightly older friend Buster, experiment with a number of meaningful identities as several events in their lives converge: the boys' recent circumcisions, the beginning of their self-imposed survival testing based on a discarded *Boy Scout's Handbook,* and the arrival of the spring carnival. Both seek the same kind of multicultural identity Ellison endorses in his essays. Their immediate goal is the circus where they hope to have their adult masculinity—figured by the phallic horns of the band—affirmed. The narrator is assisted in his quest by his older and wiser companion Buster, who is confidently multilingual: he speaks the language of white boys, colored boys, and Indians, and he even translates the "nasty" dozens-dealing language of the distant carnival band. As in the Jason section of *The Sound and the Fury,* the carnival music provides an aural backdrop to the action—the trombone, tuba, and trumpet emit homing signals that will lead the two boys to "the further edge of town . . . [where] . . . floated the tent, spread white and cloudlike with its bright ropes of fluttering flags."[11] These phallic musical instruments beckon the two boys to their manhood, the assumption of which both view as a cultural certainty once they have proved themselves worthy by accomplishing their self-appointed tasks. In the dark woods through which they must hike to reach the circus, however, the boys are separated, and the narrator has a disturbing and unexpected sexual experience with Aunt Mackie, an eccentric old black woman who lives alone in the woods. To the extent that this story is a narrative of emerging masculine identity, Aunt Mackie is posited as the intrusive feminine other whose role is to complicate Eden. To the extent, however, that this story is Ellison's assertion of the multiracial identity of the American clown, Aunt

Mackie embodies a kind of mythic representation of blackness, the hearkening toward which intermingles desire and guilt. At the end of the story, the narrator remains lost, wandering, and far short of the goal of the broadly defined self he had hoped to reach at the beginning of his journey.

Initially, the parentless narrator and his bold and imaginative friend Buster conform to the Twainian tradition of Huck and Tom, who are boyish American clowns par excellence and literary exemplars of the clownlike *eiron,* Ellison's figure of American identity. Ellison turns, however, from the circus certainty of this comic search to ambiguity as he introduces an overtly sexual element foreign to Twain's narratives of boyhood. For example, the narrator's inadvertent stumbling upon the shack of the reclusive and mysterious Aunt Mackie delays his arrival at the carnival and anticipates the challenges to his identity he might find there. Looking through the old woman's window, he is shocked by the unexpected sight of "a young, girlish body with slender, well-rounded hips" (73) moving in slow, graceful dance steps to the faraway music. When the girl, turning, reveals a "wrinkled face mismatched with [her] glowing form" (74), he realizes she is actually Aunt Mackie, and, involuntarily recoiling, he accidentally reveals his presence to her. Ordering him inside, Aunt Mackie is alternately seductress and wise woman, virgin and hag. The boy, appalled by his uncontrollable reaction to her nakedness, feels overwhelming pain, terror, and self-hatred.

Returning from the timelessness of this sexual experience to the dark woods, he finds the physical world unchanged: the carnival, the promise of the life Buster had predicted they would find when they had left their hometown and families, awaits his arrival. But Buster is no longer there to interpret "the imperious calling of the [carnival] horns" (81). Will the narrator be able to find his friend, with whom he had hoped to make a confident claim to masculine identity? Or will he dare to descend to the carnival of life by himself? Most importantly, will he reach the destination where his multiracial American identity can be confirmed? Suddenly the magnitude and difficulty of the task lying before him is clarified. The possibilities of stability and self-definition promised him through his membership in the brotherhood of American jokers diminish in the light of this newly apprehended world in which they must be claimed.

Any Ellison character who is a seeker for personal identity is a clown in this very sense: his progress toward individuation by way of his claim of multicultural self-awareness will be neither easy nor even fully accomplished. Ellison's nameless black narrator from *Invisible Man,* for example, who first appears in the 1947 publication of "Battle Royal," struggles for self-definition within the same circuslike circumstances as his fellows, the bingo game "king" and the unnamed narrator from "A Coupla Scalped Indians." The "smoker" that is the setting of "Battle Royal" and to which *Invisible Man's* narrator has been summoned has clear circus associations. Nevertheless, its uneasy balancing of the young narrator's extraordinary self-deception that he is accepted by the hierarchy with the great effort he must make to maintain the myth that feeds his self-deception reveals Ellison's own ambivalence between the cultural unities he would affirm and the social realities that stymie them.[12]

Like the white masters of ceremony from "King of the Bingo Game," the white men attending the smoker, organized (or so the narrator thinks) to showcase his prize-winning graduation speech, are clearly and cruelly in charge of the evening's events. His and his comrades' desperate eagerness for the evening's pay and for the electrified gold coins they are encouraged to gather mirrors the desperation of the main character in "King of the Bingo Game" and the consequent entertainment he provides those gathered to watch him spin fortune's wheel. The initiation to which the young black men are subjected also parallels that of the narrator of "A Coupla Scalped Indians." Like young Buster, who asserts his multicultural and multilingual know-how, these young men are toughly confident of their abilities to excel in the battle royal. Yet the sound of a sensuous clarinet initially beckons the ten young men inside the hotel ballroom, and they are appalled to find there that their first task commingles the Old South's greatest sexual taboo with its most tenaciously held stereotype: fearful of reprisals for their uncontrollable physical responses, they are forced nonetheless to gaze upon a white woman's nakedness.

Ellison's use of the circus is common to the two short stories and his first chapter of *Invisible Man*, "Battle Royal." Circus references in the previous two texts have already been examined; Ellison's use of the circus in "Battle Royal" is, if anything, more pronounced. References to the "ring" and the "canvas" in "Battle Royal" are applicable to both boxing, the literal circumstance of this chapter's plot, and the circus; they could serve merely as interesting examples of how the jargons of the two cultural phenomena intersect. Ellison's language continues to dwell on the circus aspects of this early scene in the novel, however, marking the dancer's likeness to a "circus kewpie doll" (19); the narrator's blind frustration with his fellow combatant, a "stupid clown" (25) who refuses to throw the boxing match; and one unfortunate young man whose electrified back "[glistens] with sweat like a circus seal" (27). The narrator, pushing his way through this horrific evening with no greater thought than having the opportunity of reading his high school oration, refuses consciously to acknowledge the bizarre behaviors of the white men who, with the bestowal of a calf-skin brief case and a college scholarship, will eventually pronounce themselves his benefactors. Nevertheless, he subconsciously recognizes the events for their real significance, and the presence of his long-dead grandfather in his later recurring dream confirms a subliminal awareness of what his white patrons' sponsorship really entails, a meaning safely cocooned in dream symbolism:

> That night I dreamed I was at the circus with [my grandfather] and that he refused to laugh at the clowns no matter what they did. Then later he told me to open my brief case and read what was inside and I did, finding an official envelope stamped with a state seal. . . . "Read it," my grandfather said. "Out loud!"
> "To whom It May Concern," I intoned. "Keep This Nigger-Boy Running." (33)

Appropriately, the mob scene in chapter 25 of *Invisible Man* reinforces the novel's earlier circus images. As Ellison seeks to characterize the bumbling, ineffectual actions of both black and white characters in the novel's dénouement (if such a traditional term might be used for one of literature's most conspicuously indeterminate endings), he employs a great deal of circus clown "schtick."

Chapter 25 of *Invisible Man* takes place in the midst of mindless violence that is, to the narrator's observation, both aggressive and masochistic as black looters and white policemen engage in actions that traditionally comprise the byplay of the circus clown. In this scene, Ellison includes several traditional clown gags that depend upon surprise and juxtaposition: the screaming sound effect created by an auto tire punctured by a bullet; a woman who carries a dozen dressed chickens hanging from a broomstick and another a whole side of beef on her back; Dupre's wearing three hats stacked one upon the other, several pairs of suspenders, and a shiny pair of hip boots; running looters who wear blond wigs and dress coats and others who carry dummy rifles; a woman who rides the top of a milk wagon "like a tipsy fat lady in a circus parade" (545); and even the police, who dash around Keystone Kop–like in their white helmets. The "topper" occurs when Ellison's narrator takes a tumble down an open manhole, his own version of the classic clown pratfall.

From this safe, dark cellar the Invisible Man speaks the epilogue to the novel, a hopeful yet determinedly realistic view of what awaits him when—or if—he rejoins the outside world. Indeed, his entire narrative has issued from this underground retreat during an attenuated moment of the suspended present similar to the timelessness sought by Ellison's bingo king and that which overcomes his scalped Indian. Furthermore, the Invisible Man's final words to the reader echo those of another hopeful yet determinedly realistic young man who, at the end of his own narrative, anticipates "go[ing] into the convulsion of the world, out of history into history and the awful responsibility of Time." And yet, as I have already noted in the Introduction to this study, Jack Burden's promise to himself and to his reader remains ambiguously suspended in narrative time and therefore unfulfilled—just as the promise of the Invisible Man will remain. No matter how resolutely one might assert current identity, the movement of time is inexorable. Time will carry Jack Burden into World War II, and time will carry the Invisible Man back into a culture that is just as likely to offer confusion as identity.

The hopeful promise of the circus as it appears in Ellison's essays again balances uneasily with its deconstruction in Ellison's final novel *Juneteenth,* begun even before the completion of *Invisible Man* in 1952 and compiled and published by his literary executor John Callahan in 1999. Critics see its protagonist, the young, white-skinned Bliss, as the fictional incarnation of Ellison's vision that all Americans would unite in a single multiracial culture. John Callahan, who also edited this text after Ellison's death, notes that Bliss's quest in the novel—to "[come] to grips with the fact that he is 'also somehow black,' as Ellison believed was the case for every single 'true American'"[13]—is consonant with that desire. The point at which Bliss's achievement of such self-knowledge is most gravely threatened, however, is when he attends the circus and demonstrates under its tent his growing familiarity, even at his young age, with the types of racial markers and distinctions that threaten to fragment a unified American identity rather than assert it.

In a way, the circus has been Bliss's very life. A racially ambiguous orphan, Bliss's black foster father is Daddy Hickman, a preacher who teaches him to use his prodigious speaking abilities to their fullest advantage in performances at camp meetings and revivals all over the South. Two factors, Bliss's identification with the black community who have nurtured him and Hickman's avowed purpose for Bliss—to "speak for our condition from inside the only acceptable mask" and "embody our spirit in the council of our enemies"[14]—are almost completely realized when Bliss decides to take different path toward claiming his identity.

At first the circus impresses Bliss as only a larger version of their revivalist tent show, which is, of course, generally accepted by cultural analysts as a cousin to circus spectacle. Perhaps for that reason, Bliss begins to examine his surroundings curiously for evidences that the circus also shares the father and son's mutual culture—the black culture in which he has grown up. Daddy Hickman answers his son's questions willingly, unaware at first that the boy's interest has a racial subtext: Bliss wonders why the African and Indian elephants can be differentiated by their ears and not by "the noses"; he is caught short by the information that the African lions, obviously more powerful than their white trainer, have been "mastered" by his whip and gun (246–47). This is a skill, according to Daddy Hickman, that the trainer probably had learned at Bliss's age; ironically, Bliss's own desire for a racially dominant role will burgeon with this experience of it.

Hickman begins to have a vague understanding of Bliss's purposeful questions when the clowns enter the ring. One in particular, a dwarf whose blackface evokes minstrelsy, which is the other cousin to the American circus, is the dupe of the rest, who attack and demean him as part of the act. Hickman assures Bliss that the clown is not black at all—that he wears a burnt cork mask as part of his costume—but the boy is not comforted. He seems especially troubled by his father's laughter, and Daddy Hickman, taken aback by Bliss's failure to appreciate the humor of the performance, explains that the black dwarf is "just acting his part" in the routine, "[s]o when we laugh at them we can laugh at ourselves" (250). Later however, when Bliss encounters the dwarf clown outside the circus tent, he attacks him viciously, fascinated by how the burnt cork blacking fades with every blow of his fist. His attack proves more self-directed, on the other hand, as this experience marks his tragic abandonment not only of his life with Daddy Hickman but also of Hickman's idealistic purpose for him. Bliss and his betrayal of Hickman disprove the myth Ellison had identified as the most persistent and compelling among "his people"—the myth of the flawed white southerner who challenges social and racial injustice simply because doing so is right and good, even when he has no love for the African Americans who would benefit from the changes that might result. Sadly, Bliss, who, unlike the mythic flawed white southerner Ellison describes, has every reason of love and loyalty to foster the dream for which Hickman has raised him, finds it antipathetic to his aspirations to cultural mastery. Ellison's myth of the flawed white southerner is displaced in *Juneteenth* by the myth of southern history, which has been reenacted in circus performance.

Toni Morrison

On the surface, including Toni Morrison in a study of authors of the Southern Renaissance may appear inappropriate. Not only does Morrison's career postdate that period of the rebirth of southern letters shared by the authors chosen as representative for this study—Warren, Wolfe, Faulkner, Welty, Porter, Gordon, and

Ellison—but also she has swung consciously wide of critical claims of either southern influence or intertextuality. Establishing Morrison within the tradition of the Southern Renaissance is further complicated by simple geography since she was born in Ohio. If, however, as Morrison herself claims, "roots are less a matter of geography than sense of shared history,"[15] then she and her work are just as rooted in the literary South as any of the writers we have previously examined. Morrison's sense of shared history among the writers of the Southern Renaissance is most clearly revealed in her novel *Beloved* (1987). This novel has inspired feminist and African American dialogues that, in conjunction with Morrison's own use of the southern intertext of the circus, create an intertextual bond with "The Circus in the Attic," Robert Penn Warren's own circus-centered novella, as well as with other works from the Southern Renaissance that use the circus to figure the persistence of the myth of southern history. My inclusion of Morrison's use of the circus in her fiction should not, therefore, be taken as an assertion that she is looking to white southern patriarchal structures as models and precursors merely to imitate. Her participation in the use of the southern circus intertext, however, should remind us of both Ralph Ellison's stated belief that the history of African Americans had yet to be written and the power of the black voice, like that of Ella Fitzgerald's singing the standard "Paper Moon," to offer a familiar story from an unfamiliar and underconsidered perspective.

For example, Warren's characterization of Bolton Lovehart and Morrison's treatment of her character Beloved reveal meaningful differences and similarities in the two authors' views of history, in the two primary psychoanalytic approaches used by critics to examine their texts, and in the artistic means by which Warren's and Morison's texts alternately confirm and refute hegemonic structures. In a gesture similar to those actions of her characters, who must resist the white society's cultural construction of blackness as a trope, Morrison distances herself from the modernist fathers who were the darlings of the New Critics, asserting, "I am not *like* James Joyce. . . . I am not *like* Faulkner; I am not *like* in that sense."[16] No doubt she would disclaim likeness to Robert Penn Warren with equal firmness, and, indeed, my purpose here is not served by pursuing a putative literary fathering, Warren of Morrison, where none exists, by way of establishing the influence of his text on hers. It is enough that Warren's and Morrison's common use of the circus creates an intertext; their equally marked dissimilarities within that intertext might be read by a New Critic as juxtapositions, seemingly oppositional tensions that resolve in either a single unified meaning or an equally significant ambiguity. To a poststructuralist, these same differences might be read as demonstrations of the pluralisms that produce mutually informing intertextualities. Intriguingly, then, Morrison's work invites both New Critical and poststructuralist readings. Morrison's continued "prosecution" of the myth of southern history, a favorite theme of the Southern Renaissance, is made possible by the psychological, feminist, and cultural "evidence" lately made available through poststructuralism.

Just like Bolton Lovehart, who is periodically summoned from his solitude on Rusty-Butt Hill by both actual and metaphorical circuses, Beloved's reincarnation from ghostly presence to enigmatic young womanhood is prompted by the visit Sethe, Paul D, and Denver make to the carnival. While the three living inhabitants of the house at 124 expose themselves to the paradox of community and carnival, the ghostly Beloved emerges ritualistically and fully dressed from a baptismal rebirth; similarly, as twelve-year-old Bolton Lovehart rises from his creekside immersion by a Baptist preacher, the circus images that up to that point have provided merely a backdrop to the history of Bardsville come to life. Conversely, however, when the thirty-three-year-old Bolton achieves the victory over his mother that his secret circus permits, he wanders Bardsville "with the happiness of a ghost who blesses out of his own steady peace the flickering joy of the living and wishes them well."[17] Beloved's haunting, on the other hand, confers no comparable peace; because of her and Sethe's need to confront the circumstances of her death, "124 was spiteful. Full of baby's venom."[18]

Bolton Lovehart and the character Beloved are both incarnations of the myth of southern history. Bolton, of course, perpetuates mythic southern history with every circus figure he creates in his attic. Furthermore, when he rejoins his community during World War II, he becomes the embodiment of the mythic view of history by promoting the patriotic resolve and self-sacrifice necessary to winning the war. Identified alternately with his own creations of the ring master and the clown, he is both a trope for blind acceptance of historical myth and the sense of noble purpose that the acceptance of such myth produces.

Similarly, the presence of Beloved also perpetuates the myth of southern history. But unlike Bolton Lovehart, her existence and the myth's survival are made possible through Sethe's destructive silence about the past rather than through her imaginative recreation of it. Deborah Guth's analysis of Morrison's novel confirms the important differences between characters/tropes like Warren's Bolton Lovehart and Morrison's Beloved: Beloved is "the spirit of the past . . . the demon of historic distortion which cannot be simply bracketed away in the name of renewal as Morrison feels previous generations have tried to do, but demands full recognition and understanding before it can be exorcised."[19] Bolton, on the other hand, in his role as the unofficial historian of Bardsville, may evoke the spirit of the past, but he does so as a seemingly harmless eccentric, called to service to reaffirm Bardsville's misconceptions of its role in history. Beloved is reincarnated by Sethe's refusal to tell a personal history that will challenge patriarchal myth. Sethe's silence works to confirm the myth yet proves as psychically immobilizing for her as Bolton's compulsive reiteration of his own deeply internalized "story" proves for him. Significantly, the image of the circus and the circus carnival draws these two characters together within the paralyzing myth of history.

As already established in chapters 1 and 2 of this study, Warren's use of the circus can be read to validate what critics of his canon have identified as the Freudian themes of the search for the father and the ultimate rejection of the mother. Bolton's circus begins to take shape even before his birth, when rowdy Bardsville boys, anxious to escape their "tyrannous mothers" and fight in the Civil War, are pictured as "circus performers";[20] one might even conceive that Bolton's own father was one of those romantic and rebellious boys who in later life gleans an altered version of truth from his actual war experience. As Bolton attempts to escape his own possessive mother, he runs away to an old-fashioned creek baptism, where the preacher drips with watery ring master's spangles, where a young female convert, submissive and dancerlike, hints of Bolton's ideal of the girl acrobat, and where the properly Episcopal Bolton accepts his own clown-inspired identity when he is immersed. Through the empty years of his dwindling youth, recurring visions of the three circus figures further reinforce Bolton's need to escape his mother and learn the answers to questions about the past from his emotionally distant father. Warren's narrator, inviting the reader to look back upon the three Loveharts from a vantage point of sixty years hence, notes that, as they pace themselves to Bolton's toddling steps, the three "hardly seem to move at all, to be fixed . . . in a photograph in an album to prove something sweet and sure about the past" (17). In reality troubled and illusion-riddled, the Loveharts become the perfect family only when they are frozen within the framework of that patriarchally enshadowed, mythic tableau.

Toni Morrison presents a similarly deceptive image of familial cohesion in *Beloved* as Sethe, her only remaining child Denver, and her lover Paul D walk the dusty road toward Cincinnati, where they plan to attend the circus carnival on Colored Thursday. Sethe takes it as a good sign that although she, Denver, and Paul D "were not holding hands, . . . their shadows were."[21] Like the Loveharts, this trio become the perfect family only within parameters defined by the dominant white culture. Sethe, Paul D, and Denver demonstrate the shadowy, behind-the-scenes, slave-family life which is the only one acknowledged by white masters and patriarchal myth. Sethe's hopeful but shadowy vision of family is symptomatic of her resolute denial of the past and indicative of the power the returning Beloved will later hold over the residents of 124.

Unlike Bolton, who is committed to the search for the white father, Sethe's story must assert the black mother. Thus, one of the most revealing analyses of *Beloved* emerges from Jennifer Fitzgerald's use of Kleinian objects relations theory. Using the Freudian model to read "The Circus in the Attic" asserts a patriarchal determination of what is normative and universalized among family relationships. For a text like *Beloved,* however, which asserts the cultural primacy of black motherhood over white fatherhood, the benefit of a Kleinian reading is immediately clear: instead of defining the mother according to "a very specific, restricted norm"[22] and placing responsibility and blame on her, as Freudian readings of "The Circus in the Attic" consistently do, a Kleinian approach demands that the reader observe Sethe's act of killing her own child with a cultural awareness that extends beyond the conventionally white and patriarchal. The additional considerations of race and class permitted by such an awareness will suggest factors beyond simple murderous intent. By taking into account Sethe's experiences of black slavery and their effects on her decision not to allow her children to return to a similar life, the Kleinian approach demands that readers of *Beloved* examine the white father's motives for enslavement as readily as they examine the black mother's motives for murder.

The Kleinian and Freudian approaches also place vastly different emphases on the role of community in an individual's development. In the Kleinian approach, "selfhood is socially constructed through interaction with [a community of] others, aspects of whom have been internalized by the child as part of itself."[23] Appropriately, Sethe seeks out community when she and the infant Beloved join her other children with Baby Suggs in Ohio; by killing her baby and attempting to kill her other children, she demeans the value of the socially constructed selfhood provided to her by her interaction with and dependence on community. At the novel's climax, Sethe is rescued from her fatal denial of time and self by the direct intervention of the black community, which act again demonstrates its proper place in the formation of her identity as a black woman who has escaped enslavement.

Significantly, Warren's novella draws upon Freudian texts that privilege "the healthy development of individual autonomy, highly valued by white Western capitalism."[24] "The Circus in the Attic" is consistently read as having reversed the process of identity formation. In that sense, Warren details Bolton's escape from familial and community influence to personal autonomy, his regressive return to community during World War II, and his ultimate flight from the community as he returns to his attic, his imaginative circus, and his myth of history.

Finally, a common tropic use of the circus and the carnival sideshow reveals other similarities and disparities between Warren's tale of the myth of southern history compulsively retold and Morrison's narrative of the truth of history compulsively avoided.[25] Both speak to the crippling effects of the failure to claim the present because the past has not been adequately comprehended or properly implemented, a southern theme which Morrison herself has identified by her observation that a clear understanding of the past is the only means by which one can confront the future. Yet the difficulty in achieving such an understanding is made manifest through Warren's and Morrison's mutual uses of the circus intertext; in "The Circus in the Attic" and *Beloved,* both authors reveal a patriarchal social structure seemingly invulnerable to and even reinforced by willful transgression.

Bolton Lovehart manages to escape his grasping mother by devoting his life to the secret, transgressive circus he constructs in his attic. Her death frees him of the steady, accusing gaze she has used to render him guilt-ridden and obedient; yet rather than feeling liberated and empowered, he imagines that his circus figures affix him with the same accusing gaze she had once used. Formerly, he had felt no sense of loss or fear as "the painted eyes of animals and girl acrobats and riders and ring masters and clowns circled about him, . . . [and] his world constricted to that orbit."[26] At his mother's death, however, Bolton comes to an unnerving sense of his own mortality "among the hateful, painted eyes of the creatures he had made."[27]

Bolton's experience confirms cultural critic Yorum Carmeli's assertion that although the circus is posited outside of history, outside of change, and outside of social time, it nevertheless has the effect of reifying bourgeois hegemony[28]— in Bolton's case, the myth of southern history. Spectators at the circus momentarily leave their traditional social constructs behind in order to enter a world that will parody or even destroy those constructs. After "the show" is over, however, the spectators return to their world with a reinforced and even grateful sense of what they perceive as stable and orderly there.

Correspondingly, Bolton Lovehart leaves his attic circus and reenters Bardsville as it prepares to enter the circus of World War II. There Bolton finds his girl acrobat conveniently recreated in the socially ambitious Mrs. Parton, whom he marries, and his ring master in her handsome but callow son Jasper, to whom he becomes a surrogate father. During this strangely extra-cultural interlude, Bolton again finds himself outside of history, outside of change and outside of social time. Only when time and change reassert themselves—Jasper dies an uncharacteristically heroic death in Italy, Mrs. Parton is killed with her paramour in a fiery automobile crash, and Bardsville begins to tire of its spectator's role and yearn for an end to the wartime circus—does Bolton return to his attic. He is not reconciled, perhaps, to the reminders of mortality in the eyes of his circus figures, but he is certainly now more at home among the acrobats, ring masters, and clowns whose acts of ostensible transgression actually reinforce social order and mythic history.

Sethe's experience at the traveling carnival's Colored Thursday also serves to reveal her inability and, at present, her disinclination to challenge the dominant social order. The members of the carnival sideshow, who are themselves clearly outcast and other, are nonetheless complicit with the segregation of black audiences from white ones—hence, Colored Thursday. This mandate defines the black community's otherness and intensifies it by setting it alongside the otherness of the white carnival grotesques. The carnival world may be "rootless, meaningless, and homeless"[29] in the eyes of the fixed culture, but the black community, especially as it is perceived by the dominant white culture, demonstrates those acultural qualities even more fully. As much as the black spectators anticipate "the excitement of seeing white people loose: doing magic, clowning, without heads or with two heads, twenty feet tall or two feet tall, weighing a ton, completely tattooed . . . and beating each other up," they know "none of it is true."[30] The grotesqueries the white performers assume for the carnival are less a cultural reality than the grotesqueries they seek to enforce upon the black spectators, who acknowledge even the white carnival community's perceptions of them. As Sethe herself will especially demonstrate, even black self-perceptions reflect white hegemonic thought.

This harsh lesson is reinforced when Sethe returns from Colored Thursday, not to make a home with Paul D and Denver as she had hoped to do but to have that home threatened by her refusal to tell her own Kentucky slave story. Beloved's appearance is announced by Sethe's symbolic reenactment of sudden labor and childbirth. Shocked and shamed by her body's weakness, Sethe wonders "if the carnival would accept another freak."[31] Through her continuing silence about her past, Sethe in effect accepts the freakishness of her race and gender as decreed by the white culture; she cannot and will not repudiate the white culture's myth of southern history with the reality of her own experience.

In "The Circus in the Attic," Bolton Lovehart, who cannot physically escape his region and its mythic preconceptions, attempts an imaginative escape through his circus, but even that imaginative outlet reinforces the myth he seeks to challenge. Sethe, on the other hand, achieves the physical escape that Bolton cannot effect, becoming a southern expatriate whom another—Warren himself—would have recognized and appreciated. Both escaped Kentucky physically only to realize that they each must, nonetheless, return to it through memory. Warren, who through memory produced his distinctive fiction and poetry, attributed moral significance to identity thus achieved, albeit in masculine terms: " I do attach a significance to the way a man deals with the place God drops him in. His reasons for going or staying. And his piety or impiety."[32] And, not insignificantly, Warren uses the term "piety" to suggest the morality in acknowledging one's own true father and impiety as the act of claiming a false father (Walker 156). Metaphorically, Warren, as a child of the South, is speaking of the moral necessity of choosing initiation into time over the myth of history. Similarly, Sethe's piety or impiety depends upon her choosing either to keep a silence that will affirm the false white father and deny the true black mother, or to speak the unspeakable and challenge the mythic forces that negate self and time.[33]

Sethe's and Bolton's experiences inform and corroborate Warren's conflation of history and morality. Moreover, Warren's and Morrison's individual uses of the southern intertext of the circus to voice their mutual challenges to the myth of southern history disprove the words of "the smart ones" from *Jazz* (1992), Morrison's sequel to *Beloved*. These are the southern blacks of the Great Migration of the 1920s and 1930s who relocate themselves in northern cities. Once there they make a hopeful claim: "There goes the sad stuff. The bad stuff. The things-nobody-could-help stuff. The way everybody was then and there. Forget that. History is over, you all, and everything's ahead at last."[34] Their resolute turning away from the moral task of self-definition that remains to be accomplished is similarly addressed by Warren's "Circus" narrator, who wryly notes that "people always believe what truth they have to believe to go on being the way they are."[35]

For finally, Warren's and Morrison's texts, spanning the temporal and ideological changes that separate them, speak to the viability of the circus intertext and its power to unite the authors of varying races, classes, and genders who seek to confront the myth of southern history and thus to effect the South's collective initiation into time.

Conclusion

A circus at the center

*[P]erhaps the circus seems to stand outside the
culture only because it is at its very center.*

—Paul Bouissac
Circus and Culture: A Semiotic Approach, 1976

Robert Penn Warren was born on April 24, 1905, in Guthrie,
Kentucky, a small town created only a few years earlier to serve the Louisville and
Nashville Railroad and even named for the railroad's president, a United States
congressman.[1] It is strange to think that Warren, whose writings are saturated
with a sense of the past, sprang from a setting noted for its pastlessness.[2] For
most of the residents of Guthrie, Warren's parents included, the town was a place
where they came to seek new lives and new fortunes, a place with no tradition
of its own. Warren would describe it as "a place to be from,"[3] a town "without a
sense of belonging in any particular place or having any particular history."[4]

Although Guthrie was a town noted for violence, Warren's recollections of
its harsher aspects seem deliberately understated. All the same, Guthrie's proximity to the railroad, its transient population, and the inevitability of such
small-scale lawlessness as bootlegging and cockfighting were certain to influence its character and thus Warren's memories of it. Violence spilled over into
the schoolyard when, as Warren recalls, a schoolmate, one of the "big boys,"
who had killed a carnival hand with a tent-peg, was tried for and acquitted of
the murder and allowed to return to school.[5] Warren, a studious child who was
judged a sissy by some of "the railroad boys," was the sometime target of his
classmates' antagonism.[6] Floyd Watkins speculates that the rough-and-tumble
of Guthrie may explain why the youthful Warren preferred long country rambles to in-town activities; his later poetry would certainly reflect those childhood rambles. Nevertheless, Guthrie played an important role in Warren's

109

informal education since, as Watkins notes, the "variety of cultures and of economic systems in a small geographical area may be in part responsible for Warren's knowledge of widely variant Southern ways of life as well as his lack of a strong loyalty to any one kind of Southernism."[7]

Set in the midst of the Kentucky countryside, Warren's hometown bore its own surprising brand of cosmopolitanism. Anything a train could carry came to Guthrie, including circuses and carnivals, references to which appear in such early published works as Warren's *John Brown: The Making of a Martyr* (1929) and in unpublished works such as "God's Own Time" (c1932). Then, in addition to the books that the intellectually minded Robert Franklin Warren made available to his son, Warren remembers even more wonderful possibilities at the railroad station's adjoining hotel—"a newsstand where one could buy a *Nation, New Republic, Poetry, Dial* and such—in the early 1920's."[8] Within roughly a decade, Warren's own poetry would appear in issues of the first three of those publications: "Pro Vita Sua" in the *New Republic* in 1927, "Rebuke of the Rock" in a 1928 issue of *Nation,* and "The Cardinal" in *Poetry* in 1932.

For all these reasons, Warren's boyhood was a combination of high and low cultures, played out alternately in terms of his intellectual aspirations and his observations of life's raw edge, and both of which he consciously and unconsciously blended in his later fiction, nonfiction, poetry, essays, and social commentary. Warren's artistic interest in high and low cultures reflects a life-long fascination with the interactions between the two. He would address and attempt to resolve them throughout his career, but especially in his 1974 Jefferson Lecture in the Humanities, significantly titled "Democracy and Poetry." In his fiction, he addresses the dichotomy of high and low cultures through the most seriously deluded of his characters who neglect the one, low culture, in their pursuit of the other, high culture. As an example, when in *Night Rider* Percy Munn's desire to enact noble ideals results in ignoble actions, he looks for guidance to homespun Willie Proudfit's narrative of his idealistically begun western sojourn and his sobering but gratifying return home; Ashby Wyndham's narrative plays a grim counterpoint to the idealistic but ill-fated dreams of Jerry Calhoun in *At Heaven's Gate* (1943); Jack Burden finds his escapist, scholarly distance is ineffectual in the face of Willie Stark's populist pragmatism in *All the King's Men* (1946); in *World Enough and Time* (1950), Jeremiah Beaumont learns that the West of his romantic imagination is, in actuality, the natural domain of the grossly amoral Gran' Boz, a misshapen criminal; and in *A Place to Come To* (1977), Jed Tewksbury seeks sanctuary in classical scholarship from his hardscrabble hometown and its associations with his father's ludicrous death, only to be drawn home again by the folksy, fatherly Perk Simms. All of these characters are types of Warren's semi-autobiographical protagonist Bolton Lovehart, and their collective conflicts reflect Bolton's in "The Circus in the Attic." Bolton's strange affinity for the activities his community dubs low culture—the Baptist revival meeting and silent movies to name two—puts an humble face on his thwarted yearning for intellectual identity. Thus Warren seals the irony of Bolton's romantic aspiration to a self-defining art form by giving the most satisfying metaphor at his protagonist's disposal a singularly low culture source: the circus.

The circus during the southern Renaissance

Further complicating Robert Penn Warren's and Bolton Lovehart's artistic uses of the circus image, however, is the phenomenon during Warren's lifetime of the steady cultural rehabilitation of the circus. Even before the consolidation of the Ringling Bros. Circus with the Barnum & Bailey Circus and the creation of the world-famous Greatest Show on Earth, the Ringling brothers had visually asserted their strong family tradition on their advertising handbills.[9] The name "Barnum" hearkened just as compellingly to a decades-long tradition of showmanship and family entertainment. The days when such moral arbiters as Henry Ward Beecher mourned that young people were abandoning more sober and enlightening entertainments for the circus were not completely gone by Warren's youth, but the three-ring, big top circus was well on its way to becoming a typically time-honored American custom even as early as the turn of the twentieth century.

Originally, the merging of the Ringlings with the Barnum & Bailey Circus, formalized in 1918 and effected in 1919, had been meant to serve the practical purpose of pooling the two circuses' resources during the lean days of war anticipated by circus management. With the Armistice, the consolidation proved less economically necessary, but able-bodied men were still in short supply, which may explain why women artists, especially acrobats and high-wire performers, were so prominently featured in the first season of the Ringling Bros. and Barnum & Bailey Combined Shows. Not only in the midst of war, but especially during its sobering aftermath, which would be figured by the bleak modern life-styles of the Lost Generation, the circus was a symbol of continuity and a link to a way of life many imagined was quickly disappearing. This specific role of the circus is demonstrated in the works of several artists of the Southern Renaissance. When William Faulkner sets much of the action of *The Sound and the Fury* (1929), for example, during the week "the show" is in town, he locates in the circus, which Jason Compson scornfully dismisses, a placatory, infantilizing gesture toward weary, impoverished farmers struggling with their lack of identity with the New South. Similarly, Caddie's daughter Quentin and the Rev. Shegog, who are both figured as acrobats in the novel, awe the reader with their daring circus virtuosity, but with questionable results since, in the larger Faulknerian universe, neither women nor blacks ultimately fare well. When, in *Delta Wedding* (1946), Eudora Welty invokes the image of circus acrobats to indicate the solidarity of the 1920s-era Fairchild family in the face of irresistible extracultural forces, she is taking one long, last look backward to tradition and continuity before her characters acculturate to the modern Delta. Finally, when, in Katherine Anne Porter's short story "The Circus" (1935), young Miranda's behavior is deemed inappropriate even for under the big top, she provokes disapproval from two circus clowns and realizes that these citizens of a strictly structured culture are as disappointed as her grandmother by her inability to conform to traditional southern womanhood.

The use of the circus as an ideological tool gained momentum in the 1930s and 1940s. As one of the projects of the Works Progress Administration, the circus was encouraged to continue, although on a lesser scale, even during the Depression years, when keeping people's spirits up—and thus building their confidence in the government—was high on the Roosevelt administration's list of priorities. Eudora Welty textualized her WPA experience in her photographs of southern circuses and carnivals and in her short stories from that period that allude to the circus. During World War II, however, the circus came into its own as a model for patriotic fervor, as Warren's "Circus in the Attic" illustrates. The novella is much more than Warren's reworking of a "good story" he had heard during the 1930s about eccentric Kentuckian John Wesley Venable and his collection of homemade circus figures. It took the imaginative eye of the writer, in combination with cultural associations of the 1940s, to pair Venable's circus with the three wars that shape Bolton Lovehart's life—the Civil War, World War I, and World War II. Without a doubt, Warren's choice of the circus as the cultural image Bolton Lovehart carries with him during the greatest war of the century is perfectly consistent with the propagandistic role actual circuses played from 1941 to 1945. The circus—that is, the circus management that sought to affirm the very ideals that originated with federal bureaucracy—took its job of reminding the country of wartime commitments very seriously.

Indeed, the circus of the 1930s, 1940s, and 1950s began more and more to reflect rather than to challenge the social and cultural attitudes of those decades and, in its own way, duplicated the accepted attitudes about gender, class, and race that were dominant in America at the time. For example, the ring master, who wielded a nominal authority over the show, was always a white male. Women clowns were nonexistent since women were limited to acrobatic and equestrian roles that ensured their visibility as objects of desire and display. Black participants in circus spectacle, whether those imported from Africa or hired straight from Harlem to pose as tribal peoples, were showcased in such a way as to affirm Euro-American superiority, which was accepted as a matter of course in circus life just as in the noncircus world. The paradox of the circus, structured itself as a rigid hierarchy,[10] is located in the common assumption, voiced by such circus historians as Doug Mishler, that it allowed its audiences to transcend race, class, and gender distinctions.[11] Obviously, the reality of circus structure and performance worked to affirm rather than eliminate those very distinctions.[12]

Predictably then, in the 1940s and 1950s, American circuses continued their trend toward a more conservative identity by becoming even more socially aligned with noncircus society. The circus had once been granted special status before American communities became themselves more physically and psychologically mobile. Greater social mobility after the war, however, coupled with the fact that some of the larger shows experienced a series of expensive disasters, led circuses to form coalitions with fraternal and civic organizations in the many cities they visited every season. As a result of such liaisons, the circus found a readier reception in these towns as well as better facilities in which to perform there. Many shows, like the Ringling Bros. and Barnum & Bailey Circus, had given up their big tops in favor of the safer and more permanent facilities for which groups such as the Shriners, the Lions Club, or the Rotary Club could act as guarantor.

During these decades, Ralph Ellison was one of the last of the authors of the Southern Renaissance to use the circus as an image in his canon, and in his case to demonstrate how the circus, once assumed to be a site for democracy and transgression, slavishly mirrored the society for which it performed. As revealed in chapter 4 of this study, this very knowledge informs Ellison's posthumous *Juneteenth* (1999), on which he labored for decades, having begun it even before the publication of *Invisible Man* in 1952. When Bliss, the novel's racially ambiguous preaching prodigy, goes to the circus with his black foster father, Daddy Hickman, he curiously examines the show for evidence of the father and son's mutual culture—the black culture, which the white-skinned Bliss has been encouraged to accept as his own. To his chagrin, Daddy Hickman is perfectly complacent to note that everything African about the performance, including the elephants and tigers, has been "mastered" and "tamed" by the white performers.

Even the single "black" performer, a white dwarf with skin darkened by burnt cork, has been mastered by the white clowns through their comic attacks on him. Daddy Hickman, taken aback by Bliss's failure to appreciate the humor of the performance, explains that the black dwarf is "just acting his part" in the comedy, "[s]o when we laugh at them we can laugh at ourselves."[13] Caught up short by this circus portrayal of what the black community recognizes as social reality, Bliss at first attacks the dwarf but later vents his animosity against the black community that has nurtured him.

Although the Ohio-born Toni Morrison is not a southerner, her novels examine and rework many southern themes, a fact that necessitates her inclusion in this study. By using the ideologically conservative image of the circus in *Beloved* (1987), Morrison reveals how insidiously a black community's sense of double consciousness can be heightened by even distant contact with the white community, as when Sethe and her family attend the circus freak show and, in effect, exchange roles with the freaks when they see themselves reflected through the eyes of the hostile performers. Again, circus performance reflects social reality as it is defined by the dominant white culture.

warren and "The circus in the Attic"

Warren's use of circus images in his canon and the interrelationships enacted by his three circus figures—the clown, the ring master, and the acrobat—reveal a broad range of interpretive possibilities for his previously underconsidered novella "The Circus in the Attic." The circus, filled with death defying performers whose invitations to spectacle could result happily or disastrously as chance might dictate, suggests the serious business behind play, whimsy, and creativity. When Warren's protagonist Bolton Lovehart seeks an artistic association with the circus, he reveals every artist's necessarily conflicted relationship with his community. Conflict results when, in Bolton's case, his lifetime's worth of artistry becomes alternately an object of Bardsville's admiration and a repository of its scorn.

Warren's examination of Bolton's artistic role also parallels the author's literary fascination with one of the most important influences on his canon, Nathaniel Hawthorne. A close reading of Warren's novella allows one to draw several important links between it and "Nathaniel Hawthorne," the analysis of the life and works of his nineteenth-century forebear that appears in Warren, Cleanth Brooks, and R. W. B. Lewis's anthology *American Literature: The Makers and the Making* (1973). Warren's thought-provoking introduction to Hawthorne's works is historically, psychologically, culturally, and critically informed, as one would expect from a scholar of Warren's stature.[14] It is, however, the subjective narrative quality of this twenty-nine-page introduction—one of the longest in the anthology—that evidences Warren's personal and artistic identification with the nineteenth-century literary father on whom many aspects of Bolton Lovehart's life and troubled artistry are based.

One aspect is Nathaniel Hawthorne's steady pursuit and, conversely, studied evasion of the "deep, warm secret" of humanity that results, finally, in his conviction that his alienation from the world was necessary to perfect his art. Then, in contrast to this Hawthornesque quality of Bolton's psyche is the quality best exemplified by Warren's father, Robert Franklin Warren, who sacrificed his art to accept the burdens of marriage and family life—in other words, to validate the "deep, warm secret." Bolton's attempt to resolve the conflicts inherent in combining the role of the artist with the role of the father is an action Robert Penn Warren would value since Warren, the literary son of Hawthorne and the biological son of Robert Franklin Warren, seeks to be true to the examples of both his fathers.

Hawthorne is additionally the source for the triangular geometry of the clown, the acrobat, and the ring master in "The Circus in the Attic." Their interrelationships mimic the tensions that unite Arthur Dimmesdale, Hester Prynne, and Roger Chillingworth in *The Scarlet Letter.* Moreover, Hawthorne's tale could itself be perceived as an essentially Freudian narrative in which the younger man displaces the older man to achieve the "prize"—the female component of the triangle. Both the Hawthornesque configuration and the triangular Freudian narrative are refigured several times over in "Circus," not only among the original Loveharts (Bolton, Louise, and Simon) or in the later Loveharts (Bolton, Mrs. Parton, and Jasper) but also in the primary circus threesome (the clown, the acrobat, and the ring master).

The Freudian narrative can be used to great effect to interpret "The Circus in the Attic"; applying additional psychological approaches proves equally as informative. The Lacanian narrative, for example, relies on the same triangular structure yet permits quite a different analysis of it. In this narrative, the younger man's odyssey involves a search for language that will validate not only his claim to the Name of the Father but also his ability some day to succeed the older man—with the purpose, again, of achieving all attendant patriarchal rights and privileges. Precocious as Pearl's language is in *The Scarlet Letter,* only the minister's "discovery" of language at the end of the novel can resolve the double-edged mystery of Pearl's earthly paternity and Dimmesdale's heavenly paternity. Similarly, Bolton Lovehart's receipt of numerous letters, narratives written by his stepson Jasper from the European front, bestows fatherhood on the older man in two ways: the letters give him a father by answering the "thousand questions" that Bolton never thought to ask Simon Lovehart before he died, but they also make him a father by granting him paternal rights to Jasper and his narratives.

Yet Warren's own detailed analysis of *The Scarlet Letter*, which comprises a lengthy section of his Hawthorne introduction, reads the triangular character dynamic in a way that permits contemporary critics interpretive possibilities even beyond the Freudian and Lacanian. These additional interpretations, which are equally applicable to "The Circus in the Attic," emerge with Warren's insightful observation that Hester Prynne is, for all practical purposes, written to one side as Hawthorne focuses on the relationship between Dimmesdale and Chillingworth. These male characters, Warren declares, "are more important to each other than Hester is to either; theirs is the truest 'marriage.'" This aspect of the relationship between Dimmesdale and Chillingworth is less Freudian or Lacanian than Girardian. René Girard's study of triangular desire titled *Deceit, Desire, and the Novel: Self and Other in Literary Structure* (1961, 1965) deals precisely with how the masculine components of the triangle, called the subject and the mediator, tend to claim the narrative foreground and how the feminine component, the object, takes a subordinate role to them. This dynamic is created when the subject, usually a younger man, imagines that an older, more experienced man, the mediator, is his rival for the love of a beautiful woman, the object. What initially appears to be a Freudian or a Lacanian triangle, however, masks the true desire of the subject for the mediator. Oftentimes the subject will create something akin to a Freudian narrative in which he imagines himself wronged by the mediator in order to exacerbate their "rivalry." Once again, this same dynamic is the driving force behind Bolton Lovehart's obsessive interest in Simon Lovehart and Jasper Parton, the rivals who displace Louise Lovehart and Mrs. Parton in Bolton's desire.

Still another dimension of the triangular tension among Warren's circus characters could be explained by Eve Kosofsky Sedgwick's study *Between Men: English Literature and Male Homosocial Desire* (1985). Sedgwick enhances René Girard's theory of triangular desire through her formulation of a phenomenon with cultural as well as literary manifestations. From a feminist perspective, Sedgwick refines Girard's triangular desire into male homosocial desire, which she defines not only as "men-loving-men" but also as "men-promoting-the-interests-of-men." The implicit or explicit purpose of male homosocial desire is, therefore, to dominate women. Certainly any feminist reading of Warren's thrice-repeated character triangle in "The Circus in the Attic" would need to address some aspect of Sedgwick's study.

The triangular character configuration in Warren's "Circus" novella becomes once more relevant in light of Richard King's explanation of the social, gender, and racial intricacies of the southern antebellum plantation system in *A Southern Renaissance: The Cultural Awakening of the American South, 1939–1955* (1980). The Freudian family romance, one template under which this present study organized an earlier reading of the novella, is recast in King's analysis as "the southern family romance." In this psychological narrative, the white slaveholding "father" plays a dominant role in the psychic development of his black "slave children"—terms that can have literal as well as metaphoric applications.

One might not even consider the possibility that "The Circus in the Attic" could be termed a southern family romance if it were not for Forrest Robinson's observation that considerations of black slavery are conspicuously omitted from such works as *All the King's Men,* especially from Jack Burden's final epiphany, despite his heavily researched doctoral thesis on his ancestor, the repentant slave owner Cass Mastern. Because of Jack's evasion of the issue of slavery, this racial theme "never reaches the surface of his consciousness";[15] indeed, his evasion is a moral weakness that Bolton Lovehart shares since Bolton's similar fascination for his father's Civil War service never includes a consideration of the political exigencies for which the service was required.

The subtext of black slavery emerges from *All the King's Men* through the Cass Mastern tale, the moral theme of which, according to Robinson, Jack Burden manages to ignore. The subtext of black slavery in "The Circus in the Attic" emerges in the character of Jasper Parton, who bears the stereotypical characteristics of minstrel show "blackness" as well as "secret blood" from his mother's side of the family. Critically, this secret blood connects him to Bolton's blood line, but it also suggests a darker "secret" of the blood that would realize in Jasper the black son of the South who looks to Bolton as the embodiment of every white slave-holding father who abused his paternal privilege among his black slave women. No wonder that Warren, whether consciously or unconsciously, identifies Jasper with the "sinister" ring master at the end of the novella: his heritage of illegitimacy and his true paternity, if revealed, are serious threats to the racial complacency of the modern South, which has steadily repressed acknowledgments of the southern family romance.

The circus and Modernism

Robert Penn Warren's use of the circus in "The Circus in the Attic" gains added dimension when placed alongside Thomas Wolfe's use of the circus in his short fiction "Circus at Dawn," in portions of *The Web and the Rock,* and as the centerpiece of the novel *You Can't Go Home Again.* Comparisons of these works reveal similarities and fine distinctions between the two authors' materials, methods, and literary programs. Clearly, both authors share a fascination for and a cultural familiarity with the circus. Additionally, both were greatly influenced by modernism, to which their uses of the circus pose artistic responses.

Warren was introduced to the poetry of T. S. Eliot and other modernist poets by fellow student Allen Tate while attending Vanderbilt University from 1921 to 1925. In fact, one of Warren's chief complaints about the English department at the University of California at Berkeley, where he had been admitted for graduate study in 1925, was that its faculty were stodgily uninformed about literary modernism.[16] In *A Colder Fire: The Poetry of Robert Penn Warren* (1965), Victor Strandberg establishes that T. S. Eliot had a strong poetic influence on Warren. For his fiction, Warren, like the poet Eliot and the novelist James Joyce, sought classical structures on which to base his early works. One of the most notable examples is his novel *At Heaven's Gate* (1943), for which Warren uses Dante's *Inferno* as "intellectual scaffolding."[17]

Conversely, Thomas Wolfe, who valued certain aspects of modernism, still had only a guarded admiration for a mere few of its practitioners. James Joyce was one of those few. Although the young writer's first reaction to Joyce's *Ulysses* was "whoops of joy, and . . . happy derisive laughter,"[18] he later developed an appreciation for its unusual narrative style, its use of the interior monologue, and its inventive language. Wolfe was actually disappointed to learn that scholars had discovered a discernible structure in Joyce's modernist work; he preferred, no doubt, to consider himself and Joyce kindred spirits who shared Wolfe's early tendency for monumental disorder. Even so, Wolfe composed his later works with more of a conscious sense of order as he determined to become less dependent upon his editors for eliciting coherent structures and sustained effects from his amorphous manuscripts.

In spite of Warren's youthful enthusiasm for the modernist cause, by 1935 he had made some serious reconsiderations of some of the primary tenets of the movement: its exhortation that poetry should be difficult to understand, its preference for image or effect rather than meaning, and its seeming exclusion of the reader through its intensely idiosyncratic quality of reference. These reconsiderations of modernism begin to emerge not only in Warren's own poetry and fiction but also in his critical works on other modernists' poetry and fiction. A good example of this kind of critical writing is his 1935 review of Thomas Wolfe's novel *Of Time and the River.*

Warren's stance in his review is that the poetic and the prosaic strands of Wolfe's novel should complement each other more fully, with the purpose of making the work more accessible "to the ordinary citizens of the Republic."[19] Continuing to voice critical judgments that seem antithetical to the initial spirit of modernism, Warren enlarges upon his specific review of Wolfe's *Of Time and the River* in his more generally applicable 1942 essay "Pure and Impure Poetry." In this later essay, he provides the kind of close reading of several poems that had already informed *Understanding Poetry,* the 1938 textbook he co-wrote with Cleanth Brooks. Furthermore, in the process of his own close reading, Warren implies that every reader is an active participant, although not necessarily welcomed by the artist, in determining a work's proper balance of poetic and prosaic elements. Pure poetry is effectively balanced with the impure only when the poet (or novelist or dramatist) reveals the inner workings of character and the complex accommodations to an imperfect world that inform and enrich gestures toward pure poetic transcendence. In an unbalanced system, however, the purely poetic is its own reason for being, leaving the reader unconvinced of its relevance in a world of accommodation and unconvinced of its consistency with actual experience.

According to Warren, the weakness of Wolfe's early novels lies in their insistence on the transcendent moment when the reader is still unconvinced that the protagonist has experienced enough of the world to earn and inform that moment. That Wolfe and his protagonists long to dwell in that unearned transcendent moment is revealed in his short fiction "Circus at Dawn" and in a long dream sequence from his third novel, *The Web and the Rock.* Both of these works romanticize and idealize the circus, an image that reveals Wolfe's need for unfettered self-expression and escape from time into transcendence.

Warren's Bolton Lovehart also seeks in his attic circus what Thomas Wolfe desires from his circus: unfettered self-expression and escape from time. Warren's novella, however, uses Wolfe's circus image to serve a completely different purpose: to establish fictionally, as he had earlier asserted critically, that the transcendent moment must be earned and tempered by the artist's inviting impure elements into it. In Bolton's case, the transcendent moment is earned when he willingly reveals his circus to the Bardsville community, inviting their response to it.

Tellingly, when Wolfe finally realizes the artistic necessity for incorporating impure elements in his "poetry," he lampoons the celebrated modernist circus of Alexander Calder, in which Wolfe may have recognized some of his own early artistic deficiencies. When in "The Circus in the Attic" Warren fictionalizes this same process—a pure artist's gradual acceptance of the impure into his art—he bases his depiction on an eccentric circus hobbyist, Kentuckian John Wesley Venable, who joins the series of low culture touchstones (see the aforementioned Willie Proudfit, Ashby Wyndham, Willie Stark, and Gran' Boz) who act as foils for the "purely poetic" idealism of Warren's protagonists.[20]

The circus as the south: Trope or Transgression?

The numerous creative uses of the circus in the literature of the Southern Renaissance mark it as an image heavily weighted during that era with cultural and ideological significance. Robert Penn Warren's singularly consistent use of the circus in his canon makes it a significant individual image for him, yet it also links him with southern authors such as William Faulkner, Thomas Wolfe, Caroline Gordon, Katherine Anne Porter, Eudora Welty, and Ralph Ellison. All of these major figures of the Southern Renaissance, and conceivably many other lesser lights of the period, find in the circus image something intrinsically southern, and they isolate the circus as a southern intertext through their mutual yet diverse uses of it.

To think of the circus as a southern intertext is to understand it as theorists Jay Clayton and Eric Rothstein define "intertext": as an image that demonstrates diffuseness rather than hegemony and as an image whose practitioners demonstrate inclusivity rather than evaluation. The southern circus intertext is diffuse and inclusive in that it is an image to which all writers of the Southern Renaissance feel they have a claim and on which they feel qualified to comment, regardless of gender, race, class, or historical moment. Furthermore, it is an image that writers of the Southern Renaissance use equally meaningfully to portray a southern tradition that is deficient in its provisions for personal, cultural, and ideological survival in the New South.

Because of this link between the southern circus intertext and southern tradition, it is important to differentiate between the circus as a modernist image of the carnivalesque and the circus as a modern southern image of the cultural status quo. Ordinarily, the circus is associated with the carnivalesque, the term for cultural transgression introduced by Mikhail Bakhtin in his study *Rabelais and His World* (1940, 1965). Yet in literature of the Southern Renaissance, the circus exemplifies not the kinds of carnivalesque activities that were merely permitted by the medieval church and state in Rabelais's time, but their cultural opposites, the official feasts, which were not only sanctioned but often organized by the church and the state, which had also established the dominant ideologies of the medieval culture.

I have already noted in a previous section of this chapter how, during the post–World War I years through World War II, years that roughly correspond with the height of the Southern Renaissance, the circus was slowly rehabilitated from its carnivalesque role to a role that reinforced the dominant ideology of America. In fact, the more unpredictable—one might say the more carnivalesque—social and economic conditions in the United States became during those years, the more conservative the circus became in its parallel reinforcement of traditional values. For example, as the so-called Lost Generation abandoned its faith in stability and continuity after World War I, the circuses reinforced stability and continuity by continuing their shows, despite the hardships that resulted from the harsh human and philosophical losses of the war. With WPA support during the Depression, circuses continued to raise their tents, welcome audiences, and urge Americans to think positively about the country's basic values. Finally, during World War II, circuses like the Ringling Bros. and Barnum & Bailey Combined Shows staged huge patriotic productions that prominently featured the images of President Roosevelt and Gen. Douglas MacArthur and urged audiences to buy war bonds. Encouraged to sacrificial gestures of traditional patriotism by this newly conservative circus rhetoric, North and South united successfully to weather two world wars and a severe economic depression. It is important to note, on the other hand, that when the long memory of the South casts itself back to traditional images of social and economic stability, it returns inevitably to the mythic white, patriarchal, antebellum South which, even in the early decades of the twentieth century, still had great influence over southern culture.

What made the circus a compelling image for the writers of the Southern Renaissance? One might certainly speculate that, in an era of modernist thought, they would find the circus a ready-to-hand carnivalesque trope for the low-culture transgressions often charged to the South by the mainstream North. Similarly, southern writers might have identified in the circus their own post–Civil War region, forced as it was to a status of transgressive otherness and yet honored all the more by its constituents for the very qualities that, again, set it apart from the modern mainstream. Conversely, based on my previous speculations on the way in which the circus mimics the medieval "official feast" in support of dominant ideology, one can easily see how the circus—an entity that had always been idealized and romanticized but now took on newly conservative qualities—was, to the literary eye of the Southern Renaissance, an especially appropriate image for the mythic Old South and its essentially patriarchal ideology.

Yet, as attractive as the circus—and the mythic image of the Old South it represents—could be, both the circus and the patriarchy are images that writers of the Southern Renaissance feel they must resist. In Faulkner's work, the circus provokes a sometimes regretful look backward to the familiar patriarchy of the Old South and questions what the New South can offer even once one has admitted the moral necessity of embracing it. The lure of the majestic ideals of the southern patriarchy is strong. Thus, only through the greatest of provocation does Faulkner's "Barn Burning" protagonist Sarty Snopes finally escape the cruel abuse of his father, associated as the elder Snopes is in Sarty's mind with the southern-inspired illusion of family honor. Sarty's cherished illusion of family loyalty is figured in faded circus posters of "scarlet horses . . . [and] . . . incredible poisings" that are no more real than the stories the elder Snopes tells about his days as a "professional horsetrader."[21] As for Eudora Welty, the promise of the circus is a tale told by adults, traditional keepers of myths, to avoid answering the difficult questions children ask of their uncertain world. She describes in *One Writer's Beginnings* how she learned early to interpret that promise as betrayal. Katherine Anne Porter's circus also represents patriarchal tradition and its insidious control over every aspect of the South; her Miranda finds southern myth affirmed even in "The Circus." In "A Coupla Scalped Indians," Ralph Ellison's circus is a masculine bastion of confident self-definition challenged by the threateningly unpredictable feminine. When read alongside his essay analyses of the *eiron* and its ability to unite many racial identities under one canopy of American identity, Ellison's story reveals a nagging ambivalence toward his more hopeful essay assertions. In Thomas Wolfe's *You Can't Go Home Again*, Piggy Logan's circus reminds George Webber of the South in whose mythic simplicities he has spent an attenuated adolescence that he must now sacrifice for social awareness. Finally, Warren's circus is the patriarchal image through which bloodied Civil War cavalry sabers are wiped clean, bitter war losses are repressed, and "people . . . believe what truth they have to believe to go on being the way they are," regardless of the moral imperatives of history.

Among all these writers of the Southern Renaissance and their various works, characters, and personae, however, Robert Penn Warren, through his semiautobiographical figure Bolton Lovehart and through his novella "The Circus in the Attic," makes the most comprehensive use of the circus intertext. Moreover, all that we have understood in this study's previous chapters to be true about Bolton Lovehart and his circus is equally true of Robert Penn Warren and his lifetime of artistry.

As this study has demonstrated, Warren is not only the child of the South who finds his future threatened by its historical legacy, but he is also the artist of the South whose clarity of vision threatens to set him apart from his region. Furthermore, Warren's artistic goals establish his affinity with the mainstream North even as they reveal his insights into the southern way of life. Finally, Warren's creative energies appropriate the circus, an image that had already been claimed for entirely different purposes by literary modernism, and refines it to suit his vision for southern modernism. In accomplishing this final goal, Warren achieves creatively what Paul Bouissac notes culturally about the circus in this chapter's epigraph: he shifts the circus from the social periphery to southern culture's very center.

Notes

Introduction

1. See John Culhane, *The American Circus: An Illustrated History* (New York: Henry Holt, 1990) and Don B. Wilmeth, "Circus and Outdoor Entertainment," in *Handbook of American Popular Culture,* vol. 2, ed. M. Thomas Inge (Westport, Conn.: Greenwood Press, 1980), 51–77.

2. See, for example, James Carlyon's biography of the popular clown Dan Rice, *Dan Rice: The Most Famous Man You've Never Heard Of* (New York: Public Affairs, 2001). One aspect of Carlyon's work is to establish Rice's role in the formation of middle-class values during the nineteenth-century antebellum period.

3. George L. Chindahl, *A History of the Circus in America* (Caldwell, Idaho: Caxton, 1959), 45.

4. See Janet M. Davis, *The Circus Age: Culture and Society under the American Big Top* (Chapel Hill: Univ. of North Carolina Press, 2002) for further discussions of changes in gender expectations facilitated by the twentieth-century circus.

5. Frank Gado, "A Conversation with Robert Penn Warren," in *Talking with Robert Penn Warren,* ed. Floyd C. Watkins, John T. Hiers, and Mary Louise Weaks (Athens: Univ. of Georgia Press, 1990), 78.

6. Doug A. Mishler, "'It Was Everything Else We Knew Wasn't': The Circus and American Culture," in *The Culture of Celebration,* ed. Ray B. Browne and Michael T. Marsden (Bowling Green: Bowling Green State Univ. Press, 1994), 139. Not surprisingly during this time, other out-of-work artists such as Eudora Welty and Ralph Ellison swelled the ranks of various WPA programs. Welty's WPA experience was responsible, in part, for her artistic fascination with the circus. See chapter 4 of this study.

7. Whereas Kelly's hobo clown appears to have been borrowed from Chaplin's screen persona, Chaplin's Little Tramp in turn had adapted performance elements of the circus clown, the mime, and even the acrobat, as Chaplin's wobbly gait and signature cane might attest. These traits of his comic persona made his performance in the full-length film *The Circus* (1928) particularly appropriate.

8. Mishler, "'It Was Everything,'" 128.

9. John Ringling North and Alden Hatch, *The Circus Kings: Our Ringling Family Story* (Garden City, N.Y.: Doubleday, 1960), 238.

10. Howard Loxton, *The Golden Age of the Circus* (New York: Smithmark Press, 1997), 104.

11. North and Hatch, *Circus Kings,* 325.

12. Fred Bradna, *The Big Top: My Forty Years with The Greatest Show on Earth* (New York: Simon and Schuster, 1952), 118–20. Actually, as Bradna points out, the word "ringmaster" is a misnomer used only by circus outsiders to refer to the "equestrian director," the actual master of ceremonies. Please note that for the sake of consistency, I will defer to Robert Penn Warren's spelling—"ring master"—in the remaining chapters of this study.

13. North and Hatch, *Circus Kings,* 320.

14. Bradna, *Big Top,* 263.

15. Marcello Truzzi, "Introduction: Circuses, Carnivals and Fairs," *Journal of Popular Culture* 6, no. 3 (Winter 1972): 533.

16. Robert C. Sweet and Robert W. Haberstein, "Some Perspectives on the Circus in Transition," *Journal of Popular Culture* 6, no. 3 (Winter 1972): 587–88.

17. Mikhail Bakhtin, *Rabelais and His World,* trans. Helene Iswolsky (Cambridge: MIT Press, 1965), 9.

18. Robert Penn Warren, "The Circus in the Attic," in *The Circus in the Attic and Other Stories,* by Robert Penn Warren (New York: Harcourt Brace Jovanovich, 1975), 3–62.

19. Joseph Millichap, *Robert Penn Warren: A Study of the Short Fiction* (New York: Macmillan, 1992), 10.

20. Richard King, *A Southern Renaissance: The Cultural Awakening of the American South, 1930–1955* (New York: Oxford Univ. Press, 1980).

21. René Girard, *Deceit, Desire, and the Novel: Self and Other in Literary Structure,* trans. Yvonne Freccero (Baltimore: Johns Hopkins Press, 1965).

22. Robert Penn Warren, "Nathaniel Hawthorne," in *American Literature,* bk. B, ed. Brooks, Lewis, and Warren, 451.

23. For a detailed analysis of the Eliotian influence on Warren's early poetry, see Victor Strandberg, *A Colder Fire: The Poetry of Robert Penn Warren* (Lexington: Univ. of Kentucky Press, 1965).

24. Joseph Blotner, *Robert Penn Warren: A Biography* (New York: Random House, 1997), 71.

25. Robert Penn Warren, "A Note on the Hamlet of Thomas Wolfe," in *Thomas Wolfe: Three Decades of Criticism,* ed. Leslie A. Field (New York: New York Univ. Press, 1968).

26. John L. Idol Jr., "Thomas Wolfe Attends a Performance of Alexander Caulder's Circus," in *Thomas Wolfe: A Harvard Perspective,* ed. Richard S. Kennedy (Athens, Ohio: Croissant, 1983), 43–52.

27. Jay Clayton and Eric Rothstein, "Figures in the Corpus: Theories of Influence and Intertextuality," in *Influence and Intertextuality in Literary History,* ed. Jay Clayton and Eric Rothstein (Madison: Univ. of Wisconsin Press, 1991), 3–36.

Chapter 1

1. Quoted in Ruth Fisher, "A Conversation with Robert Penn Warren," in *Talking with Robert Penn Warren,* ed. Floyd C. Watkins, John T. Hiers, and Mary Louise Weaks (Athens: Univ. of Georgia Press, 1990), 178.

2. Richard B. Sale, "An Interview in New Haven with Robert Penn Warren," in *Talking with Robert Penn Warren,* ed. Floyd C. Watkins, John T. Hiers, and Mary Louise Weaks (Athens: Univ. of Georgia Press, 1990), 130.

3. Fisher, "Conversation," 178.

4. David Farrell, "Poetry Is a Way of Life: An Interview with Robert Penn Warren," in *Talking with Robert Penn Warren,* ed. Floyd C. Watkins, John T. Hiers, and Mary Louise Weaks (Athens: Univ. of Georgia Press, 1990), 371.

5. Allen G. Shepherd, "Prototype, Byblow, and Reconception: Notes on the Relation of Warren's *The Circus in the Attic* to His Novels and Poetry," *Mississippi Quarterly* 33 (1979): 4.

6. Ibid., 12.

7. Randolph Runyon, "The View from the Attic: Robert Penn Warren's *Circus Stories,*" *Mississippi Quarterly* 38 (1985): 119–35.

8. Millichap, *Robert Penn Warren,* 9–10.

9. Luke 2:42–49 (AV).

10. Again, as noted in the Introduction, note 12, although the dictionary standard is "ringmaster," I will defer to Warren's spelling, "ring master," throughout this study.

11. Appropriately for this text, cultural historian Marcello Truzzi, who himself comes from a circus family background, includes in the category of circuses and carnivals "the tented revival meetings of evangelists" (Truzzi, "Introduction," 531).

12. Bolton's failure to learn the proper lesson from his circus experience is greatly at odds with the intent of popular circus literature of the nineteenth century. See, for

example, Richard W. Flint, "The Evolution of the Circus in Nineteenth Century America," in *American Popular Entertainment: Papers and Proceedings of the Conference on the History of American Popular Entertainment,* ed. Myron Matlaw (Westport, Conn.: Greenwood Press, 1977), 187–96. Flint cites the example of the anti-circus tract *Slim Jack: or, The History of a Circus-Boy,* first published in 1847, in which a poor orphan boy's cruel treatment by his abusive employers is meant to make boys think twice about running away to the circus (187). James Otis Kaler's *Toby Tyler or Ten Weeks with a Circus* (New York: Harper & Bros., 1880) is a similar cautionary tale. Toby comes to appreciate his churchgoing Uncle Daniel all the more when he falls under the control of a wicked concessions operator. Despite Toby's surprising rise to stardom as the trick rider Monsieur Ajax, his return to Uncle Daniel and into "the presence of Him who is ever a father to the fatherless" (252) ensured steady sales of this book to sober parents and their recalcitrant sons for more than four decades.

13. Once more, Warren's narrator briefly conflates the image of the circus with the related images of more traditional theatrical entertainment and religious gatherings, noting, "There had been moving pictures before, in tents, with the . . . tinkle of the piano like the moment in a revival meeting when the piano strikes a few notes, waiting in the eddy of silence for the singers to catch breath and drown the music . . . ("Circus," 37).

14. One of the silent films which Bolton introduces to appreciative Bardsvillians is *Ben Hur* (1926), which was adapted from the 1880 novel by Lew Wallace (1827–1905). This work is significant to Warren's circus image since in the film version, the climactic chariot scene was filmed in a backlot Circus Maximus, the original of which many consider (probably erroneously) the origin of the modern circus. The conjunction of this cinematic horsemanship with the rowdy Bardsville horsemen on their way to the "circus" of the Civil War should remind the reader of the earliest beginnings of Philip Astley's British Hippodrama in 1768 and of Bill Ricketts's later American circus in 1793 (see Antony Hippisley Coxe, *A Seat at the Circus* [London: Evans Brothers, 1951], 22 and 26). Their primary acts were equestrian in nature; in fact, the person modern audiences think of as the "ring master" was originally the "equestrian director" in the days when trick riding acts were the raison d'être of circus spectacle.

15. For a similar image, see W. B. Yeats's "The Circus Animals' Desertion," in *The Collected Poems of W. B. Yeats,* ed. Richard J. Finneran (New York: Macmillan, 1989), 346–48. As unsympathetic as Warren's portrait of Mrs. Parton is, she remains the epitome of the person who, unlike the artist, must daily face a life of harsh experience, "the foul rag and bone shop of the heart" (40).

16. Joseph Millichap, "'The Circus in the Attic' and Robert Penn Warren's Romance of Southern History" (paper presented at the Robert Penn Warren Hometown Symposium, Clarksville, Tenn., Oct. 15, 1987).

17. See note 27 for the Introduction above.

18. Robert Penn Warren, *John Brown: The Making of a Martyr* (New York: Payson & Clarke, 1929; Nashville: J. S. Sanders, 1993).

19. Joseph Blotner adds that "troubled romantic and marital relationships are presented together against scenes Warren knew from childhood: the visiting carnival and the railroad depot" (*Robert Penn Warren,* 129). Blotner further notes that Warren salvaged three stories, later included in *The Circus in the Attic and Other Stories,* from these unpublished manuscripts (*Robert Penn Warren,* 148); more than likely, he is referring to "Christmas Gift," "The Love of Elsie Barton: A Chronicle," and "Testament of Flood." For an in-depth discussion of the other cultural marker of Warren's youth that Blotner mentions—the railroad—see Joseph Millichap's *Dixie Limited: Railroads, Culture, and the Southern Renaissance* (Lexington: Univ. Press of Kentucky, 2002).

20. Robert Penn Warren, *At Heaven's Gate* (New York: Harcourt, Brace, 1943; New York: New Directions, 1985), 359–60, 61.

21. Robert Penn Warren, *All the King's Men* (New York: Harcourt, Brace, 1946; New York: Harcourt Brace Jovanovich, 1975), 196–200.

22. Randolph Runyon, *The Taciturn Text: The Fiction of Robert Penn Warren,* (Columbus: Ohio State Univ. Press, 1991), 79.

23. See chapter 2 of this study for a more detailed examination of Warren's relationship with his mother Anna Ruth Penn Warren as well as more lengthy analyses of the ways in which the circus image makes itself known in Warren's novels.

24. Robert Penn Warren, *The Collected Poems of Robert Penn Warren,* ed. John Burt (Baton Rouge: Louisiana State Univ. Press, 1998), 441.

25. Robert Penn Warren, "Ballad of Your Puzzlement," in *The Collected Poems of Robert Penn Warren,* ed. John Burt (Baton Rouge: Louisiana State Univ. Press, 1998), 423.

26. See James H. Justus's *The Achievement of Robert Penn Warren* (Baton Rouge: Louisiana State Univ. Press, 1981), in which this "ambiguous second-person pronoun" is identified as a "virtual signature of Warren's poetry." Justus further suggests that Warren's "you" is directed collectively to "the poet himself, to the individual reader, and to the corporate reader" (58).

27. Robert Penn Warren, "Aspen Leaf in Windless World," in *The Complete Poems of Robert Penn Warren,* ed. John Burt (Baton Rouge: Louisiana State Univ. Press, 1998), 430.

28. Chapter 2 of this study will examine in greater detail the role Robert Franklin Warren plays in a psychological interpretation for "The Circus in the Attic." Chapter 3

of this study will trace the role played by yet another father, Hopkinsville eccentric John Wesley Venable, in shaping the fictional Bolton Lovehart.

29. Robert Penn Warren, "Hawthorne, Anderson, and Frost," review of *Nathaniel Hawthorne: A Study in Solitude,* by Herbert Gorman; *Robert Frost: A Study in Sensibility and Common Sense,* by Gorham Munsun; *Sherwood Anderson,* by Cleveland B. Chase; and *The Phenomenon of Sherwood Anderson: A Study in American Life and Letters,* by N. Bryllion Fagin, *New Republic,* May 16, 1928, 399.

30. Robert Penn Warren, "Hawthorne *Was* Relevant," *Nathaniel Hawthorne Journal* 2 (1972): 87.

31. Cleanth Brooks, R. W. B. Lewis, and Robert Penn Warren, eds., *American Literature: The Makers and the Making* (New York: St. Martin's, 1973).

32. See R. W. B. Lewis's "Warren's Long Visit to American Literature," *Yale Review* 70, no. 4 (Summer 1984): 589; of special interest is what Lewis reveals of the writing assignments among the three editors for the anthology. See as well Hyatt Waggoner, *The Presence of Hawthorne* (Baton Rouge: Louisiana State Univ. Press, 1979) for his analysis of the literary and psychic affinities between Warren and Hawthorne.

33. Lewis, "Long Visit," 587.

34. Warren, "Nathaniel Hawthorne," 432–33.

35. More recent Hawthorne scholars, most prominently Nina Baym, have challenged as literary myth the longstanding narrative of Hawthorne's isolation and estrangement from his mother; nevertheless, what interests me for this study is Warren's *perception* of Hawthorne's psychic and artistic state of mind and how Warren's critical narrative of Hawthorne parallels his artistic narrative of Bolton Lovehart. For Nina Baym's analysis of the relationship between the Hawthornes, mother and son, see her "Nathaniel Hawthorne and His Mother: A Biographical Speculation," *American Literature* 54, no. 1 (Mar. 1982): 1–27.

36. If we doubt Warren's reading of Emerson as Hawthorne's "father," we have only to consult the essay "Hawthorne *Was* Relevant," *Nathaniel Hawthorne Journal* 2 (1972): 85–89. In this essay, Warren envisions Emerson and Hawthorne meeting "on the wood paths of Concord, . . . Emerson with his head full of bright futurities and relevances, Hawthorne with his head full of the irrelevant past" (86). As evocative as this scenario is of a much earlier one on the road to Thebes, however, Warren replaces violent parricide with a philosophical tone, noting elsewhere, "I'm strictly for Hawthorne. I have . . . a pathological flinch from Emersonianism, . . . from oversimplifications . . . of the grinding problems of life and of personality." See Marshall Walker, "Robert Penn Warren: An Interview, in *Talking with Robert Penn Warren,* ed. Floyd C. Watkins, John T. Hiers, and Mary Louise Weaks (Athens: Univ. of Georgia Press, 1990), 155.

37. Warren's later disavowed segregationist views are voiced in his essay "The Briar Patch," in *I'll Take My Stand: The South and the Agrarian Tradition* (New York: Harper & Bros., 1930), 246–64.

38. Shepherd, "Prototype," 8.

39. Joseph Blotner notes that after age sixteen, Warren had effectively left his Guthrie home for good; sixteen is, of course, Bolton Lovehart's age when he stages his short-lived escape with the circus (Blotner, *Robert Penn Warren*).

40. Robert Penn Warren, *Portrait of a Father* (Lexington: Univ. Press of Kentucky, 1988), 7.

41. Millichap, *Robert Penn Warren*, 9.

42. Robert Penn Warren, "In the Time of *All the King's Men*," *New York Times Book Review,* May 31, 1981, 9.

Chapter 2

1. Warren, "Nathaniel Hawthorne," 440n.

2. Justus, *Achievement,* 124. Justus further notes two themes Warren discusses in his critical writings that also appear in his own fiction, especially in "The Circus in the Attic": "the quality of success in America [. . . and . . .] the thrust and drag of individualism as opposed to community" (124).

3. See, for example, Colette Soler, "Literature as Symptom," in *Lacan and the Subject of Language,* ed. Ellie Ragland-Sullivan and Mark Bracher (New York: Routledge, 1991), 213–19. As Soler and others illustrate, Freud's reaction to the novel is to lapse "into applied psychoanalysis, treating the artist's know-how as equivalent to what he himself called the work of the unconscious, putting artistic and literary works on the same level as dreams, slips of the tongue, bungled actions, and symptoms, all of which are interpretable" (213).

4. Warren, "Nathaniel Hawthorne," 442.

5. Terry Eagleton, *Literary Theory: An Introduction* (Minneapolis: Univ. of Minnesota Press, 1983), 155.

6. Compare this passage with the passage in *All the King's Men* that describes Cass Mastern's realization that "the world is all of one piece," cast in the image of an enormous spider web that, when even lightly touched, sends vibrations to its furthest edges (188). Mastern's understanding of this fact of life impresses on him the knowledge that his kinsman Jack Burden seeks to escape: "the awful responsibility of Time" (438). That Simon Lovehart shares Mastern's awareness of the web suggests that he might also share his sense of guilt and complicity for the wide-ranging power he wields, as a man of privilege, over innocent lives. Rather than live without the

illusion that how they conduct their lives has no effect for good or ill on those around them, both men allow themselves to be overtaken by death.

7. Blotner, *Robert Penn Warren,* 25.

8. Robert Penn Warren, "The Return: An Elegy," in *The Collected Poems of Robert Penn Warren,* ed. John Burt (Baton Rouge: Louisiana State Univ. Press, 1998), 33–35.

9. Pursued in another direction, Warren's claim of an artistic "breakthrough" leads us back to Warren's literary father, Nathaniel Hawthorne, about whom Warren remarks that the death of his mother "made certain forces available to the labor" he subsequently put toward his masterpiece *The Scarlet Letter* ("Nathaniel Hawthorne," 445n). Bolton Lovehart similarly achieves his masterpiece—the integration of his disparate artistic and social selves—at the death of his mother.

10. Victor Strandberg, "Robert Penn Warren and the Poetic Afterlife" (address presented at the Robert Penn Warren 11th Annual Symposium, Bowling Green, Ky., Apr. 26, 1998).

11. Meredith Anne Skura, *The Literary Uses of the Psychoanalytic Process* (New Haven: Yale Univ. Press, 1981), 22.

12. Eagleton, *Literary Theory,* 164.

13. See, for example, Joyce McDonald's "Lacan's Mirror Stage as Symbolic Metaphor in *All the King's Men,*" *Southern Quarterly* 34, no. 4 (1996): 73–79, of interest here because of the novel's function as a companion piece in theme, structure, and image to "The Circus in the Attic." The similarities between the two works are more fully explored in chapter 1 of this study.

14. Anthony Wilden, "Lacan and the Discourse of the Other," in *The Language of the Self: The Function of Language in Psychoanalysis,* by Jacques Lacan, trans. Anthony Wilden (Baltimore: Johns Hopkins Press, 1968), 174.

15. Christine Van Boheemen, *The Novel as Family Romance: Language, Gender, and Authority from Fielding to Joyce* (Ithaca: Cornell Univ. Press, 1987), 31.

16. Girard, *Deceit,* 2–3.

17. Quoted in Girard, *Deceit,* 47–48.

18. As Girard explains, internal mediation occurs when the distance between the subject and the mediator is negligible enough to allow them ready interaction; conversely, external mediation occurs when physical contact between the subject and mediator is precluded but the influence still exists (ibid., 9); in Bolton's case, the deaths of Simon and Jasper produce the movement from internal to external mediation.

19. Robert Penn Warren, *World Enough and Time: A Romantic Novel* (New York: Vintage Books, 1979).

20. Robert Penn Warren, *A Place to Come To* (New York: Random House, 1977).

21. Warren, *Portrait,* 7.

22. Blotner, *Robert Penn Warren,* 172.

23. Warren's *Portrait of a Father* does include a postscript of sorts to this episode. Thirty years later, when Robert Franklin Warren was in his seventies, he sent an original typescript of one of his poems to his son, with the scribbled admonition, "Do not answer" (42).

24. Blotner, *Robert Penn Warren,* 207.

25. See chapter 1 of this study for a lengthier analysis of this poem.

26. Robert Penn Warren, "Afterthought," in *The Collected Poems of Robert Penn Warren,* ed. John Burt (Baton Rouge: Louisiana State Univ. Press, 1998), 441.

27. Robert Penn Warren, "October Picnic Long Ago," in *The Collected Poems of Robert Penn Warren,* ed. John Burt (Baton Rouge: Louisiana State Univ. Press, 1998), 381.

28. Eve Kosofsky Sedgwick, "Introduction to *Between Men: English Literature and Male Homosocial Desire,*" in *Feminisms,* ed. Robyn R. Warhol and Diane Price Herndl (New Brunswick, N.J.: Rutgers Univ. Press, 1991), 463–77.

29. Quoted in Sedgwick, "Introduction to *Between Men,* 464. To forestall accusations of a homophobic agenda behind this definition of patriarchy, Sedgwick makes this disclaimer: "I am not assuming or arguing either that patriarchal power is primarily or necessarily homosexual (as distinct from homosocial), or that male homosexual desire has a primary or necessary relationship to misogyny. Either of those arguments would be homophobic and, I believe, inaccurate" (477).

30. King, *Southern Renaissance,* 28.

31. Forrest G. Robinson, "A Combat with the Past: Robert Penn Warren on Race and Slavery," *American Literature* 67, no. 3 (1992): 512.

32. Robinson faults *All the King's Men* protagonist Jack Burden, and thus Warren, for never achieving the same conviction of moral and ethical complicity in black slavery as Cass Mastern does.

33. Robert C. Toll, "Showbiz in Blackface: The Evolution of the Minstrel Show as a Theatrical Form," in *American Popular Entertainment: Papers and Proceedings of the Conference on the History of American Popular Entertainment,* ed. Myron Matlaw (Westport, Conn.: Greenwood Press, 1977), 23. Although Toll does not pursue the idea, the prominence of female impersonation in minstrel shows could correspondingly indicate an acting out of gender fantasies in stereotypes of women.

34. Michael Kreyling, *Inventing Southern Literature* (Jackson: Univ. Press of Mississippi, 1998), 34.

35. Robert Penn Warren, *Flood: A Romance of Our Time* (New York: Signet Books, 1965).

36. Robert Penn Warren, *Meet Me in the Green Glen* (New York: Random House, 1971).

37. King, *Southern Renaissance,* 37.

Chapter 3

1. "Prime Leaf" appeared first in *American Caravan IV,* ed. Alfred Kreymborg et al. (New York: Macauley, 1931), 3–61; "Unvexed Isles" appeared in *Magazine* 2 (July–Aug. 1934): 1–10; "Testament of Flood" was published in *Magazine* 2 (Mar.–Apr. 1935): 230–34; and "Her Own People" was published in *Virginia Quarterly Review* 11 (Apr. 1935): 289–304. These short fictions were later republished in 1947 in *The Circus in the Attic and Other Stories,* Warren's only short fiction collection.

2. The essay "A Note on the Hamlet of Thomas Wolfe" first appeared in *American Review* 5 (May 1935): 191–208 and later in Warren's *Selected Essays* (New York: Random House, 1958), 170–83. For the purposes of this chapter, I will cite the reprint of the essay included in Leslie A. Field's *Thomas Wolfe: Three Decades of Criticism* (New York: New York Univ. Press, 1968), 205–16.

3. David Herbert Donald, *Look Homeward: A Life of Thomas Wolfe* (Boston: Little, Brown, 1987), 360. Wolfe ultimately never took the *Southern Review* editors up on their offer of publication.

4. Warren, "Hamlet," 216.

5. Wolfe biographer David Herbert Donald confirms the reason for Warren's confusion, a reaction shared by many readers of the first edition of *Of Time and the River.* At the time, Wolfe was disinclined to read his own galley proofs as carefully as he should have, due in part over his unhappiness with the massive cuts made to the manuscript. For that reason, and others beyond his control, the first edition contained many confusing first-person references that were inconsistent with the later decision to make the novel a third-person narrative (Donald, *Look Homeward,* 303, 317).

6. Other critics were equally disapproving of Wolfe's autobiographical preoccupations and even less kind in their examinations of them. Bernard DeVoto's "Genius Is Not Enough," *Saturday Review* 13 (Apr. 25, 1936): 3–4, 14–15 was one of the most famous attacks against Wolfe's work. In it, DeVoto deplores "the frequent recurrence of material to which one must apply the adjective placental" (4).

7. It is very unlikely that Warren, who memorized huge passages of *The Waste Land* when he was a student at Vanderbilt, would not also have read T. S. Eliot's

1919 essay "Hamlet," eventually included in *Selected Essays* (New York: Harcourt, Brace & World, 1960), in which Eliot criticizes Shakespeare for not having established a satisfactory "objective correlative" for the puzzling behaviors of his protagonist: "[I]n other words, a set of objects, a situation, a chain of events which shall be the formula of that *particular* emotion; such that when the external facts, which must terminate in sensory experience, are given, the emotion is immediately evoked" (125). What Eliot requires is simply that the experiential cause show more relation to the emotional effect and, further, that the cause be worthy of the effect. Eliot's request that what Hamlet has experienced in the world be consistent with his emotional response to it is not all that different from Warren's judgment that Wolfe's protagonist earn through experience the poetic stances he takes toward life. The Hamlet of Thomas Wolfe, like the Hamlet of Shakespeare, is too heavily determined by emotional response (that yearning for the poetic vision in Wolfe), unconvincingly contextualized in a setting that fails to explain and validate the strength of his poetic yearning or its subsequent impassioned expression. Such intense feeling in the absence of an object, according to Eliot, "often occurs in adolescence" (126). Eliot admits that Hamlet does not have that excuse; perhaps Warren is suggesting that Wolfe does.

8. Robert Penn Warren, "Pure and Impure Poetry," in *New and Selected Essays,* by Robert Penn Warren (New York: Random House, 1989), 3–28.

9. "Democracy and Poetry" was first delivered in 1974 as the second of that year's Thomas Jefferson Lectures. It was subsequently published in the *Southern Review* 11 (1975): 1–28.

10. Ibid., 16–17.

11. Warren, "Pure and Impure," 15.

12. Warren neglects here the play's canny audience, who know from previous scenes that Romeo is prone to falling in and out of love with the least provocation. They too demand that Romeo earn the right to his romantic but ultimately empty phrases by undertaking a more serious-minded study of the nature of love.

13. Warren, *All the King's Men,* 438.

14. Perhaps Warren's essay reveals his own sense of the temptations of pure poetry. In an interview with Warren, Marshall Walker suggests that "what is lacking in [Warren's novels] *Wilderness* [1961] and *Band of Angels* [1955] is this Mercutio in the underbrush. There's something, somehow, too *straight,* too 'pure' about them" (Walker, "Interview," 160). Warren does not disagree with Walker's evaluation, even though he is quick to point out other, more specific technical failings of the two works.

15. Warren, "Pure and Impure," 2. See chapters 1 and 2 of this study for these varieties of analyses of "The Circus in the Attic."

16. See Joy Bale Boone, "A Circus at the Top," *Courier-Journal Magazine,* June 4, 1978, 10–15, and Will Fridy, "Peering into the Pure Imagination: Robert Penn Warren's 'The Circus in the Attic,'" *Mississippi Quarterly* 45, no. 1 (1992): 69–75. Neither Boone nor Fridy, Warren scholars who have written extensively on this Kentucky source for "The Circus in the Attic," can identify the date of Warren's first encounter with the Venable story more exactly than this.

17. Boone, "Circus at the Top," 13 and 11. In this respect, Warren could certainly identify with Thomas Wolfe, whose editors lived in constant fear of libel suits when he included characters into his works who were only thinly disguised versions of real and readily identifiable people from Asheville and later New York. Other than this initial reaction to Warren's novella, however, neither Venable nor his family seemed interested in proceeding legally against the author, who, after all, had the word of an Episcopal minister that he had not knowingly included uncomplimentary aspects of the Venables' home life in his story.

18. Warren, "Circus," 56.

19. Ibid., 61–62.

20. Ironically, Wolfe was invited to replace Bernard DeVoto at the 1935 Writers Conference as the "visiting novelist" when DeVoto unexpectedly withdrew. The next year, DeVoto would write his stinging critique of Wolfe's *Story of a Novel* entitled "Genius Is Not Enough"; see Donald, *Look Homeward,* 335.

21. Thomas Wolfe, "Circus at Dawn," in *From Death to Morning,* by Thomas Wolfe (New York: Scribner's, 1935), 205–11.

22. Yorum S. Carmeli, "Text, Traces, and the Reification of Totality: The Case of Popular Circus Literature," *New Literary History* 25, no. 1 (1994): 176.

23. While the circus motif in several of Wolfe's works reaffirms the patriarchal, carnival images, especially in *Look Homeward, Angel* reassert, through Eugene, Wolfe's hatred for the seedy life-style enforced upon his family by his mother's desire to run a boardinghouse. Indeed, when Eugene's father W. O. scorns his wife Eliza's decision to open a boardinghouse, he uses a telling carnivalesque comparison: "She'll have the place filled with all of Barnum's freaks the next thing you know"; see Wolfe's *Look Homeward, Angel* (New York: Simon and Schuster, 1995), 165.

24. Wolfe's implied comparison is especially appropriate since the decline in the popularity of the circus can be directly traced, in part, to the growing popularity of motion pictures.

25. Carmeli, "Text," 195.

26. Thomas Wolfe, *The Web and the Rock* (New York: Harper & Row, 1967).

27. In his memoirs, for example, W. C. Coup, a circus showman who at one time partnered with P. T. Barnum, recalls the regional antagonism circuses often experienced in the South, even as late as the 1890s, since they were presumed to originate in the North and to operate under northern management. See Coup's *Spangles and Sawdust: Stories and Secrets of the Circus* (Washington, D.C.: Paul A. Ruddell, 1901).

28. Thomas Wolfe, *You Can't Go Home Again* (New York: Signet, 1968).

29. Idol, "Thomas Wolfe Attends," 43. Examining this lengthy episode from the novel has recently been complicated by the resurfacing of an old argument in Wolfe scholarship—that is, to what extent his books were the edited creations of Maxwell Perkins and Edward Aswell—and by the resurgence of interest in Wolfe's manuscripts prompted by the recent publication of *O Lost!*, the original version of *Look Homeward, Angel.*

30. This lengthy center section of *You Can't Go Home Again* went through several transformations before, through the editing prowess of Edward Aswell, it became the anchor to Wolfe's final novel. Wolfe's notebook contains references to this story line as early as 1930, and he continued to work on it off and on until 1938; see Suzanne Stutman and John L. Idol Jr.'s introduction to *The Party at Jack's*, by Thomas Wolfe (Chapel Hill: Univ. of North Carolina Press, 1995), ix.

31. Donald, *Look Homeward*, 77.

32. Ibid., 175. In Alexander Calder's own account of the performance, included in his autobiography, the sculptor remembers that he had arrived at the Bernsteins' apartment with "five valises and a very small gramophone"; see Alexander Calder, *Calder: An Autobiography with Pictures* (New York: Pantheon, 1977), 106.

33. Thomas Wolfe, *The Letters of Thomas Wolfe,* ed. Elizabeth Nowell (New York: Scribner's, 1956), 764.

34. Thomas Wolfe, *The Party at Jack's,* ed. Suzanne Stutman and John L. Idol Jr. (Chapel Hill: Univ. of North Carolina Press, 1995), 118. One of the tasks that Edward Aswell and Wolfe's agent Elizabeth Nowell set for themselves in editing this section for *You Can't Go Home Again* was to change the descriptions of characters that were too faithful to their originals. Wolfe also had a tendency to use actual or thinly disguised names in his drafts; Aswell changed several characters' names for this reason. In the final novel version, Piggy Logan is described as balding with freckled hands.

35. Wolfe, *You Can't*, 175.

36. Alexander Rower documents Alexander Caulder's personal commentary on the modern artist's use of the "found object": "Sculptors of all places and climates have used what came readily to hand. They did not search for exotic or precious materials. It was

their knowledge and invention which gave value to the result of their labors"; see Rower's *Caldersculpture* (New York: Universe Press, 1998), 45. Calder's own philosophy of the "found object" is equally applicable to Wolfe's own choice of autobiographical materials to inform his fiction. Wolfe also insisted (albeit somewhat more defensively) that the artist's ability took precedence over his choice of materials, humble and autobiographically familiar as they may be.

37. Wolfe, *Letters,* 707.

38. Quoted in Calder, *Autobiography,* 106. Calder was, for many years afterward, ignorant of his brush with greatness. As he recorded in his autobiography, "I was never aware that the great Wolfe—that is, Thomas Wolfe, the writer—was present at my circus performance. He did not have the good sense to present himself and I only heard from him much later—some nasty remarks on my performance, included in a long-winded book" (107). Unlike John Wesley Venable's circus, currently housed in the Pennyroyal Museum in Hopkinsville, Kentucky, Calder's circus is permanently on display in the Whitney Museum of American Art in New York.

39. A textual comparison of Stutman and Idol's "Party at Jack's" and the Aswell version included in *You Can't Go Home Again* will reveal significant narratological differences between the two. Wolfe's harsh and defensive reactions to the rich and talented guests gathered in the Jack home are attributed to George Webber in the novel, but in the absence of George's filtering consciousness in "The Party at Jack's," they become more clearly Wolfe's own. For the purposes of this chapter, I will not dwell on Wolfe's obvious anti-Semitism, homophobia, or misogyny, which are extensively dealt with elsewhere.

40. Wolfe's original, unedited language, revealed in Idol and Stutman's recovery of the original version of "The Party at Jack's," is much more blunt; this trio, whose "carnal history . . . [is] written with such brutal nakedness," provoke virtuous feelings of wonder, revulsion, and amusement among their fellow party-goers (184). This language, not surprisingly, also characterizes the reactions of audiences at a circus sideshow.

41. Warren, "Pure and Impure," 8.

42. Ibid., 26.

Chapter 4

1. Wilmeth, "Circus," 54.

2. Paul Bouissac, "Semiotics and Spectacles: The Circus Institution and Representations," in *A Perfusion of Signs,* ed. Thomas A. Sebeok (Bloomington: Indiana Univ. Press, 1977), 144.

3. Blotner, *Robert Penn Warren,* 79.

4. See Robert Penn Warren, "Katherine Anne Porter (Irony with a Center)," in *Critical Essays on Katherine Anne Porter,* ed. Darlene Harbour Unrue (New York: G. K. Hall, 1997).

5. Sale, "Interview," 143.

6. Katherine Anne Porter, *Letters of Katherine Anne Porter,* ed. Isabel Bayley (New York: Atlantic Monthly Press, 1990), 331.

7. Warren also wrote "Uncorrupted Consciousness: The Stories of Katherine Anne Porter," *Yale Review* 55 (1965): 265–74, as part of a special supplement on her work. Porter's regard for Warren was both personal and professional, as his was for her. She considered him an "old valued friend and most-loved and admired poet and critic"; see Porter, *Letters,* 614.

8. George Cheatham, "Death and Repetition in Porter's Miranda Stories," in *Critical Essays on Katherine Anne Porter,* ed. Darlene Harbour Unrue (New York: G. K. Hall, 1997), 159.

9. Robert Penn Warren, "Irony with a Center: Katherine Anne Porter (1941–52)," in *Selected Essays,* by Robert Penn Warren (New York: Random House, 1958), 153–54.

10. Suzanne W. Jones, "Reading the Endings in Katherine Anne Porter's 'Old Mortality,'" in *Critical Essays on Katherine Anne Porter,* ed. Darlene Harbour Unrue (New York: G. K. Hall, 1997), 179.

11. Katherine Anne Porter, "The Circus," in *The Leaning Tower and Other Stories* (New York: Harcourt Brace, 1944), 25.

12. Janis Stout, "Katherine Anne Porter and Mark Twain at the Circus," *Southern Quarterly* 36, no. 3 (Spring 1998): 113–23. Stout provides a more traditional Bakhtinian reading of both Twain's and Porter's texts to establish the influence of Twain's *Adventures of Huckleberry Finn* on Porter's "The Circus."

13. Circus historian John Culhane traces Dan Rice's adaptation of just such an act. As Culhane explains, "[M]any don't know that the clown Huck [Finn] sees at the circus is almost certainly Rice" (*American Circus,* 47), the nineteenth-century American clown whose adaptation of a classic British clown act is strikingly similar to the one Mark Twain describes in his 1885 novel. In his routine, Rice played a drunken backwoodsman who first angers the crowd by delaying the show with his ridiculous assertions of equestrian prowess only to endear himself to them when he doffs his rags and his drunken demeanor to reveal himself as a star equestrian.

14. The conclusion Bouissac draws from this observation certainly applies in this context: "[T]he theme of the circus is generally used by literary works only inasmuch as it provides opportunities for dramatic accidents" ("Semiotics and Spectacles" 147).

15. Robert F. Heilman's use of the circus intertext in his analysis of Porter's style suggests the possibility of reading the acrobat's performance in "The Circus" as meta-narrative: "'Stylist' is likely to call up unclear images of coloratura, acrobatics, [and] elaborateness of gesture. . . .[Yet] there is nothing of arresting façade in [Porter's] style, nothing of showmanship. . . . She does not introduce herself or present herself. Much less does she gesticulate. . . . She does not cry 'Look, ma, no hands.'" See Robert F. Heilman, "*Ship of Fools:* Notes on Style," in *Critical Essays on Katherine Anne Porter,* ed. Darlene Harbour Unrue (New York: G. K. Hall, 1997), 222–23.

16. Paul Bouissac, *Circus and Culture: A Semiotic Approach* (Bloomington: Indiana Univ. Press, 1976), 164–65.

17. Katherine Anne Porter, "The Old Order," in *The Leaning Tower and Other Stories* (New York: Harcourt Brace, 1944). In this story, five-year-old Sophia Jane, who grows up to become the Grandmother of "The Circus," claims the slave Nannie with the words "'I want the little monkey'" (40).

18. George Cheatham, "Death and Repetition," 162.

19. Ann Waldron, *Close Connections: Caroline Gordon and the Southern Renaissance* (New York: G. P. Putnam's Sons, 1987), 31.

20. Quoted in Waldron, *Close Connections,* 247.

21. John Crowe Ransom, "The Equilibrists," in *The South in Perspective: An Anthology of Southern Literature,* ed. Edward Francisco, Robert Vaughan, and Linda Francisco (Upper Saddle River, N.J.: Prentice Hall, 2001), 589–90.

22. Sale, "Interview," 141.

23. Robert Penn Warren, Introduction, *Collected Stories of Caroline Gordon,* by Caroline Gordon (New York: Farrar, Straus, Giroux, 1981), ix.

24. Nancylee Jonza, *The Underground Stream: The Life and Art of Caroline Gordon* (Athens: Univ. of Georgia Press, 1995), 269.

25. Caroline Gordon, "The Petrified Woman," in *The Collected Stories of Caroline Gordon,* by Caroline Gordon (New York: Farrar, Straus, and Giroux, 1981), 3–15.

26. Joseph Blotner, "William Faulkner and Robert Penn Warren as Literary Artists," in *Faulkner and the Artist: Faulkner and Yoknapatawpha, 1993,* ed. Donald M. Kartiganer and Ann J. Abadie (Jackson: Univ. Press of Mississippi, 1996), 22–40.

27. William Faulkner, *Selected Letters of William Faulkner,* ed. Joseph Blotner (New York: Random House, 1977), 239.

28. See chapter 1 of this study for a discussion of the parallels and intersections of these two important Warren texts.

29. André Bleikasten, "Introduction to *The Sound and the Fury,* 1933," in *William Faulkner's The Sound and the Fury: A Critical Casebook,* ed. André Bleikasten (New York: Garland Press, 1982), 7.

30. Faulkner, *Selected,* 74.

31. Ibid., 236.

32. Bleikasten, "Introduction," 7.

33. William Faulkner, "An Introduction to *The Sound and the Fury,*" *Mississippi Quarterly* 26, no. 3 (Summer 1973): 410.

34. Quoted in Bleikasten, "Introduction," 12.

35. William Faulkner, *The Sound and the Fury* (New York: W. W. Norton, 1994), 117.

36. Fred Chappell, "The Comic Structure of *The Sound and the Fury,*" in *William Faulkner's The Sound and the Fury: A Critical Casebook,* ed. André Bleikasten (New York: Garland Press, 1982), 36.

37. Quoted in Chappell, "The Comic Structure of *The Sound and the Fury,*" 139.

38. S. Tarachow, "Circuses and Clowns," in *Psychoanalysis and the Social Sciences,* ed. G. Roheim (New York: International Universities Press, 1951), 179.

39. Bouissac, *Circus and Culture,* 25–26.

40. Cheryl Lester, "Racial Awareness and Arrested Development: *The Sound and the Fury* and the Great Migration," in *The Cambridge Companion to William Faulkner,* ed. Philip Weinstein (New York: Cambridge Univ. Press, 1995), 129.

41. William Faulkner, "Barn Burning," in *Collected Stories of William Faulkner,* by William Faulkner (New York: Random House, 1950), 20.

42. Duncan Aswell, "The Recollection and the Blood: Jason's Role in *The Sound and the Fury,*" in *William Faulkner's The Sound and the Fury: A Critical Casebook,* ed. André Bleikasten (New York: Garland Press, 1982), 119–20.

43. John Sykes, *The Romance of Innocence and the Myth of History: Faulkner's Religious Critique of Southern Culture* (Macon, Ga.: Mercer Univ. Press, 1989); see especially 42–45.

44. Peggy Whitman Prenshaw, "Eudora Welty," in *The History of Southern Literature,* ed. Louis D. Rubin Jr. et al. (Baton Rouge: Louisiana State Univ. Press, 1985), 470.

45. Robert Penn Warren, "The Love and the Separateness in Miss Welty," *Kenyon Review* 6 (Spring 1944): 246–59.

46. Eudora Welty, *One Writer's Beginnings* (New York: Warner Books, 1984), 40.

47. Ibid., 41. Welty continues this thought by noting the "distrust and apprehension" with which we greet processions and spectacles: "their intent is still to be revealed. (Think what it was in 'My Kinsman, Major Molineux')" (41). I find it significant that Welty as well as Warren notes this tale's circus subtext. See chapter 1 above on Hawthorne.

48. Ruth Vande Kieft, *Eudora Welty*, rev. ed. (New York: Twayne, 1987), 5.

49. Hunter Cole and Seetha Srinivasan, "Eudora Welty and Photography: An Interview," in *More Conversations with Eudora Welty*, ed. Peggy Whitman Prenshaw (Jackson: Univ. Press of Mississippi, 1966), 197–98.

50. The photographic records of Welty's WPA experience are included in her *Photographs* (Jackson: Univ. Press of Mississippi, 1989), especially numbers 126–42 and in her *One Time, One Place: Mississippi in the Depression. A Snapshot Album* (New York: Random House, 1971). Jan Nordby Gretlund's study *Eudora Welty's Aesthetics of Place* (Newark: Univ. of Delaware Press, 1994) also includes Welty's photograph of a trapeze artist from 1935 to 1936, which was not later included in the photograph collections.

51. See Eudora Welty's "Retreat," *River* 1 (Mar. 1937): 10–12. "Lily Daws and the Three Ladies," "Petrified Man" and "Keela, the Outcast Indian Maiden" appeared in *A Curtain of Green* (1941) and were later published in *The Collected Stories of Eudora Welty*, by Eudora Welty (1980).

52. Eudora Welty, "Keela, the Outcast Indian Maiden," in *The Collected Stories of Eudora Welty*, by Eudora Welty (New York: Harcourt, Brace, 1980), 44.

53. See Jan Nordby Gretlund's introduction to "Acrobats in a Park" titled "Remember How It Was with the Acrobats," *South Carolina Review* 11, no. 1 (Spring 1978): 22–25.

54. Welty, *One Writer's*, 93.

55. Ibid., 94.

56. Michael Kreyling, *Eudora Welty's Achievement of Order* (Baton Rouge: Louisiana State Univ. Press, 1980), 76. Both Vande Kieft and Kreyling seem to be voicing reactions to what they see as several unflattering misreadings of Welty's novel in which her seeming indifference to the harsh realities of the mid-1940s and her seeming nostalgia for the less socially responsible way of life of the 1920s—not to mention her departure from a traditional linear narrative—are taken to task. See also Vande Kieft's *Eudora Welty* (Boston: Twayne, 1962), 108–9, in which she cites reviews by Isaac Rosenfeld (*New Republic*, Apr. 29, 1946), Diana Trilling (*Nation*, May 11, 1946), and John Crowe Ransom (*Sewanee Review*, Summer 1946).

57. Joseph R. Millichap, "Eudora Welty's Real and Recreated Railroads," in *Dixie Limited: Railroads, Culture, and the Southern Renaissance,* by Joseph R. Millichap (Lexington: Univ. Press of Kentucky, 2002), 77.

Chapter 5

1. Quoted in Blotner, *Robert Penn Warren,* 307.

2. Ralph Ellison, Introduction to *Invisible Man,* by Ralph Ellison (New York: Vintage Books, 1972), xxiii.

3. Ralph Ellison, "On Initiation Rites and Power: Ralph Ellison Speaks at West Point," in *Going to the Territory,* by Ralph Ellison (New York: Random House, 1986), 50. Ellison's experience is not to suggest that the circus as an institution did not engage in racism; personal accounts such as Fred Bradna's *Big Top* reveal that racism was common among management and performers.

4. Ralph Ellison, Introduction to *Shadow and Act,* by Ralph Ellison (New York: Random House, 1964), xiv.

5. Ralph Ellison, "Change the Joke and Slip the Yoke," in *Shadow and Act,* by Ralph Ellison (New York: Random House, 1964), 52.

6. Ralph Ellison, "What's Wrong with the American Novel," in *Conversations with Ralph Ellison,* ed. Maryemma Graham and Amritjit Singh (Jackson: Univ. Press of Mississippi, 1995), 60.

7. Ralph Ellison, "The Little Man at Chehaw Station: The American Artist and His Audience," in *Going to the Territory* (New York: Random House, 1986), 21.

8. Ralph Ellison, "The Uses of History in Fiction," in *Conversations with Ralph Ellison,* ed. Maryella Graham and Amritjit Singh (Jackson: Univ. Press of Mississippi, 1995), 153.

9. Ralph Ellison, "The Myth of the Flawed White Southerner," in *Going to the Territory,* by Ralph Ellison (New York: Random House, 1986), 86–87.

10. Willi Real links the two works as he explores how "King of the Bingo Game" anticipates the main themes of *Invisible Man,* which Ellison began in 1945. See Real's "Ralph Ellison: 'King of the Bingo Game' (1944)," in *The Black American Short Story in the 20th Century: A Collection of Critical Essays,* ed. Peter Bruck (Amsterdam: B. R. Gruner, 1977), 111–12.

11. Ralph Ellison, "A Coupla Scalped Indians," in *Flying Home and Other Stories,* by Ralph Ellison (New York: Random House, 1996), 64.

12. Ralph Ellison, *Invisible Man* (New York: Vintage Books, 1972).

13. John Callahan, Introduction to *Juneteenth,* by Ralph Ellison (New York: Vintage Books, 2000), xxviii.

14. Ralph Ellison, *Juneteenth,* ed. John Callahan (New York: Vintage Books, 2000), 271.

15. Quoted in Ashraf H. A. Rushdy, "Daughters Signifyin(g) History: The Example of Toni Morrison's *Beloved,*" *American Literature* 64, no. 3 (1992): 575.

16. Nellie McKay, "An Interview with Toni Morrison," in *Conversations with Toni Morrison,* ed. Danille Taylor-Guthrie (Jackson: Univ. Press of Mississippi, 1994), 152.

17. Warren, "Circus," 43.

18. Toni Morrison, *Beloved* (New York: Plume Books, 1988), 3.

19. Deborah Guth, "A Blessing and a Burden: The Relation of the Past in *Sula, Song of Solomon,* and *Beloved,*" *Modern Fiction Studies* 39, no. 3/4 (1993): 589.

20. Warren, "Circus," 6.

21. Morrison, *Beloved,* 47.

22. Quoted in Jennifer Fitzgerald, "Selfhood and Community: Psychoanalysis and Discourse in *Beloved,*" *Modern Fiction Studies* 39, no. 3/4 (Fall/Winter 1993): 669.

23. Ibid., 672.

24. Ibid., 669.

25. Patrick Easto and Marcello Truzzi write that the sideshow display is the single factor common to both circuses and carnivals, which fact they note to explain the greater number of fictional treatments of the circus that focus on the sideshow. They also note that the American carnival was a development of the World's Columbian Exposition in Chicago in 1893 (554). This fact might indicate Morrison's conscious artistic choice of the carnival despite the anachronism produced by its use. See Patrick C. Easto and Marcello Truzzi, "Towards an Ethnography of the Carnival Social System," *Journal of Popular Culture* 6 (Winter 1972): 550–66.

26. Warren, "Circus," 43.

27. Ibid., 45.

28. Yorum S. Carmeli, "The Invention of the Circus and Bourgeois Hegemony: A Glance at British Circus Books," *Journal of Popular Culture* 29, no. 1 (1995): 218.

29. Ibid., 215.

30. Morrison, *Beloved,* 48.

31. Ibid., 51.

32. "Interview with Eleanor Clark and Robert Penn Warren," in *Talking with Robert Penn Warren,* ed. Floyd C. Watkins, John T. Hiers, and Mary Louise Weaks (Athens: Univ. of Georgia Press, 1990), 329.

33. The entry into time that Bolton Lovehart is unable to effect is ultimately attempted by another Warren protagonist: Amantha Starr in *Band of Angels* (1955). She, like Sethe, escapes northward, transcending enslavement in Kentucky and Louisiana, and seeks to forget her past through marriage to a white man in Ohio and Kansas; once freed, Amantha, like Sethe, also encounters her own moral discomfort with having failed first to resolve the myth of southern history.

34. Toni Morrison, *Jazz* (New York: Plume Books, 1993), 7.

35. Warren, "Circus," 8.

Conclusion

1. Floyd C. Watkins, *Then & Now: The Personal Past in the Poetry of Robert Penn Warren* (Lexington: Univ. Press of Kentucky, 1982), 31.

2. Warren would, of course, seek out his past in tales told by his maternal grandfather, Gabriel Penn, and from other, more obscure sources. The fruits of his search for a personal past are revealed in his memoir *Portrait of a Father.*

3. Blotner, *Robert Penn Warren,* 26.

4. Quoted in Watkins, *Then & Now,* 32.

5. Ibid., 33.

6. Blotner, *Robert Penn Warren,* 26.

7. Watkins, *Then & Now,* 34.

8. Ibid.

9. See Charles Philip Fox and Tom Parkinson, *Billers, Banners, and Bombast: The Story of Circus Advertising* (Boulder, Colo.: Pruett, 1985). According to Fox and Parkinson, the Ringlings traded on the distinguished family ownership of their circus quite early, as seen in a series of advertising pictorials featuring the oval portraits of Alf T., Al, John, Otto, and Charles Ringling (44). By the 1930s, popular and effective circus bills featuring the three-quarter profiles of "the circus kings"—the five Ringling brothers and their partners P. T. Barnum and James Bailey—asserted the dignity and tradition of the Greatest Show on Earth (48).

10. Bradna, *Big Top,* 40, 213. The biography of Fred Bradna, who was associated for forty years with the Ringling Bros. as their ring master, reveals that a strict hierarchy was observed even in as simple a thing as eating arrangements. Owners ate at

the first table, the ring master at the second, and so on down to the clowns, who were assigned an area distant from the rest of the show population.

11. Mishler, "It Was Everything," 128.

12. Recently organized feminist circuses attest to the patriarchal mode of the traditional circus, which was challenged in yet another way in 1998 when the Ringling Bros. and Barnum & Bailey Circus hired its first black ring master.

13. Ellison, *Juneteenth*, 250.

14. On the other hand, Warren's approach is not consistent with what many understand of the New Critical approach, for which Warren—along with Brooks, Tate, and others—is often credited (or criticized).

15. Robinson, "Combat," 512.

16. Blotner, *Robert Penn Warren*, 62.

17. See Joseph Millichap's "Robert Penn Warren's Divine Comedy," *Kentucky Philological Review* 8 (1993): 36. Warren noted that *At Heaven's Gate* was his most carefully outlined novel, perhaps because of his having borrowed its structure from a classical source. The novel is also an intriguing example of how low culture inserts itself into Warren's high culture considerations since the plot line involving Ashby Wyndham, the grim foil to Jerry Calhoun, was not part of Warren's original plan; Wyndham came to the author in a "fevered dream" as Warren was recovering from typhus ("Divine Comedy," 36).

18. Donald, *Look Homeward*, 78.

19. Warren, "Hamlet," 214.

20. I also find it significant that Calder's circus is permanently housed in the Whitney Museum of American Art in New York, while Venable's circus is featured in the more humble Pennyroyal Museum in Hopkinsville, Kentucky.

21. Faulkner, "Barn Burning," 20.

Bibliography

Aswell, Duncan. "The Recollection and the Blood: Jason's Role in *The Sound and the Fury.*" In *William Faulkner's The Sound and the Fury,* ed. Bleikasten, 115–22.

Bakhtin, Mikhail. *Rabelais and His World.* Translated by Helene Iswolsky. Cambridge: MIT Press, 1965.

Bleikasten, André. "Introduction to *The Sound and the Fury,* 1933." In *William Faulkner's The Sound and the Fury,* ed. Bleikasten, 7–14.

———, ed. *William Faulkner's The Sound and the Fury: A Critical Casebook.* New York: Garland, 1982.

Blotner, Joseph. *Robert Penn Warren: A Biography.* New York: Random House, 1997.

———. "William Faulkner and Robert Penn Warren as Literary Artists." In *Faulkner and the Artist: Faulkner and Yoknapatawpha, 1993,* edited by Donald M. Kartiganer and Ann J. Abadie, 22–40. Jackson: Univ. Press of Mississippi, 1996.

Boone, Joy Bale. "A Circus at the Top." *Courier-Journal,* June 4, 1978, 10–15.

Bouissac, Paul. *Circus and Culture: A Semiotic Approach.* Bloomington: Indiana Univ. Press, 1976.

———. "Semiotics and Spectacles: The Circus Institution and Representations." In *A Perfusion of Signs,* edited by Thomas A. Sebeok, 143–52. Bloomington: Indiana Univ. Press, 1977.

Bradna, Fred. *The Big Top: My Forty Years with the Greatest Show on Earth.* New York: Simon and Schuster, 1952.

Brooks, Cleanth, R. W. B. Lewis, and Robert Penn Warren, eds. *American Literature: The Makers and the Making.* New York: St. Martin's Press, 1973.

Calder, Alexander. *Calder: An Autobiography with Pictures.* New York: Pantheon, 1977.

Callahan, John. Introduction to *Juneteenth,* by Ellison, xix–xxxi.

Carmeli, Yoram S. "The Invention of Circus and Bourgeois Hegemony: A Glance at British Circus Books." *Journal of Popular Culture* 29, no. 1 (1995): 213–21.

———. "Text, Traces, and the Reification of Totality: The Case of Popular Circus Literature." *New Literary History* 25, no. 1 (1994): 175–205.

Chappell, Fred. "The Comic Structure of *The Sound and the Fury.*" In *William Faulkner's The Sound and the Fury,* ed. Bleikasten, 135–39.

Cheatham, George. "Death and Repetition in Porter's Miranda Stories." In *Critical Essays on Katherine Anne Porter,* ed. Unrue, 158–69.

Chindahl, George L. *A History of the Circus in America.* Caldwell, Idaho: Caxton Printers, 1959.

Clayton, Jay, and Eric Rothstein. "Figures in the Corpus: Theories of Influence and Intertextuality." In *Influence and Intertextuality in Literary History,* edited by Jay Clayton and Eric Rothstein, 3–36. Madison: Univ. of Wisconsin Press, 1991.

Cole, Hunter, and Seetha Srinivasan. "Eudora Welty and Photography: An Interview." In *More Conversations with Eudora Welty,* edited by Peggy Whitman Prenshaw, 188–213. Jackson: Univ. Press of Mississippi, 1996.

Coup, W. C. *Spangles and Sawdust: Stories & Secrets of the Circus.* Washington, D.C.: Paul A. Ruddell, 1961.

Coxe, Antony Hippisley. *A Seat at the Circus.* London: Evans Brothers, 1951.

Culhane, John. *The American Circus: An Illustrated History.* New York: Henry Holt, 1990.

DeVoto, Bernard. "Genius Is Not Enough." *Saturday Review of Literature* 13 (Apr. 25, 1936): 3–4, 14–15.

Donald, David Herbert. *Look Homeward: A Life of Thomas Wolfe.* Boston: Little, Brown, 1987.

Eagleton, Terry. *Literary Theory: An Introduction.* Minneapolis: Univ. of Minnesota Press, 1983.

Easto, Patrick C., and Marcelo Truzzi. "Towards an Ethnography of the Carnival Social System." *Journal of Popular Culture* 6 (Winter 1972): 550–66.

Eliot, T. S. "Hamlet." In *Selected Essays,* by T. S. Eliot, 121–26. New York: Harcourt, Brace & World, 1960.

Ellison, Ralph. "Change the Joke and Slip the Yoke." In *Shadow and Act,* by Ellison, 45–59.

———. "A Coupla Scalped Indians." In *Flying Home,* by Ellison, 63–81.

———. *Flying Home and Other Stories,* edited by John F. Callahan. New York: Random House, 1996.

———. *Going to the Territory.* New York: Random House, 1986.

———. Introduction to *Invisible Man.* In *Invisible Man,* by Ellison, vii–xxiii. New York: Vintage Books, 1972.

———. Introduction to *Shadow and Act.* In *Shadow and Act,* by Ellison, xi–xxiii. New York: Random House, 1964.

———. *Invisible Man.* New York: Vintage Books, 1972.

———. *Juneteenth.* Edited by John Callahan. New York: Vintage Books, 2000.

———. "King of the Bingo Game." In *Flying Home,* by Ellison, 123–36.

———. "The Little Man at Chehaw Station: The American Artist and His Audience." In *Going to the Territory,* by Ellison, 3–38.

———. "The Myth of the Flawed White Southerner." In *Going to the Territory,* by Ellison 76–87.

———. "On Initiation Rites and Power: Ralph Ellison Speaks at West Point." In *Going to the Territory,* by Ellison, 39–63.

———. *Shadow and Act.* New York: Random House, 1964.

———. "The Uses of History in Fiction." In *Conversations with Ralph Ellison,* ed. Graham and Singh, 141–72.

———. "What's Wrong with the American Novel." In *Conversations with Ralph Ellison,* ed. Graham and Singh, 20–62.

Ellison, Ralph, and Eugene Walter. "Warren on the Art of Fiction." In *Talking with Robert Penn Warren,* ed. Watkins, Hiers, and Weaks, 25–51.

Farrell, David. "Poetry Is a Way of Life: An Interview with Robert Penn Warren." In *Talking with Robert Penn Warren,* ed. Watkins, Hiers, and Weaks, 357–73.

Faulkner, William. "An Introduction to *The Sound and the Fury.*" *Mississippi Quarterly* 26, no. 3 (Summer 1973): 410–15.

———. "Barn Burning." In *Collected Stories of William Faulkner,* by William Faulkner, 3–25. New York: Random House, 1950.

———. *The Sound and the Fury.* New York: W. W. Norton, 1994.

———. *Selected Letters of William Faulkner,* edited by Joseph Blotner. New York: Random House, 1977.

Fisher, Ruth. "A Conversation with Robert Penn Warren." In *Talking with Robert Penn Warren,* ed. Watkins, Hiers, and Weaks, 170–89.

Fitzgerald, Jennifer. "Selfhood and Community: Psychoanalysis and Discourse in *Beloved.*" *Modern Fiction Studies* 39, no. 3/4 (Fall/Winter 1993): 669–87.

Flint, Richard W. "The Evolution of the Circus in Nineteenth-Century America." In *American Popular Entertainment,* ed. Matlaw, 187–96.

Fox, Charles Philip, and Tom Parkinson. *Billers, Banners, and Bombast: The Story of Circus Advertising.* Boulder, Colo.: Pruett, 1985.

Fridy, Will. "Peering into the Pure Imagination: Robert Penn Warren's 'The Circus in the Attic.'" *Mississippi Quarterly* 45, no. 1 (1992): 69–75.

Gado, Frank. "A Conversation with Robert Penn Warren." In *Talking with Robert Penn Warren,* ed. Watkins, Hiers, and Weaks, 68–85.

Girard, René. *Deceit, Desire, and the Novel: Self and Other in Literary Structure.* Translated by Yvonne Freccero. Baltimore: Johns Hopkins Press, 1965.

Gordon, Caroline. "The Petrified Woman." In *The Collected Stories of Caroline Gordon,* 3–15. New York: Farrar, Straus, Giroux, 1981.

Bibliography

Graff, Gerald, and James Phelan, eds. *Adventures of Huckleberry Finn: A Case in Critical Controversy.* New York: St. Martin's Press, 1995.

Graham, Maryemma, and Amritjit Singh, eds. *Conversations with Ralph Ellison.* Jackson: Univ. Press of Mississippi, 1995.

Gretlund, Jan Nordby. "Remember How It Was with the Acrobats." *South Carolina Review* 11, no. 1 (1978): 22–25.

Guth, Deborah. "A Blessing and a Burden: The Relation of the Past in *Sula, Song of Solomon,* and *Beloved." Modern Fiction Studies* 39, no. 3/4 (1993): 575–96.

Heilman, Robert F. "*Ship of Fools:* Notes on Style." In *Critical Essays on Katherine Anne Porter,* ed. Unrue, 222–32.

Idol, John L., Jr. "Thomas Wolfe Attends a Performance of Alexander Calder's Circus." In *Thomas Wolfe: A Harvard Perspective,* edited by Richard S. Kennedy, 43–52. Athens, Ohio: Croissant, 1983.

"Interview with Eleanor Clark and Robert Penn Warren." In *Talking with Robert Penn Warren,* ed. Watkins, Hiers, and Weaks, 318–35.

Jones, Suzanne W. "Reading the Endings in Katherine Anne Porter's 'Old Mortality.'" In *Critical Essays on Katherine Anne Porter,* ed. Unrue, 177–92.

Jonza, Nancylee. *The Underground Stream: The Life and Art of Caroline Gordon.* Athens: Univ. of Georgia Press, 1995.

Justus, James H. *The Achievement of Robert Penn Warren.* Baton Rouge: Louisiana State Univ. Press, 1981.

[Kaler], James Otis. *Toby Tyler or Ten Weeks with a Circus.* New York: Harper & Bros., 1880.

King, Richard. *A Southern Renaissance: The Cultural Awakening of the American South, 1930–1955.* New York: Oxford Univ. Press, 1980.

Kreyling, Michael. *Eudora Welty's Achievement of Order.* Baton Rouge: Louisiana State Univ. Press, 1980.

———. *Inventing Southern Literature.* Jackson: Univ. Press of Mississippi, 1998.

Lester, Cheryl. "Racial Awareness and Arrested Development: *The Sound and the Fury* and The Great Migration." In *The Cambridge Companion to William Faulkner,* edited by Philip Weinstein, 123–45. New York: Cambridge Univ. Press, 1995.

Lewis, R. W. B. "Warren's Long Visit to American Literature." *Yale Review* 70, no. 4 (Summer 1984): 568–91.

Loxton, Howard. *The Golden Age of the Circus.* New York: Smithmark Press, 1997.

Matlaw, Myron, ed. *American Popular Entertainment: Papers and Proceedings of the Conference on the History of American Popular Entertainment.* Westport, Conn.: Greenwood Press, 1977.

McKay, Nellie. "An Interview with Toni Morrison." In *Conversations with Toni Morrison,* edited by Danille Taylor-Guthrie, 138–55. Jackson: Univ. Press of Mississippi, 1994.

Millichap, Joseph R. "'The Circus in the Attic' and Robert Penn Warren's Romance of Southern History." Paper presented at the Robert Penn Warren Hometown Symposium, Austin Peay State Univ., Clarksville, Tenn., Oct. 15, 1987.

———. "Eudora Welty's Real and Recreated Railroads." In *Dixie Limited: Railroads, Culture, and the Southern Renaissance,* by Joseph R. Millichap. Lexington: Univ. Press of Kentucky, 2002.

———. *Robert Penn Warren: A Study of the Short Fiction.* New York: Macmillan, 1992.

———. "Robert Penn Warren's Divine Comedy." *Kentucky Philological Review* 8 (1993): 34–40.

Mishler, Doug A. "'It Was Everything Else We Knew Wasn't': The Circus and American Culture." In *The Culture of Celebration,* edited by Ray B. Browne and Michael T. Marsden, 127–44. Bowling Green: Bowling Green State Univ. Press, 1994.

Morrison, Toni. *Beloved.* New York: Plume Books, 1988.

———. *Jazz.* New York: Plume Books, 1993.

North, John Ringling and Alden Hatch. *The Circus Kings: Our Ringling Family Story.* Garden City, N.Y.: Doubleday Press, 1960.

Porter, Katherine Anne. "The Circus." In *Leaning Tower,* by Porter, 21–29.

———. *The Leaning Tower and Other Stories.* New York: Harcourt Brace, 1944.

———. *Letters of Katherine Anne Porter,* edited by Isabel Bayley. New York: Atlantic Monthly Press, 1990.

———. "The Old Order." In *Leaning Tower,* by Porter, 33–56.

Prenshaw, Peggy Whitman. "Eudora Welty." In *The History of Southern Literature,* edited by Louis D. Rubin Jr. et al., 470–75. Baton Rouge: Louisiana State Univ. Press, 1985.

Ransom, John Crowe. "The Equilibrists." In *The South in Perspective: An Anthology of Southern Literature,* edited by Edward Francisco, Robert Vaughan, and Linda Francisco, 589–90. Upper Saddle River, N.J.: Prentice Hall, 2001.

Real, Willi. "Ralph Ellison: 'King of the Bingo Game' (1944)." In *The Black American Short Story in the 20th Century: A Collection of Critical Essays,* edited by Peter Bruck, 111–27. Amsterdam: B. R. Gruner, 1977.

Robinson, Forrest G. "A Combat with the Past: Robert Penn Warren on Race and Slavery." *American Literature* 67, no. 3 (1995): 511–30.

Rower, Alexander S. C. *Caldersculpture.* New York: Universe, 1998.

Runyon, Randolph. *The Taciturn Text: The Fiction of Robert Penn Warren.* Columbus: Ohio State Univ. Press, 1991.

———. "The View from the Attic: Robert Penn Warren's *Circus* Stories." *Mississippi Quarterly* 38 (1985): 119–35.

Rushdy, Ashraf H. A. "Daughters Signifyin(g) History: The Example of Toni Morrison's *Beloved.*" *American Literature* 64, no. 3 (1992): 569–97.

Bibliography

Sale, Richard B. "An Interview in New Haven with Robert Penn Warren." In *Talking with Robert Penn Warren,* ed. Watkins, Hiers, and Weaks, 110–46.

Sedgwick, Eve Kosofsky. Introduction to *Between Men: English Literature and Male Homosocial Desire.* In *Feminisms,* edited by Robyn R. Warhol and Diane Price Herndl, 463–77. New Brunswick, N.J.: Rutgers Univ. Press, 1991.

Shepherd, Allen G. "Prototype, Byblow, and Reconception: Notes on the Relation of Warren's *The Circus in the Attic* to His Novels and Poetry." *Mississippi Quarterly* 33 (1979): 3–17.

Skura, Meredith Anne. *The Literary Uses of the Psychoanalytic Process.* New Haven: Yale Univ. Press, 1981.

Soler, Colette. "Literature as Symptom." In *Lacan and the Subject of Language,* edited by Ellie Ragland-Sullivan and Mark Bracher, 213–19. New York: Routledge Press, 1991.

Stout, Janis P. "Katherine Anne Porter and Mark Twain at the Circus." *Southern Quarterly* 36, no. 3 (Spring 1998): 113–23.

Strandberg, Victor. "Robert Penn Warren and the Poetic Afterlife." Paper presented at the Robert Penn Warren 11th Annual Symposium, Western Kentucky Univ., Bowling Green, Ky., Apr. 26, 1998.

———. *A Colder Fire: The Poetry of Robert Penn Warren.* Lexington: Univ. of Kentucky Press, 1965.

Stutman, Suzanne, and John L. Idol Jr. Introduction to *The Party at Jack's,* by Thomas Wolfe, ix–xxv. Chapel Hill: Univ. of North Carolina Press, 1995.

Sweet, Robert C., and Robert W. Haberstein. "Some Perspectives on the Circus in Transition." *Journal of Popular Culture* 6, no. 3 (1972): 583–90.

Sykes, John. *The Romance of Innocence and the Myth of History: Faulkner's Religious Critique of Southern Culture.* Macon: Mercer Univ. Press, 1989.

Tarachow, S. "Circuses and Clowns." In *Psychoanalysis and the Social Sciences,* edited by G. Roheim, 171–85. New York: International Universities Press, 1951.

Taylor, Robert Lewis. *Center Ring: The People of the Circus.* Garden City, N.Y.: Doubleday, 1956.

Toll, Robert C. "Showbiz in Blackface: The Evolution of the Minstrel Show as a Theatrical Form." In *American Popular Entertainment,* ed. Matlaw, 21–32.

Truzzi, Marcello. "Introduction: Circuses, Carnivals and Fairs." *Journal of Popular Culture* 6, no. 3 (Winter 1972): 531–34.

Unrue, Darlene Harbour, ed. *Critical Essays on Katherine Anne Porter.* New York: G. K. Hall, 1997.

Van Boheemen, Christine. *The Novel as Family Romance: Language, Gender, and Authority from Fielding to Joyce.* Ithaca: Cornell Univ. Press, 1987.

Vande Kieft, Ruth. *Eudora Welty.* Rev. ed. New York: Twayne, 1987.

Waldron, Ann. *Close Connections: Caroline Gordon and the Southern Renaissance.* New York: G. P. Putnam's Sons, 1987.

Walker, Marshall. "Robert Penn Warren: An Interview." In *Talking with Robert Penn Warren,* ed. Watkins, Hiers, and Weaks, 147–69.

Warren, Robert Penn. "Afterthought." In *Collected Poems of Robert Penn Warren,* by Warren, 441.

———. *All the King's Men.* New York: Harcourt, Brace and Company, 1946; New York: Bantam, 1974.

———. "Aspen Leaf in Windless World." In *Collected Poems of Robert Penn Warren,* by Warren, 430.

———. *At Heaven's Gate.* New York: Harcourt, Brace,1943; New York: New Directions, 1985.

———. "Ballad of Your Puzzlement." In *Collected Poems of Robert Penn Warren,* by Warren, 423–25.

———. "The Circus in the Attic." In *The Circus in the Attic and Other Stories.* New York: Harcourt Brace Jovanovich, 1975.

———. *The Collected Poems of Robert Penn Warren.* Edited by John Burt. Baton Rouge: Louisiana State Univ. Press, 1998.

———. "Democracy and Poetry." *Southern Review* 11 (1975): 1–28.

———. *Flood: A Romance of Our Time.* New York: Signet, 1965.

———. "Hawthorne, Anderson, and Frost." Review of *Nathaniel Hawthorne: A Study in Solitude,* by Herbert Gorman; *Robert Frost: A Study in Sensibility and Common Sense,* by Gorham B. Munson; *Sherwood Anderson,* by Cleveland B. Chase; and *The Phenomenon of Sherwood Anderson: A Study in American Life and Letters,* by N. Bryllion Fagin. *New Republic,* May 16, 1928, 399–401.

———. "Hawthorne *Was* Relevant." *Nathaniel Hawthorne Journal* 2 (1972): 85–89.

———. "In the Time of *All the King's Men.*" *New York Times Book Review,* May 31, 1981, 9.

———. "Irony with a Center: Katherine Anne Porter (1941–52)." In *Selected Essays,* by Warren, 146–56.

———. Introduction to *The Collected Stories of Caroline Gordon,* by Caroline Gordon, ix–xiii. New York: Farrar, Straus, Giroux, 1981.

———. *John Brown: The Making of a Martyr.* New York: Payson & Clarke, 1929; Nashville: J. S. Sanders, 1993.

———. *Meet Me in the Green Glen.* New York: Random House, 1971.

———. "Nathaniel Hawthorne." In *American Literature,* ed. Brooks, Lewis, and Warren, B: 432–61.

———. "A Note on the Hamlet of Thomas Wolfe." In *Thomas Wolfe: Three Decades of Criticism,* edited by Leslie A. Field, 205–16. New York: New York Univ. Press, 1968.

———. "October Picnic Long Ago." In *Collected Poems of Robert Penn Warren,* by Warren, 381.

———. *A Place to Come To.* New York: Random House, 1977.

———. *Portrait of a Father.* Lexington: Univ. Press of Kentucky, 1988.

———. "Pure and Impure Poetry." In *New and Selected Essays,* by Robert Penn Warren, 3–28. New York: Random House, 1989.

———. "The Return: An Elegy." In *Collected Poems of Robert Penn Warren,* by Warren, 33–35.

———. *Selected Essays.* New York: Random House, 1958.

———. *World Enough and Time: A Romantic Novel.* New York: Vintage Books, 1979.

Watkins, Floyd C. *Then & Now: The Personal Past in the Poetry of Robert Penn Warren.* Lexington: Univ. Press of Kentucky, 1982.

Watkins, Floyd C., John T. Hiers, and Mary Louise Weaks, ed. *Talking with Robert Penn Warren.* Athens: Univ. of Georgia Press, 1990.

Welty, Eudora. "Acrobats in a Park." *South Carolina Review* 11, no. 1 (1978): 26–33.

———. "Keela, the Outcast Indian Maiden." In *The Collected Short Stories of Eudora Welty,* by Eudora Welty, 38–45. New York: Harcourt Brace, 1980.

———. *One Writer's Beginnings.* New York: Warner Books, 1983, 1984.

Wilden, Anthony. "Lacan and the Discourse of the Other." In *The Language of the Self: The Function of Language in Psychoanalysis,* by Jacques Lacan, translated by Anthony Wilden, 159–311. Baltimore: Johns Hopkins Press, 1968.

Wilmeth, Don B. "Circus and Outdoor Entertainment." In *Handbook of American Popular Culture,* edited by M. Thomas Inge, 2: 51–77. Westport, Conn.: Greenwood, 1980.

Wolfe, Thomas. "Circus at Dawn." In *From Death to Morning,* by Thomas Wolfe, 205–11. New York: Scribner's, 1935.

———. *The Letters of Thomas Wolfe,* edited by Elizabeth Nowell. New York: Scribner's, 1956.

———. *Look Homeward, Angel.* New York: Simon and Schuster, 1995.

———. *The Party at Jack's,* edited by Suzanne Stutman and John L. Idol Jr. Chapel Hill: Univ. of North Carolina Press, 1995.

———. *The Web and the Rock.* New York: Harper & Row, 1967.

———. *You Can't Go Home Again.* New York: Signet, 1968.

Yeats, W. B. "The Circus Animals' Desertion." In *The Collected Poems of W. B. Yeats,* edited by Richard J. Finneran, 346–48. New York: Macmillan, 1989.

Index